INTEGRATED INDIAN
PUBLIC LIBRARY SYSTEM

INTEGRATED INDIAN
PUBLIC LIBRARY SYSTEM

Dr. Kapil Singh Hada/
Dr. R. P. Bajpai

PARTRIDGE
A Penguin Random House Company

To order additional copies of this book, contact
Partridge India
000 800 10062 62
orders.india@partridgepublishing.com

www.partridgepublishing.com/india

"To My Parents and
Grand Father (Nana Jee)"

"Om Vaakdeviyai cha Vidhmahe
Virinji Pathniyai cha Dheemahe
Thanno Vani Prachodayath".

"Om, Let me meditate on the goddess of speech,
Oh, wife of Lord Brahma, give me higher intellect,
And let Goddess Vani illuminate my mind".

Foreword

(With a Foreword by Prof. Umesh Chandra Sharma)

I am most gratified to place in the hand of the teachers, researchers and students of Library and Information Science, this work on *"Integrated Indian Public Library System", as* book brought by Dr. Kapil Singh Hada and Dr. R. P. Bajpai, I am confident that, this will serve as firm and accurate base for research and study and teaching on the subject.

Public library plays a crucial role in the society as a centre for education, information, recreation and culture. Because of these functions, Alvin Johnson rightly calls public library as "People's University". It is said that a public library should render free service to all without any discrimination based on caste, creed, age, sex or any other consideration. The role of public library is great indeed in the changing educational and societal circumstances in the third world countries like India, in order to achieve such a multifarious goal, a public library system should be brought under the mandate of law. This aspect has been emphasized in the official document called UNESCO manifesto.

The information explosion and ICT has led to the emergence of the electronic information. We live today in an information era wherein information as a commodity is increasingly playing a central role in our daily life. The digital revolution has alerted the way of societies function at the global, local, and personal level. We have entered the third millennium with the promise of new infrastructures and capabilities to handle information in ways the 21st century might have imagined. Libraries have changed with time from mere static storehouse of interested collections of documents to dynamic service centers, serving all professionals utilizing useful and need-based collection of documents. The medium of information storage has changed from clay tablets to paper and now to electronic and optical media of CD-ROMs. The library building is not limited just to a library, now we have digital library/electronic library, virtual library and a library without walls. Digital libraries provide instant access to digitize information by utilizing avenues of information communication technology. Today's electronic library based on digitized data is gradually replacing paper-based records and by means of networking one can have access to resources 24*7.

The rapid technological developments have opened up additional facilities by providing multiple choice of media, showing improved performance and assuring greater economy in time, money and effort. At the same time here is an increasing complexity in selecting the right, useful, authoritative information from vast available information sources.

However, a library cannot save itself as a switching centre. To justify its existence in the electronic world, the Library must continue to perform one of the most important functions it now performs in the print-on-paper worlds to organize the universe of resources in such a way that those most likely to be of value to the user community are made most accessible to the community, physically and intellectually. For libraries to stay in the game, they will not only need to become learning centre's and make their collections and stack available electronically over the World Wide Web and other online services to people, who want to get their information and knowledge from their office or home, but they will also have to contend with documents in the new media. There will be a new role and skill for library and information professionals, who will need to investigate the future of library and information services.

The aim of this book is to bring out the role of public library in modern society as well as role of technologies in libraries, in the present day information environment and their new challenges and promises for library services and information science. The book consist following chapters, Chapter One, Introduction Chapter Two Genesis and Development of Public, Libraries in India, Chapter Three Administrative Organization, Chapter Four Status of Collection of Reading Materials, Chapter Five Status of Manpower, Chapter Six Status of Financial Organization, Chapter Seven Status of Infrastructure, Chapter Eight Services Offered, Chapter Nine Resource Sharing and Network, Chapter Tenth: Historical Background of GIAN (General Information Access Network), Chapter Eleventh Sarve Shiksha Mission, Chapter Twelve Model for Integrated Public Libraries System, Chapter Thirteen Suggestions and Recommendations, book also include list of tables, maps, and glossary, which is helpful for information retrieval.

Hope, this book is useful for the students, Professionals, Researchers and Teachers of the library and information Science.

Prof. U. Chandra. Sharma
Professor,
Dept. of Library and Information Science,
Dr. H. S. Gour Vishwavidyalaya, Sagar (M.P.)

Preface

In modern society which is a knowledge based society depends on the production and efficient use of information through the libraries, specially developing country like India, where 70% population were living in rural areas, so public libraries plays a significant role to collect, storage and dissemination of information in ICT's age.

It had been dreams came true to present a book on Integrated Public Library System for India, especially the heart of India Madhya Pradesh and the role of concern authorities.

In this book, I have tried to touch various aspects of public library development in Madhya Pradesh, the role of public libraries in modern society, collection development, status of manpower, financial Organisation, status of infrastructure (Physical and ICT's), uses of computers, services provision, technical status of Divisional and District public libraries in state and also including comparative study for financial aspects, various committees and its recommendations on public library, which was appointed by Government of India and state governments. I also planned this volume to serve as a handbook for library professional to various queries regarding comprehensive information of public libraries in a state.

Electronic library are also established and working at District levels in state, these libraries are established under the Sarve Shiksha Mission, Madhya Pradesh under the General Information Access Network (GIAN) in the year of 2002 and financial assistance given by 12th year plan, both libraries are compared different parameters by IFLA standards for Public Library services and RRRLF Guidelines for Public Libraries.

In Madhya Pradesh both libraries established and have different collection formats, but it governed by two different entities i.e. Public Libraries under the Directorate of Public Instruction (DPI) and Electronic libraries the Sarve Shiksha Mission, so for these problem, proposed a Integrated Public Library System for Madhya Pradesh or GIAN Network, it should be applicable entire our country. If merge the both libraries in one entity in proposed plan, The proposed plan is totally based on the recommendation of National Knowledge Commission, 2005. so well called Public E-Library, The Public Libraries is offered different *fundamental services* like lending document for home reading, lending within the libraries, reference service, searching through catalogue cards and referral services to their users, but it can't offered *applied services like or IT based information services like* Current Awareness Service (CAS), Selective Dissemination of Information (SDI), Bibliography, Inter Library Loan, Online Searching, Indexing Service, Abstracting Service, Document Delivery Service, Translation Service, Online Services, Bibliography information of document, Blogs, feedback of library and Resourcing Sharing resource sharing among the libraries in entire state and create a consortia among the public libraries in state and as well as India. The library can be an effective facilitator of self learning through its extension service activities. It formed on the basis of experience and knowledge gained in the entire study.

Dr. Kapil Singh Hada

Acknowledgements

I would like to express my deep and heartfelt gratitude to the '*Almighty GOD*' for giving me health, wealth, strength and mind to accomplish this venture.

This humble attempt of mine owes. Its origin mainly to the inspiration and encouragement, I received from **Prof. V. N. Gautam, Vice Chancellor, Mahatma Gandhi Chitrakoot Gramodaya Vishwavidayalaya, Chitrakoot, Satna (Madhya Pradesh)**.

I am pleased to place my special debt of gratitude to **Prof Aditya Shastri, Vice Chancellor, Banasthali Vidyapith, Banasthali, Rajasthan,** for gave me a chance working at *Banasthali Vidyapith, Banasthali (Rajasthan)* is the Women University.

I would like to express my immensely thanks and respect to *Mr. Ramraj Karsoliya sir, Chairman, TIT Group of Institutions, Bhopal,* **Madhya Pradesh** to his support and encouragement to complete my project *(where, I was working from 2003 to 2010 as a Librarian)*. I can not express my regards and respect in words.

Dr. B. K. Dubey, Director-*TIT College of Pharmacy, Bhopal* to his support and encouragement to entire my project;

I must express my heartfelt for love, support, encouragement of my *Parents.* The accomplishment could not been achieves without unconditional love, support and prayer from them. Thank you, I have reached this place not my efforts alone, but also throughout yours support, love, guidance, patience and best wishes. To my precious Patricia your patient ears, interesting eyes and loving heart meant the world to me throughout this endeavor, you are my strength, love and you truly bring me a special meaning to the depth to my heart.

My heartfelt thanks to my wife *Nitu* for providing me moral support, everlasting encouragement is generous help for the success of my project and how can I forget to my son *Master Diviz ,* who bearing with equal measures of acceptance and irritation the presence of the project in my life, where my cheering squeal urging me toward.

I proudly place my accord to **Keith and keen** for their support, constant encouragement and eternal patience, without which this work would not have been possible.

I would like to special thanks to **Archna** for her support, guidance and encouragement in my entire work.

I thank all those who have helped me directly and indirectly in my pursuit and also all librarian and professional colleagues, who spent their precious time to fulfilling the questionnaires.

I am also indebted to the various authors, whose books and papers I have consulted or quoted in this work. I am thankful to all those seen or unseen hands and heads that have rendered direct or indirect help in the completion of this project.

Lastly, I would not be doing full justice without expressing my admiration and feeling towards the great ideals to **Mahatma Gandhi Chitrakoot Gramodaya Vishwavidyalay, Chitrakoot (M.P.),** institution, where I got the opportunity to study. I would make every attempt to imbibe and cherish the memories the same throughout my life.

Finally, I thank the publisher **Partridge Indian,** *A Penguin Random House Company, Bloomington IN 47 403,* who have willingly agreed to take up the work of this publication and also **Bert Solit**, Publishing Consultant and *Ann Minoza*, Publishing Service Associate, Partridge India, a Penguin Random House Company, Bloomington IN 47 403.

Dr. Kapil Singh Hada

List of Abbreviations

ADINET	: Ahmedabad Library Network
ASP	: Active Server Pages
BALNET	: Bangalore Library Network
BONET	: Bombay Library Network
CALIBNET	: Calcutta Library Network
CAN	: Cluster Area Network
CAN	: Controller Area Network
DAN	: Desk Area Network
DPL	: District Public Library
DELNET	: Developing Library Network
DYRC	: District Youth Resource Centres
e-Library	: Electronic Library
LAN	: Local Area Network
IFLA	: International Federation of Library Associations
IITA	: Information Infrastructure Technology and Applications
HTML	: Hyper Text Markup Language
IPLS-MP	: Integrated Public Library System-Madhya Pradesh
LAN	: Local Area Network
MAN	: Metropolitan Area Network
MALIBNET	: Madras Library Network
MAYIBNET	: Mysore Library Network
NAPLIS	: National Policy for Library & Information System
NLI	: National Library of India
PAN	: Personal Network

POTS	: Plain Add Telephone System
PUNNET	: Pune Library Network
RAM	: Random Access Memory
SAN	: Server Area Network
SAN	: Small Area Network
SAN	: Storage Area Network
SAN	: System Area Network
SLC	: State Library Committee
SSA	: Sarve Shiksha Mission
RRRLF	: Raja Rammohun Rai Foundation for Library
UEE	: Universal Elementary Education
UPS	: Uninterruptible Power Supply
WAN	: Wide Area Network

CONTENTS

List of Tables

List of Map

Chapter One

Library

Library is the giant brain of the humanity. It preserves the various thoughts of different minds, the lovely imaginings of sensitive brains, the wise and weighty counsels of sound and sagacious heads, in short, all the accumulated wisdom and knowledge of the hoary, dim and distant past. It links up hundreds and thousands of generations with one another and thus provides a panoramic picture of the humanity.

"A library is an institution charges with the
- Maintain a collection of documents;
- To making them accessible to those who require;
- Function of persuading every person within its jurisdiction to accept and continuously use its service.
- It is essentially a trinity of Document, Library Staff and Reader".[1]

Purpose of Library

"A library is a social institution. As such, it has to serve several purposes:
- Should help in life long learning, self education;
- Should provide up to date and pin pointed data and information on required subject or area;
- Disseminate and store all records, views, information and thoughts and discharge on local, national and international affairs;
- It should provides the latest trends in diversification of information to the researchers, designers, and technologies and also store every new thoughts, promptly and pin pointedly;
- It should encourage and provide use of leisure in library;

- It should preserve literary remains of humanity for posterity, as a vehicle of culture and as source material for antiquarian research; and in general;

It should work for continued social well-being as the agency in charge of all socialized recorded thought. Thus a library has educational, informational, political, economic, industrial, cultural and antiquarian research functions".[2]

The Public Library

A library established by the Government and which collects fees is considered to be a subscription library, although it serves the public as a public library. In order to function as a true public library, it must have two characteristics—it must render free services to all and it must be established from the public funds. We can't say that library serving the general public are public libraries. They could be either private or subscription libraries owned by voluntary organizations. Such libraries can also be classified as aided and non aided libraries. Some such libraries charge a membership fee and take deposits for home lending of library resources. These types of libraries extend their services to all its community members.

The public library acts as a catalyst for socio-economic development by providing facilities for acquiring knowledge, education, information recreation and research. It is rightly believed that where formal education ends, informal education begins and this life-long learning process continues with the support of public library services. The focus of a modern public library therefore remains on dissemination of information to the common man.

Definitions of Public Library

The phrase public libraries denotes, differently to different authors, which could be seen from the following definitions:

"William Ewart—The Libraries, which are established by the public, for the public and entertain the people with certain rules and regulations, are called Public Libraries".[3]

"Prof. Vishwanathan–The public provide free library service to all local community without any discrimination of color, caste and management is working under the local government with own expenditure and run by the appointed staff or committee by the local administration.".[4]

Ranganathan, S. R. (1960)—The term Public Library codified that:

- Any library established or maintained by a local library authority, including the traveling and service libraries;
- Any library open to the public free of charge and maintained and managed by the Government or by any local body;
- Any library notified by the Government as Public Library". [5]

"IFLA/UNESCO Public Library manifesto (1994)—depicts the meaning of the Public library as follows; "The Public Library is the local gateway and centre of information making all kinds of knowledge and information readily available to its users. The services of the public library are provided on the basis of equality of access for all regardless of age, race, sex, religion, nationality, language or social status, specific services and materials must be provided for those users who cannot for whatever reason, use the regular services and materials. All age group must find materials relevant to their needs. Collections and services have to include all types of appropriate media and modern technologies as well as traditional materials. High quality and relevant to local needs and conditions are fundamental. Material must reflect current trends and the evolution of society; as well as the memory of human endeavor and imagination".[6]

"The Sinha Committee (1959) placed Public Libraries in India as follows, "Public Libraries" is used in a very loose sense. It is used to denote any library which permits members of the public to use its materials for reference or borrowing on payment of fees or rent".[7]

"Johnson, Gerald—wrote in books Public Libraries Services – The quickest and easiest access to the world's best thought is through public library".[8]

"Encyclopedia of Library and Information Science (Kent and Lancour; 1987)—state that, "Public library is a public institution, supported by taxation, one that opens its collections, facilities and services without distinction to all citizens".[9]

"IGNOU 2003—Public library has been emerged as an important social institution. This social institution's set up and working is based on the definition of 'democracy'. It is for the people, by the people and of the people. In other words, a public library is freely open to all irrespective of age, race, sex, color, creed or religion and provides free access to each and every-one".[10]

"Thomas (1997)—"one which is authorized by legislation, open to the public without charge and financed out of public fund".[11]

"Librarian's Glossary defines Public Library as "a library provided wholly or partly from public funds, and the use of which is not restricted to any class of persons in the community best of freely available to all".[12]

The internationally accepted definition of a public library, It read as—it is a library which:
- It is totally depends on the public funds;
- No fee charges from the readers and it open for the public on equal basis;
- Is introduced, provide and prmote of self education;
- To provide information freely and without partiality on each and every subject and it will satisfy the interests of readers;

After the analysis of definition of public library, we can say that public library offers a wide range of reading material to fullfils every individual in the community or society. It is an institution which is promoting self-education and preserves our cultural heritage on priority basis. A public library called a "People's University", for it provides information to every citizen of the state and it has two important functions to entertain and to educated. Thus, the true concept and character of a public library can be summed up in the words of William Ewart who considered public library as that library is which if funded by the people;

supported by the people; and enjoyed by the people; and is established by the people; at public expense out of local rates and sometimes by state taxes. Hence, a library is a service institution.

The Objectives and Functions of Public Libraries

The primary objectives of establishing the public libraries or running Public library services in the country are to the achieve the following purposes:
- Preserve, store and promoting the knowledge, education and culture;
- To promote and strengthening the socialism, secularism, democracy and rule of law among the society;
- To free access to the users of without discrimination of race, colour, age, sex, nationality and language.

S. R. Ranganthan describes the following function of Public Library:
- Help in life-long education for all;
- To provide up-to-date data and information on all subjects;
- To distribute all sources of information which is available in recorded reviews and thoughts;
- To contribute in produced of information and management of latest trends to help for researchers, designers and technologists, every piece of relevant new thoughts promptly;
- Preserve and dissemination of literary remains the humanity for posterity as vehicles of culture and source materials for antiquarian research;
- Provide to one and all worthy and elevating use of leisure;
- To continued social well-being as the agency in-charge of all socialized thoughts".[13]

"**American Library Association** in its publication entitled Public Library Services. A guide to evaluation with minimum standards, points out the function of a Public Library as follows;
- To provide and promote information of all people in the community;
- To promote formal education those who involve in it and also enrich and further develop of the subjects;

- To meet the information need of all;
- To support the educational, civic, and cultural activities of groups and organization;
- To encourage whole some recreation and constrictive use of leisure time".[14]

"Public Library Enquiry Committee (UK) opines the following three functions like;

- To gather resources in order to promote and enlightened citizenship and enrich personal life;
- To provide reliable information to the community and
- To provide opportunities for self-education to children, young people, men and women".[15]

"The Robert Committee Ministry of Education (1959), UK enumerates the functions of the Public Library as follows;

- To provide to any reader or group the books and other related materials for which they wants;
- It is the function of the public library not only to satisfy, but to promote the desire for books . . . ;
- It is a centre for exhibition, lectures, adult education classes and discussion groups . . . ;
- The success of any library depends on properly qualified staff working in suitable premises and finally public library should be free libraries . . ."[16]

Types of Public Libraries

The public libraries can be classified according to their targets users, their level of operations and types of services offered to the public. The UNESCO Public library Manifesto states that, the public library network must be designed in relation to national, regional, research and special libraries as well as libraries in schools, colleges and universities. The public libraries however can be divided as follows:

- **National Library**
- **State Central Library**
- **Regional/Divisional Library**
- **District Central Library**
- **Taluk Library**
- **Branch Library**
- **Village/Town Library**
- **Delivery Station/Book Deposit Centre.**

National Library

It is the apex public library of a nation. The national library, Kolkatta (India) serves as the permanent repository all reading materials and information produced in India, as well as printed materials written in Indian and concerning India written by foreign wherever published and in whichever language.

State Central Library

It is the apex library of state located in the capital of the state. It has to play the role of a leader among the public libraries of the state. It should strive to establish standard procedures and guidelines for the effective functioning in the state. The State Central Library has to be the coordinating authority for the public libraries of the state. A State Central Library is a replica of a National Library. It performs the same functions and provides the same services for a State as a National Library does for the nation, except being different is its geographical character.

Regional/Divisional Libraries

It established to cater to the reading needs of a particular region division of a state, roughly comprising of an area of three to seven districts.

District Central Library

It is the apex libraries of a District, usually located in District headquarter. Books and other reading materials are purchased, technically processed and distributed to all public libraries in District by the District Library. The administration, inspection and monitoring of various public libraries located in the district are carried out by the District Central Library Authority. The District Central Library is the central hub of all the libraries located in the District.

Taluk Library

It is situated in a Taluk headquarter, serves the users living in any part of Taluk, a Branch Library is established in village/towns, which are exceeding a specified population limit say 5000. A Branch library caters to the reading needs of several other villages situated around the place in which the library is located.

Village/Town Library

It is being run for the benefit of the people living in a particular village/town.

The Delivery Station/Book Deposit Centre

It is an extension library of the nearby public library without any permanent stock of books. The libraries of the Delivery Station/Book Deposit Centre borrow a limited number of books around 500 from the parent public library which are lent to the members of Delivery Station/Book Deposit Centre. After utilization by the members, the borrowed books are returned to the parent public libraries and other set of books are borrowed for distribution to the members of respective Delivery station.

Conclusion:

It may be consider that the present chapter gave the basic information about the public libraries as per definitions, function, objective and types of public libraries.

References:

1. Thomas, V. K. *Public Libraries in India: Development and Finance* (New Delhi: Vikas Publishing House. 2006), 1.
2. Ibid., 1-2.
3. Sharma, S. K. *Pushkalaya Aur Samaj* (New Delhi: Granth Academic: 1998), 12.
4. Vyas, S. D. *Pushkalaya Aur Samaj* (New Delhi: Panchsheel Prakashan: 1998), 5
5. Ibid., 5
6. United Nations *Educational Scientific and Cultural Organisation. Public Library Manifesto*: Paris UNISIST Newsletter. 23(1), 1994.
7. *Advisory Committee for Libraries*, 1959 prepared by the Department of the Education Youth Affairs, (New Delhi, 1959).
8. Ibid., 1-2.
9. *Encyclopedia of Library and Information Science*, 24th ed., s.v. "salvation".
10. 1*Indira Gandhi National Open University*, 2003.
11. 1Ibid., 1-2.
12. 1Doerschuk, Ernest and Palmer, "Current Conceptions in State Aid to Public Libraries". *Library Trends* no. 9: 35-49.
13. 1Ibid., 1-2.
14. 1Ibid., 4.
15. 1Ibid., 5.
16. 1Ibid., 5.

Chapter Two

Genesis and Development of Public Libraries in India

Introduction

India is one of the most ancient of human civilization; thousands of years ago the built up a tradition of intellectual activity and developed great system of philosophy. It was on this soil that the great philosophical work like Vedas was composed. It was here the noble ideas expressed by great teachers of India found expression in stone and bronze in some of the artistic wonders that have inspired artistic traditions in various part of the world. The world and Asia in particular owe a great cultural debt to India.

"In the Buddhist period manuscripts were prepared with great care and it was deposited for preservation in libraries and the libraries were attached with temple, places or private houses of rich peoples. During 6th century B. C. Taxila was the main centre of learning and the library at Nalanda was the best equipped. The ancient India could boast of very rich and resourceful libraries"[1]. "Tipoo Sultan who was a linguist established a library containing many books in European languages. This library now part of the India office Library at London[2]. "In 1724, Maharaja Sowai Jai Singh of Jaipur was established a library which contained important books on astronomy"[3]. "Tanjore Saraswati Mahal Library which was established by Maratha Kings. The libraries contain 20,000 manuscripts written in Devnagri, Telegu, Malayalam, Bengali, Punjabi, Kashmiri and Uriya scripts, Out of this collection 8,000 volumes are on palm leaves"[4].

"The fashion of commercial circulating libraries went on well in the first three decades of the 19th century. The term 'Public Library' in the 19th century was used to denote 'only a subscriber or as a public project promoted by the Government'. Up to 1817, there were very few printing presses in India and consequently many libraries could be set up due to non-availability of published material. The era of transformation of libraries in India began towards the middle of the 19th century. During the first half of this century public libraries were established in the three presidency cities of Bombay, Calcutta and Madras. The libraries were mainly meant for British residents in India. These library were not free, but was supported by subscriptions and provided information and entertainment for thin upper layer of the society". [4]

"The fashion of commercial circulating libraries went on well in the first three decades of the 19th century. In fact, the seeds of the modern library movement can be seen in the first half of the 19th century. It was during this period that public libraries were established with the support of Europeans at Calcutta, Madras and Bombay". [5] "The term "Public Library" in the 19th century was used to denote "only a subscriber or as a public project promoted by the Government". [6] "These libraries were, however, mainly meant for British residents in India, and were not free, but supported by subscription and provided information and entrainment for the "thin upper layer of society". [7]

"In Bombay the movement began in 1808 when the Bombay government takes a proposal to register libraries which were to be given copies of books published from the funds for the encouragement of literature. In various state capitals of Saurashtra (now part of Gujarat) rulers and Europeans established or helped in establishing public libraries." [8] "The Indore General Public Library was founded in 1854. The credit of starting the public library movement of Indore, credit goes to Maharaja Tukoji Rao Holkar II. He founded the present Indore General Library in the Huzuriya Mahal of the Old Place and provided a donation of Rupees 500 and a recurring grant of Rupees 12 per month". [9]

"The oldest and premier public library known as a Kitab Ghar 1866, the rules of library were first published in 1884 and a catalogue of 2507 book printed in 1891. In 1909, occupies the present building situated in the heart of the city the Rajwada Chowk and finally June 8, 1948 the State Government handed over the building to the library".[10]

"The Khuda Baksh Oriental Public Library, founded at Patna in 1876. The library was owes its origin to Maulvi Muhammad Baksh Khan, who at the time of his death in July 1876 left a collection of 14,000 volumes".[11]. The Library has one of the richest collections in the world of ancient Persian, Arabic Manuscripts and Chinese, Central Asian, Persian and Indian Paintings. It was opened to public in 1891, in 1969, Government of India passed the Khuda Baksh Library Act, declaring it as an institution of national importance, took full financial and administrative responsibilities for it. The total collection of library is over 16,000 manuscripts, 90,000 old and rare printed books and over 2,000 paintings of the Mughal, Rajput, Iranian and Turkish Schools. Two others libraries deserving mention at this stage are the Hindi Sangrahalaya established in 1935 and having collection of 45,000 books and 5,000 manuscripts and the India Office Library located in London which had a collection of 70,000 valuable reference books in English and other languages.

"The Punjab Public Library, Lahore was set up in 1900. Being the first Central Library in Punjab, it occupies the most significant place in the history of libraries in India. The movement for the establishment of a public library system was first initiated in India in 1910, in the State of Baroda. To Sayajirao Gaikewad of Baroda, goes the credit for initiating a programme of free public library service throughout the state in the first decade of this century. The system consisted of a State Central Library, many branch libraries and traveling libraries with special provision for women and children and audio-visual section for the semi literates. Shri Motibhai Amin had already started the public libraries and reading rooms called "Mitra Mandal", libraries with the help of teachers in the year of 1906 and within two years 150 such libraries were established. Gandevi Public Library is the oldest library of Baroda State. It was established in 1865 and Baroda State library was founded in 1877".[12]

"In 1910, Dr. Wiliiam Alanson Borden spent three years in Baroda, where in addition to developing libraries, he started a library school, the first of its kind. It conducted the first ever formal library training course in India. A central library was established in the state capital, besides a network of rural and mobile libraries. By 1930, 85 % of Baroda's urban and rural population obtained access to libraries. In 1907 Sayajirao Gaikewad introduction of free primary compulsory education and linked every primary school with a free public library. It has also usual service section, including children's corners. This was the first children's library in India. It had a separate ladies section, under the system every town has a library and every village with a primary school also had a library".[13] "The Calcutta Public Library which had been functioning since 1835. The Calcutta Public Library was renamed as the Imperial Library (now the National Library of India) and was accessible to the general public".[14]

"Another important public library of this era was the Central Jain Oriental Library of Sri. Jain Siddhant Bhagwan at Patna (Bihar) founded in 1906. As one of the major Jainological research institute of northern India. It has one of the greatest collections of old manuscripts of rare religious books and is a notable centre for academic and research work".[15] "The Bhandarkar Oriental Research Institute, Pune was established in 1917. The institute is one of the pioneering institutes of Indology in India. The library of the Institute is specially known for its manuscripts collection. The society started publications of a journal entitled "The journal of the Bihar and Orissa Research Society", which was renamed as "The Journal of the Bihar Research Society".[16]

The All India Public Library Association was set up in 1920. The first all India Public Library Conference (in association with the Indian National Congress) was held in 1926 at Calcutta and first library van in India was inaugurated in 1931 in Mannargudi. "Bombay Presidency Public Library Bill empowering local bodies to levy a library cess and start libraries, but the bill was not taken up for consideration".[17]

In 1935, Andhra Pradesh started library service in boats instead of motor vans and this service was later extended to passengers traveling by boats in 30 villages. The service is called "Floating Library Service", and has produced good results. The government of Bengal sanctioned grants for rural and regional libraries in 1946-47 and a central library was set up in Banikpur. The first time in 1936 Government of Travancore allotted grants to libraries. The education minister of Cochin created a full-fledged Department of Libraries under a Director of libraries independent of the Department of Education, perhaps for the first time in the history of any Government in India.

The Connemara Public Library in Madras became the State Central Library in 1950 under the provision of Madras Public Libraries Act 1948, and became one of the three depository libraries in 1955. Delhi Public Library was established in 1951 as the first UNESCO Public Library Pilot Project under the joint auspices of UNESCO and Government of India to adopt "Modern Techniques to Indian Conditions" and to 30 serve as a model public library for Asia. (Kumbar). In 1954, the Delivery of Book Act was passed to include newspaper. The act obligated every publisher in India to deposit one copy each of its publications to the National Library in Calcutta, the Asiatic Society Library in Bombay, Connemara Public Library in Madras, and Delhi Public Library in New Delhi. Delhi Public Library became a copyright library in 1982.

"National Literacy Mission was adopted in 1986, which emphasized education for women and also establishment of rural libraries. Library networks and systems were strengthened at the national level institutions in the development of literature in neo-literates".[18]

The National Book Policy, 1986 also had an impact on libraries;

- Provision of reading material for children by all the agencies involved;
- That 10 percent of the annual education budget of the governments be used to purchase books for libraries.

These goals are to be achieved by using formal, non-formal, and open channels of earning. Rural libraries should become the focal point for post literacy and continuing educational programs. Publishers, voluntary organizations, and school library programs undertaken as part of the "Operation Blackboard Scheme" of the National Education Policy on Education, 1986 were given assistance. The following five libraries were regarded as national importance and may be stated in a very brief manner:

"National Library, Kolkata was established in 1836 name was Calcutta Public Library, when it was not a Government institution. Governor General, Lord Metcalf transferred 4,675 volumes from the library College of Fort William to the Calcutta Public Library. This and donations of books from individuals formed the nucleus of the library. Prince Dwarkanath Tagore was the first proprietor of the Calcutta Public Library. Both the Indian and foreign books, especially from Britain, were purchased for the library. In the report of 1850 we find that the library started collecting books in Gujarati, Marathi, Pali, Ceylonese and Punjabi. The Government of Bengal and North Western Provinces regularly made by individuals as well as donations. The Calcutta Public Library had the first public library in this part of country. Such a well-organized and efficiently run library was rare even in Europe during the first half of the 19th century, because of the efforts of the Calcutta Public Library. The Imperial Library was formed in 1891 by combining a number of Secretariat libraries. The most important library was Home Department, which contained many books formerly belonging to the library of East India College, Fort William and the library of the East India Board in London. But the use of the library was restricted to the superior officers of the Government. Lord Curzon, the then Governor General of India, was the person who conceived the idea of opening a library for the use of the public. He noticed both the libraries, Imperial Library and Calcutta Public Library, were under-utilized for the want of facilities or restrictions. So, he decided to amalgamate the rich collection of both of libraries. He was successful in effecting the amalgamation of Calcutta Public Library with the then Imperial Library under certain terms. The library, called Imperial Library, was formally opened to the public on 30ᵗʰ January 1903 at Metcalf Hall, Kolkata. The aims and objectives of the Imperial Library, well defined in a Notification in the 'Gazette of India' *as ' It is intended that it should be a library of reference, a working place for students and a repository of material for the future historians of India, in which, so far as possible, every work written about India, at any time, can be seen and read.*

John Macfarlane, the Asst. Librarian of the British Museum, London, was appointed as the first Librarian of the Imperial Library. After his death, the famous scholar and linguist Harinath De took over the charge of the library. After his death J. A. Chapman became the librarian. Mr. Chapman showed keen interest in the affairs of the library and worked hard to improve its status. After his retirement, Khan Bahadur M.A. Asadulla was appointed as the librarian and he continued as the librarian till July 1947. The policy of acquisition broadly adhered to by the Imperial Library was enunciated by Lord Curzon in his speech at the opening ceremony of the library, "The general idea of the whole Library is that it should contain all the books that have been written about India in popular tongues, with such additions as are required to make it a good all-round library of standard works of reference."

After the independence the Government of India changed the name of the Imperial Library as the National Library, with an enactment of the Imperial Library Act 1948 and the collection was shifted from the Esplanade to the present Belvedere Estate. On 1st February 1953 the National Library was opened to the public, inaugurated by Maulana Abul Kalam Azad. Sri B.S. Kesavan was appointed as the first librarian of the National Library. The reviewing Committee in its report of 1969 suggested that the following should be the basic features of the National Library; Acquisition and conservation of all significant printed materials produced in the country to the exclusion of ephemera:

Collection of printed materials concerning the country wherever published and also acquisition of photographic record of such materials that is not available within the country;

- Acquisition, preservation and conservation of manuscripts having national importance;
- Acquire foreign reading materials those required by the country;
- To provide and arrange bibliographical and documentation service of retrospective materials, both general and specialized;
- Acting as a referral centre to provide full and accurate knowledge of all sources of bibliographical activities;
- Provision of photocopying and reprographic services;
- Acting as the main centre for international book exchange and international loan. (National Library 2003)".[19]

"Khuda Bakhsh Oriental Public Library, Patna was open for the public in October 1891 with 4000 Oriental manuscripts. Maulvi Khuda Bakhsh donated his entire collection to the nation by a deed of trust. Acknowledging the immense historical and intellectual value of its rich and valued collection, the Govt. of India declared the Library as Institution of National Importance by an act of Parliament in 1969. The Library is now fully funded by the Ministry of Culture (Govt. of India). This autonomous institution is being governed by a Board with the Governor of Bihar as its ex-officio Chairman and Director is carrying the responsibility of day to day management of Library affairs."[20]

Rampur Raza Library, Rampur was founded by Nawab Faizullah Khan in 1774 AD. It was brought under the management of a Trust till the Government of 34 India took over the library on 1 July 1975 under the Act of Parliament, which declared it as an institution of National importance. It contains very rare and valuable collection of manuscripts, historical documents, specimens of Islamic calligraphy, miniature paintings, astronomical instruments and rare illustrated works in Arabic and Persian languages besides 80,000 printed books. Nawab Faizullah Khan who ruled the state of Rampur, from 1774 to 1794, established the library with his personal modest collection kept in the Tosha Khana of his Palace. Now the Library occupies the position of an autonomous institution of national importance under Department of Culture, Government of India and is fully funded by Central Government. The Library has now attained an International status of higher studies".[21]

"Thanjavur Maharaja Serfoji's Sarasvati Mahal Library, Thanjavur is one among a few medieval libraries existing in the world. It contains very rare and valuable collections of manuscripts, books, maps and paintings on all aspects of Art, Culture and Literature. The Encyclopedia Britannica in its survey of the Libraries of the world mentions this as "the most remarkable Library in India". The Library houses a rich and rare collection of manuscripts on art, culture and literature. Conceived and christened as the Royal Palace Library by the Nayak Kings of Thanjavur (1535-1675 AD). And the Maratha rulers (1676-1855) nourished it for intellectual enrichment. In 1918 this Library was made as a public Library. A body constituted by the Government and financed by the Central and State Governments now administers the library. During the reign of Nayaks of Thanjavur (1535-1675 A.D.), "Sarasvati Bhandar"(Collection place of Manuscripts) was formed and developed. The Maratha rulers who captured Thanjavur in 1675 A.D. patronized the culture of Thanjavur and developed the Royal Palace Library till 1855 A.D. The Sarasvati Bhandar was situated within the Palace campus and the Manuscripts used for the purpose of reading by the Royal personages. Among the Maratha Kings, King Serfoji II (1798—1832), was an eminent scholar in many branches of learning and with great enthusiasm he took special steps for the enrichment of the Library. It is a fitting tribute to the great collector Serfoji that the Library is named after him. Till the survival of the last Maratha Queen, the Library was the Palace property. After that, 35 the Library together with the Palace properties formed the subject of litigation in Civil Courts. The Royal Family members voluntarily came forward to delete this Library from the suit properties formed an Endowment and dedicated this Library to the public with one lakh rupees for its maintenance and upkeep. Accordingly, the Government of Madras in their G.O. Ms. No.1306 Home (Education) dated 5th October 1918, took possession of the Library under the Charitable Endowment Act and framed scheme for the Library management. In 1983, the Library was declared as an Institution of National Importance. The Government of Tamil Nadu abolished the Five Member Committee of administration and made it as a Registered Society as per G.O. 209 (EST) dated 1-2—83. The Society was constituted and got registration on 9-7-1986 under the Tamil Nadu Registered Societies Act of 1975. The Society consists of ex-officio members of Central and State Governments, nominated Scholars, Member from the Royal family and the Director of the Library. The Hon'ble Education Minister of the Government of Tamil Nadu is the ex-officio Chairman of this society".[22]

Harekrushna Mahtab State Library, Bhubaneswar was conceived during 1st Five Year Plan under the advice of Government of India and was completed in 1959, enshrined within a beautiful land of 3 acres in a prime location of Capital City of Bhubaneswar. In 1967, it was named as Gandhi Bhawan commemorating birth centenary of Mahatma Gandhi, the father of the nation. In 1987 it was renovated and entire space of the four storied building was utilized for the functioning of two Libraries i.e. State Library for the entire State of Orissa and another Public Library for Bhubaneswar City. In 1987, Government decided to rename the State Library and the Public Library as Harekrushna Mahtab State Library (in memory of Dr. Harekrushna Mahtab, the builder of modern Orissa) and the Bhubaneswar Public Library respectively. The former is a Reference Library and lending of books is not permitted whereas the latter is a Lending Library for the public of Bhubaneswar City. These two Libraries have managed to function over the limited space. Total readers seats available are about 350 against the present demands of 600-700 readers per day".[23]

After 1979 many state have taken initiatives in establishment of library legislation for providing public library services to the common citizens. A list mentioning the public libraries Act passed by states and UTs as per the official record is. Andhra Pradesh (Hyderabad) (1960) Arunachal Pradesh (2009); Bihar (2007); Chattisgarh (2007); Goa (1993); Gujarat (2001); Haryana (1989); Karnataka (Mysore) (1965); Kerala (1989); Maharashtra (1967); Manipur (1988); Mizoram (1993); Orissa (2001); Pondichery (2007); Rajasthan (2006); Tamil Nadu (Madras) (1948); Uttar Pradesh (2005); Uttarakhand (Uttaranchal) (2005) and West Bengal (1979).

Present Status of Public Libraries in India

The overall number of public libraries in India is 24 State Central Libraries, 451 Divisional and District Public Libraries, Sub-Divisional/Taluka/Tehsil Libraries 501, 1798 Development Block 5027 have Villages Libraries and 1280 towns have Town Libraries. Madras, Hyderabad, Bangalore and Delhi have City Public Library Systems with Central Libraries, their Branches and Deposit centres.

Growth and Development of Public Library in Five Year Plans:

All Five Year plans in India have emphasized the importance and necessity of education, especially higher education. There is brief information about the five year plan wise development in India.

First Five Year Plan: In First Five Year Plan of the Education Department, 1951-56, included the scheme of 'Improvement of Library Service'. This scheme envisaged a network of libraries spread all over the country. The proposal setting up at New Delhi a National Central Library was also made.

Second Five Year Plan: Under the Second Five Yeas Plan (1956-61) allocated 140 lakh for setting a countrywide network of libraries in 320 at district levels. As a result of this plan most of the States had several State Central Libraries and District Libraries as the main distributing centres and the Institute of Library and Information Science at the University of Delhi was also established.

Third Five Year Plan: In the Third Five Year Plan (1962-67) the Government of India has recognized that "an adequate system of any well-organized system of India further agreed that during current Plan steps were taken to set up or develop all the four national libraries at Delhi, Calcutta, Madras and Bombay. In this plan there were provisions also for strengthening libraries at District and Taluka levels. Other universities were provided with facilities for research in Library and Information Science and facilities for training the library personnel.

Fourth Five Year Plan: Under the current Plan the Planning Commission made an appointment of a working group on libraries consisting of eminent librarians and educationists of India with Professor V. K. R. Rao as its chairman to evolve a second programme of library development consistent with the needs and requirements of the country as well as it resources. This group prepared a scheme of a phased and coordinated programme for the foundation of a public library system, wherein the library was given the status of a sub sector.

Fifth and Sixth Five Year Plan: Under the Fifth and Sixth Five Year Plan, (1971-75) and (1976-80), subsequently, no working group for libraries was constituted.

Seventh Five Year Plan: During the Seventh Five Year Plan (1985-90), the Indian Governments, s proposed library development, stressed on the appointment of a working group on the modernization of the library services and informatics, under the Chairmanship of Dr. N. Seshagiri. The report was which was submitted in July 1984, has two parts, the first dealing the requirement of public, academic, special and national libraries, information centres and systems. The second parts deals with Informatics and computer applications; recommendation on computers culture in the library community; education and training, computerization of major libraries, constitution of a group to plan, design, monitor, and evaluate computerization of libraries-software development, a computer-based union catalogue, national bibliography, and developing a library network using computer and communication technologies. A provision of 996 crore was made for this purpose out of which 10 crore were made available for public, academic and special libraries; Rs. 70 –of Library Directorate and library association and its publications. Many of these proposals are being implemented.

Eight, Ninth and Tenth Five Year Plan: In the Eight Five Year Plan (1992-1997) the Government of India gave Rs. 2, 18,001 millions, Rs. 249084 million in Ninth Five Year Plan and Rs. 4, 38,250 million in Tenth Five Year Plan for the development of higher education in India but unfortunately nothing specific was mentioned shall be provided for the development of libraries of these institutions as compared to the first seventh fifth year plan. However, a new boast for the development of libraries can be seen in the recommendation made by the National Knowledge of Commission set up by the Government of India in 2005.

Recommendations of Various Library Committees

It is important to note the work and recommendations of various committees and commissions of the public libraries. A brief account of the recommendations of some important committee of public libraries is given below:

"The Sinha Committee: In 1957, the Government of India appointed an Advisory Committee, for Libraries under the Chairmanship of K. P. Sinha. The Committee submitted its report in 1958-59, which was published in 1961. The Committee reviewed the Library movement in India and added the following words. "The Mardas Library Act has justified the wisdom of those who brought it on the status book. The organization of library service appears to be more effective in Madras than in any other part of India, mainly on account of Library Act", with these words the committee has recommended library legislation for all the states and also recommended an integrated library services to be provided within 25 years is by 1984. It recommended for setting up a National Central Library at the apex with three National Libraries functioning at Calcutta, Madras and Bombay and it would be linked with the state central libraries and district libraries".[24]

"Report of Advisory Committee for Libraries 1970: It was suggested that "the needs for public libraries so conceived and dedicated has been felt all the more keenly in India after independence. There is a remarkable unanimity of opinion among all national leaders that facilities for reading books must be brought within the means of all citizens and particularly of villages. It is believed that this will prevent their world of learning from being limited to personal experiences and observations. Reading will widen their horizon beyond the barriers of space and time".[25]

"Gopal Rao Ekbote Committee: In Andhra Pradesh, a Committee was appointed in February, 1976 under the Chairmanship of justice Gopal Rao Ekbote, to review the working of the Andhra Pradesh Public Libraries Acts 1960 and to suggest necessary amendments to the Act. The Committee submitted its report in 1977. The committee also made several worthwhile recommendations on various aspects of public library system, in the light of experience of working of the Andhra Pradesh Public Library Act 1960. The Government of Andhra Pradesh has accepted the report of this Committee, but did not implement the recommendations.

"Shri Vavilala Gopalkirshnayya Committee: There was yet another committee appointed by Government of Andhra Pradesh in July 1978, under the Chairmanship of Shri Vavilala Gopalkirshnayya, to suggest measures for the improvement of private libraries (added libraries) and to evolve a system of grant-in-aid to the private libraries. It has suggested norms and procedures for identification, grant-in-aid, inspection, etc. of private libraries. The Government had accepted a majority of the recommendations of this Committee in 1982".[26]

"V. N. Subharayan Committee: In Tamil Nadu, a Library Reorganizing Committee was appointed in 1974, under the Chairmanship of Shri V. N. Subharayan. The Committee made valuable recommendations, following which a separate full time District Library Officer for each district has been provided to a administer the district library system. An official level committee headed by Sri S. Srinivasan, examined the implications of the recommendations of the Subharayan Committee and proposed in November 1978, sanction of family benefir fund, retirement fund and integrated library personal for the public library system in state".[27]

"M. S. Randhava Committee: The Government Jammu and Kashmir appointed a Commission vide its order no. 1867 CD in 1975 under Chairmanship of Prof M. S. Randhava, Department of Libraries, Research and Museum and also recommend improvement which is necessary to run the department on scientific lines. The Commission submitted its report on 10th August 1975. Unfortunately the Government did not take action on the report".[28]

"National Policy on Library & Information System (NAPLIS): In 1985, a committee was set up under the chairmanship of Prof. D.P. Chattopadhyay to formulate a National Policy on Library & Information System (NAPLIS). The Committee submitted its report in May 1986. The Empowerment Committee submitted its report in April 1988 and an Implementation Cell was formed to implement its recommendations within a period of six months. Yet another Working Group, under the Joint Secretary to the Government of India in the Department of Culture, was constituted to examine its recommendations for implementation. The Working Group submitted its report in July 1993 and suggested implementing only 29 of 60 recommendations made by the NAPLIS.

The following are some of the recommendations of NAPLIS related to Public Libraries:

- The maintenance and development of public libraries should come from State Legislative Enactment. The Central Government may revise the Model Public Library Bill. Funds for library development and it should be discussing with each state, either from general revenue or from local taxation. Central Government must provide funds under Plan Expenditure;

- Should emphasize on rural public libraries. Every village should have a community library/rural community centre cum information centre. Resources from various agencies engaged in the public health, adult education, State and central government, etc., should be used to build up and maintain this centre;

- The central government increases its assistance to state governments in the development of public libraries. The RRRLF, as the national agency for coordinating and assisting the development of public libraries, should be suitably strengthened in order to do this.

- Standards and guidelines for library service should be created;

- There should be a system of national libraries consisting of National Library, Calcutta (Now Kolkatta) as the National Library of India, National Depository libraries in Delhi, Bombay (Now Mumbai), Madras (now Chennai), National Subject Libraries, and others. These national libraries should form part of one integrated system;

- National Commission on Libraries and Information System or National Commission on Informatics and Documentation may be constituted by an Act of Parliament to serve under the Ministry of Human Resource Development. The Commission will have representation from appropriate central and state agencies and could provide guidance and coordinate library development programmes in all sectors and it will have the primary responsibility for the implementation of NAPLIS programmes;

- National Depository libraries; Connemara Public library, Chennai; Central Library (Asiatic Society), Bombay; and Delhi Public Library, Delhi should concentrate on development of collections and preservation of Indian culture produced in the languages of their regions, supplementing and complementing the efforts of the Indian National Library;

- Should be preparing an Indian National Bibliography and should be updated regularly and National Library should responsible for it;

- Government should create a national awareness of the need to preserve the nation's cultural heritage. National libraries should be responsible, with preservation facilities created there. Links between

46

libraries, archives, and museums should be established for the purpose of national preservation;

- Should be eastalibshed a community centre in every Panchayat Centre and Ministry of Rural Development is responsible.
- Should be established a link between community centre library and primary schools. If the schools do not have libraries of their own, the community centre library should provide children with adequate services and it should plays a important role in adult education programmes;
- District library should provide facilities and recreation for the disabled and low-income people.
- Libraries should be built in areas of tribal and minority communities to help in developing and sustaining their distinctive cultures;
- Libraries should be equipped with relevant resources, such as publications covering Open University and vocational educational courses, for their supportive role in distance education;
- Should be form a library network for public library with in a state and it extending up to village library cum community centre and district library, and should be linked to the national network;[13]

National Knowledge Commission"[29]

The following are some of the recommendations National Knowledge Commission for Libraries:

Library and Information Science Policy:
- Libraries should be included in Concurrent List of the Constitution of India by an Act passed by Parliament and the development of public library is a state subject, the legislative framework in many states is not enough support to provide the required legal support and financial;
- Should be forming a National Commission on Libraries for a period of three years, which should be converted into a permanent Commission.
- Data on the status of libraries at the national level is largely lacking, making any kind of realistic planning impossible, so for this purpose

a national census of all libraries should be prepared by undertaking a nationwide survey under the Department of Culture;

- A survey of user needs and reading habits should be conducted at the national level;
- The LIS education and training (including in-service) should be revised as per new education policy and environment and NML must assess manpower requirements for the LIS education, and take necessary measures to meet out the requirement for future;
- An Institution for Advanced Training and Research in LIS and Services should be set up.

Finance:
- A specified percentage of the Central and State education budgets must be allocated for libraries. A Central Library Fund should be instituted to take care of upgrading existing libraries over a period of 3-5 and around must be Rs. 1,000 crores and fund should be administered by NML

Library Management:
- All institutions/ organizations that run their own libraries to ensure that they meet the objectives and compile a library charter for each library;
- Each library must have a collection relevant to its user community and e-resources are also essential part of collection.

The basic expectations from libraries of all types (public, academic, national, and special) include:
- identifying potential users;
- analyzing users' needs;
- developing services for groups and individuals;
- introducing customer-care policies;
- promoting user education;
- cooperating and sharing resources;
- developing electronic network-based services;
- To provide attractive and functional library buildings with Pleasant, aesthetic and functional ambience;

- To provide access to knowledge and resources of a diverse user community.

All libraries in India must have the following facilities:
- Trained and adequate staff
- Easy access and user-friendly retrieval systems;
- Appropriate furniture, stacking and display facilities;
- Effective signboard for library;
- Internet access, scanners, photocopiers, etc.;
- Drinking water, cafeteria (for larger libraries) and clean toilets.
- All libraries should collect and maintain data on various activities and submit the data periodically to a central evaluation agency.
- It is necessary to involve different stakeholders, including civil society and user groups, in the managerial decision-making;
- Libraries should develop special collections and services for the disables;
- To prepare the Union Catalogue of reading materials books, journals, magazine;
- To promote exchange of information between the public libraries and as well as national and international level networks;
- To offer computerized services to users, participating libraries and cumulative effort for collection development for unnecessary duplication;
- In rural areas Community Knowledge Centre should be established in each and every library;
- Recognizing the role of reference service for the information needs of individuals and set up a centralized collaborative virtual enquiry handling system using ICT;

Private Collections:
- Should be set up a National Committee for identification, documentation and preservation of the private collections;
- it is suggested that Ten Regional Centres be set up by the Government of India in different parts of India to house selected and approved private collections. These centres should be located in Delhi, Kolkata,

Guwahati, Pune, Bangalore, Hyderabad, Chennai, Ahmedabad, Patna and Jammu.

Digitization and Open Access:
To create digital resource of historical important this can be shared among the public

Peer-reviewed published research papers which funded by publicly must be made available through open access;

- All pre-independence periodicals and newspapers in all Indian languages and in English must be digitized;
- State should establish archives of knowledge-based digital resources and make it accessible.
- **Staffing Pattern**

It is necessary to assess the manpower requirements for different types of libraries and departments of library and information science, keeping in mind job descriptions, qualifications, designations, pay scale, career advancement, service conditions, etc.

Public Private Partnerships
Philanthropic organizations and other private agencies should be encouraged to support existing libraries set up by the government or set up new libraries.

"Raja Rammohan Roy Library Foundation and Public Libraries"[30]

The Genesis
Raja Rammohun Roy Library Foundation (RRRLF) was established in May, 1972 by the Department of Culture, Govt. of India to spread library services in the country and that year was also celebrating silver jubilee of our independence and also year of birth Raja Rammohun Roy, a social reformer who had stressed the need for modern education for the progress of the nation and was being celebrated as an International Book Year with the slogan BOOKS FOR ALL to promotion of reading habit among the masses.

The Foundation

RRRLF is an autonomous organization established and fully funded by Government of India and it registered under the West Bengal Societies Registration Act, 1961. It is the nodal agency to support library services, systems and promote public library movement in the country. The committee is called foundation, which consists of 22 members nominated by the Government of India from amongst eminent educationists, librarians, administrators and senior officials. The Minister of the Department of Culture is nominees the Chairman of RRRLF. The Foundation works with State Library Planning Committee (SLPC/SLC) set up in each State and Union Territory. To participate in Foundation's programmes, a State Government/U.T. is required to contribute a certain amount to the Foundation. Since 2005-06 it is also develop District Youth Resource Centre in collaboration with Nehru Yuvak Kendra Sangathana, under the Ministry of Sports & Youth Affairs.

Objectives of RRRLF

RRRLF has function as a promotional agency, an advisory and consultancy organization a funding body for public library development in India. The listed 29 objectives are:

- to promote the library movement in the country;
- to form a library policy and to work towards its adoption by the Central and State governments;
- to help build up a national library system by integrating the services of the National libraries, the state central libraries, the district libraries, and other types of libraries children's, academic and special) through inter-library lending system;
- to promote awareness adoption of library legislation in those states, where it is not adopted ;
- to provide financial and technical assistance to libraries, library association and NGO, who engaged promotion library development in the country;
- to support compilation and publication of directory of libraries, union catalogue, Subject bibliographies and documentation lists;
- to establish regional library service centers;

- to advice the Government of India on all matters pertaining to library development in the country.

Activities:

Assistance Programme: RRRLF promotes public library services book and financial assistance under different schemes of assistance, schemes is known as matching and non-matching schemes.

District Youth Resource Centres (DYRCs): The DYRCs is assisted for the following purpose:
- To building up adequate stock of books.
- To acquiring storage materials and library furniture, computers.
- To construction library building.

Promotional Activities: It is also responsible to promote for qualitative improvement of library services, to organize seminars and conferences and also to prepare a National Policy on Library and Information System. It has issued guidelines on public library systems and services. RRRLF have also cooperation and collaboration with many national and international professional associations like IFLA, ILA, IASLIC and different state level library associations. The Foundation introduced Annual Raja Rammohun Roy Award to the best contributor of an article related Public Library Systems and Services or suggesting measures for promotion of reading habit. The Foundation has also giving seven awards one for the best State central Library and six for the best District Libraries of six regions in the country. Since 2005 the Foundation also introduced RRRLF Best Rural Library Awards-one per each state. The Foundation provide "RRRLF Fellowship" to offer fellowship five eminent men and women, who have contributed to the library movement in the country through active involvement in the movement, organizational initiative, leadership and reading habit among the masses.

Research Project: A research cell along with a special library on Library & Information Science and a statistic unit supported by a computer unit are providing necessary input to its various activities. About 5000 important books and journals on Library & Information Science and allied fields have been acquired in the library, besides carrying on Research Projects on public library or allied subject, the Research Cell renders advisory and consultancy services whenever required. It has prepared and published a report on loss of books in libraries for the Government of India.

Publication of RRRLF: The publications are;
- Indian Libraries : Trends and Perspectives;
- Raja Rammohun Roy and the New Learning;
- Directory of Indian Public Libraries;
- Granthana, Indian Journal of Library Studies (bi-annual);
- RRRLF Newsletter (bi-monthly);
- Annual Report;
- Books for the Millions at their Doorsteps (Information Manual)

Modernization Programme: The Foundation have a computer lab with latest ICT equipment to data-bank of Public Libraries for the country. It connected via inter office LAN with Internet facilities.

The Foundation has taken long strides in promoting library services in the country. With the expanded activity during the 9th Five Year Plan (1997-2002) the total Plan grant reaches Rs. 3233.00 lakh against Rs. 1175.70 lakh during the 8th Five Year Plan from the Govt. of India with an average annual plan grant @ Rs.646.60 lakh and state contribution reaches Rs. 1977.00 against Rs. 645.97 lakh during the 8th Five Year Plan with an average annual contribution @ Rs.395.40 lakh. During the year under report, the third year of the 10th Five year Plan, the plan grant stepped up to Rs.1150.21 lakh including a special grant of Rs.150.21 lakh for North-Eastern states and contribution received from various state governments also reached Rs.769.59 lakh. Consequently the amount of assistance rendered to libraries during the year under report also reached Rs.1756.29 lakh against the annual average of Rs.701.20 lakh during the 9th Five Year Plan.

At the instance of the Foundation, every State/U.T. has set up State Library Planning or State Library Committee

The SLCs will particularly decide:

- The number and categories of libraries for assistance under different schemes, mode of preparation of consolidated list(s) of books for different categories of libraries;
- To purchase of books to be selected under different subject headings;
- Collection of books through advertisement of physical verification and other related matters;
- Setting up of a committee or sub-committee for book selection, if considered necessary.
  (i) The SLCs will approve list(s) of books and the list of libraries at the second meeting. The mode of purchase, rate of discount and distribution of books will also be decided at this stage taking into consideration the guidelines of the Foundation in this regard.
  (ii) Selection of books and libraries shall be the responsibility of the State Library Committee and this fund is allotted by foundation to each and every SLC.
  (iii) The Convener of SLC shall forward the following documents to the Foundation:
- Copy(s) of the Minutes of SLC;
- List of selected libraries together with full postal address under the seal and signature of the convener;
- Copy(s) of the valid order placed on the supplier(s);
- Certified bill(s) or bill with acknowledgements;
- List of selected titles duly signed on each page by the convener with office seal."

Panchayats and Public Libraries

The Panchayat is one of the most gross root levels of government authorities and it is also one of the rare groups, which communicates directly to the people also, hence there is a certain amount of vigilance and alertness levels which the Panchayat should maintain as a legal authority. For these reference and queries related to the people the government has made provisions for the setting up of libraries across the country. These libraries are the centres of learning for the people of the village and also for the Panchayat.

The subjected as listed in the 11ᵗʰ Schedule for Panchayats include also **'Libraries' (item no 20) which obviously means 'Public Libraries'.** The state governments have been empowered to decide whether Public Libraries will be placed under the Village Panchayat, Samiti Panchayat or the Parishad Panchayat under the all the three in their respective areas.

After X Schedule in the Constitution, Schedule XI (Article 243 G) shall be treated as included, Agriculture. Including agricultural extension; Land improvement, implementation of land reforms, land consolidation and soil conservation; Minor irrigation, water management and watershed development; Animal husbandry, dairy and poultry; Fisheries; Social forestry and farm forestry; Minor forest produce; Small-scale industries, including the food processing industries; Khadi, village and cottage industries; Rural housing; Drinking water; Fuel and fodder; Roads, culverts, bridges, ferries, waterways and other means of communications; Rural electrification, including distribution of electricity; Non-conventional energy sources; Poverty alleviation programme; Education, including primary and secondary schools; Technical training and vocational education; Adult and non-formal education; **Libraries;** Cultural activities; Markets and fairs; Health and sanitation, including hospitals, primary health centres and dispensaries; Family welfare; Women and child development; Social welfare, including welfare of handicapped and mentally retarded; Welfare of weaker section and in particular of the SC/STs; Public distribution system; Maintenance of community assets.

The Panchayat is also able to enhance the knowledge of the members of their groups along with providing fair judgment to the people of the village. Also these libraries contain books on history, medicine, legalities and other story and fiction books also. The collection of books here are usually in the native language and even though the books her are limited they provide some knowledge to the people in the village. These books can help the villagers as sources of entertainment or for providing valuable information. These books are usually in the native languages of the district to ensure that more people are able to read the same. It is not possible to remember every small thing that you learn from school or college. Hence the library is the ideal method of encouraging that knowledge and also for finding various aspects of life, subject and issues, which are of the past or present also, and for the villagers these libraries are the god of knowledge.

For the present study gave related some review of literature in given below:

Review of literature is an essential requirement for any field of research as it is necessary for a scholar to know well in advance the quantum of literature unfolded on a particular subject. This helps the scholar to be aware of the ground already covered, so that he may proceed further in the right direction.

"In the words of Berg "the literature in any field forms the foundation open which future work will be built. The author further observes that if we fail to avoid this foundation of knowledge provided by the review of literature, our work is likely to be shallow is naïve will often duplicate work that has already been done better by someone else".[31]

"According the Best "Since effective research is based upon past knowledge, this step helps to eliminate the duplication of what has been done and provides useful hypothesis and helped and helpful suggestion for significant investigation".[32]

"Review according to West Dictionary (1987) is to "examine again, study critically, general survey, critiqued. In research, review of related literature means to conduct general survey of related studies, to analyze then critically and put them logically such that certain form works dimensions can emergence based the a research can look for missing limit in the chain of knowledge continuum".[33]

The purpose of review of literature:

- It shows whether the evidence already available serve the problem adequately without further investigation and thus to avoid the risk of duplication;
- It provides ideas, theories, explanation hypothesis valuable in formulating the problem;
- It suggest the methods of research appropriate to the problem;

- It locates comparative data useful in the interpretational research;
- Review bridges the gap between the new and the old knowledge. This bridging helps the researcher to have a certain uses systematic knowledge about the content and make his/her concepts clear;
- Review of a good no of area based studies can prove to be very helpful in enabling a researcher to understand how various issues have been studied by research in different part of the world.

Review of Literature

Thus keeping in view the above mentioned advantage the researcher has reviewed the related literature of this study are conducted in India. Through a few studies on e-library and digital libraries, most of these studies seem to have been done on public libraries. **Some of such studies that deserve mention are as under:**

"**Lajari, Somraya Rayappa (1983)** finds that the present public library System is not good for further development for Public Library in the state, so find some new developmental plan for the Public Library System in the state".[34]

"**Singh, Jagtar (1986)** was tried to propose and established a rural public library system, suggested a model for these and also gave direction to further development a network. The proposed network should be connect public library and as well as rural public library within state".[35]

"**Padhi and Panda (1988)** Apprising the origin and development of Harekrushna Mehtab Public Central Library of Orissa, have informed that "the incidence of use of the library is unprecedented in the annals of public library development since perhaps no other library in the country can claim to have attracted 4 to 5 hundred readers per day within a few days of its opening".[36]

"**Konar, Satyaangsu Sekhar (1990)** attempt to find out come what are the changes in the development and progress of public libraries in the state after the implementation Library Act, critical study of present public library Act and also further gave suggestion to improvement in the public library Act".[37]

"Singh, Thaunaojam khomdon (1991) find that present system of public library in the state, what is future planning for the further development of the present public library system and also proposed the library legislation for the state".[38]

"Nigam, Bir Singh (1993) described that what the public library is and emphasized on the important of mass communication in library and information science. It is further find that impact of mass communication on the libraries, library services, library staff and we improve our library system, library services help of mass communication".[39]

"Chandra, H. (1994) Rural Information System: Design and Development. In this study we know about the rural libraries their objective, aim, working pattern of this libraries, and also get information about rural information system. This system is useful for get information about the rural area of India. We know about the social problems, their requirement, and present condition of rural area. This system is beneficial for the government planning and implementing their policies, schemes for rural area".[40]

"Nanddwana, H. A. (1994) find that what is public library and their services, mission and objectives and social contribution in the development of society, and also found the public library system of Madhya Pradesh, how is the works, how we improvement the public library system of Madhya Pradesh".[41]

"Ijari and Khan (1996) have informed that through the State Central Library of Karnataka State of Bangalore was providing lending facilities in the beginning as per the provisions of the Karnataka Public Library act, 1965, the State Central Library was designed as State Central Reference Library by the State Government in 1986 and the lending facilities were discontinued".[42]

"Ohdedar (1996) has made a critical analysis of the establishment and functioning of the State Central Library of West Bengal at Kolkata and laments that "Obviously, from the very start, the Sate Central Library has deviated from its intended function and carried on only as reference library without any connection with the state Library System".[43]

"Khanna (1996) in his study summarizes the past and present of the Delhi Public Library and argues that since no public library in India has as many multifarious activities as Delhi Public Library has its ambit which certainly entitles Delhi Public Library to be the National Public Library of India".[44]

"Bajpai, R. P. (1998) in this study we know about the rural libraries their objectives and services also get information about the rural libraries of Madhya Pradesh. In Madhya Pradesh what is the purpose behind the established the rural library. How these libraries are beneficial of our community in the development".[45]

"Shukla, S. P. (1998) in this study we find that public libraries is play vital role in adult education services for their community. The adult education is very essential part of new education system. With the help of public library, we can do aware to masses about the adult education".[46]

"Sharma, R. K. (1999) in this study it found what is the public library, their services, their mission and vision, social responsibilities of public library and present status of public library in Madhya Pradesh and also found proposed networking plan for resource sharing and their services".[47]

"Kumar, Sunil (2003) it gave information about the role and important of rural library in India and discuss particularly states, where public library acts is implemented. The rural libraries play an important role in development of rural community. It is also discussing that problem of rural libraries in these states also".[48]

"Majumdar, Swapna (2003) it gave information about the state where public library acts is implementing and also gave comparative study of all public library acts. It is gave information about efforts to implementing public library acts in all state of India, where the public library act is implemented".[49]

"Manjunatha and Shivalingaiah (2003) revealed that in the age of digital evaluation escalating price of electronic information, resource sharing is critical for effective functioning of libraries. Increased availability of information in digital format and high costs of journal subscription compels the libraries to work together. Technical advancements provide a platform for digital resource sharing and offer many opportunities for librarians to become more technical and professional. His work also attempted to identify the needs and factors influencing the electronic resource sharing and presented requirements and strategies for effective resource sharing in academic libraries".[50]

"Tiwari, Ramakant (2003) it gave information about the state where public library acts is implementing and also gave comparative study of all public library acts. It is gave information about efforts to implementing public library acts in Madhya Pradesh".[51]

"Umajee, P. Nelha (2003) in this study we find that about finance pattern of public library in Nagpur District of Maharashtra. The finance is playing a crucial role of development and strengthens for the public libraries. It also finds service of the library and also improving in the future".[52]

"Inamdar (2004) stated that the conventional libraries are now in transforming phase. The techniques of accumulation / gathering of information, processing it and way of disseminating it among the readers have also drastically been changed. The librarians, there for, have to get acquainted with the new trends of fruitful training on library automation and electronic information handling which they are lacking. An attempt has been made to draw a strategic plan for electronic information handling for library professionals. He also suggested some points to the librarian for information handling technology strategy are undertake a systematic assessment of readers information competence to develop a bench mark, develop a model list of information competence skills for readers, develop pilot information competence programs of course, utilize computer software that enables the librarians for information competence and develop a workbook and checklist to assist the subordinates for information competence".[53]

"Pandey, Vinita (2004) in this study we find that what is the public library and role of these libraries in the development of the nation. How the public libraries are beneficial for rural development programmes of the government. Also know the about the particular area of Jabalpur, these area are benefited from the public library and information centre".[54]

"Ghosh (2005) The current situation of Indian public libraries has been viewed by some as follows: the public library system in India is condemned to remain peripheral to the actual information needs of the masses; that it is in a depressed state, and serves as little more than a warehouse of recreational reading materials, a majority of which are in regional languages. This paper suggests possible remedies on how to transform the situation, and details new technological developments which are already showing the potential to change public libraries in rural India for the better".[55]

"Mishra, Jagdish Kumar (2006) in this study we find that historical background effort to implementing library legislation in Madhya Pradesh, get the information about different library act in India and model library act for Madhya Pradesh".[56]

"Talakeer, A. (2006) It find that the ICT's is very essential for any community in present time and it is also affect the every aspects of life so libraries is change their role, so Information Technology is very beneficial for the development of rural population and as well as the Rural community".[57]

"Singh, Kapila and Pateria (2007) stated that the concept of library is changing very fast due to impact of ICT. Now the libraries will not have only printed collections but also digital resources, which are not seen physically. The technology has forced the library to digitize information. Keeping in view of all this libraries will need redefining or reengineering as they may be named as Knowledge Management Centers, Cyberary, Ebrary, Virtual library, Digital Library. No doubt technology will play major role in changing the shape of libraries in the time to come yet basic material will remain the same. Whatever the technology may come and find use in the library for the benefit of users to access the information as a fast mode of communication and whatever nomenclature may be given to library, but it is a hardly matter that the print media will hold the vein of library for the society".[58]

"Kumar, Ashok (2007) ascertains the present status of public libraries in the state with special reference to the rural libraries of the state. In the study also find the services given by rural libraries and how beneficial for their users".[59]

"Imchen, A. I. (2007) it is describe the how the public library system works in state and further explain the role of public library as a Community Information Centre in state, further it was also explained the how public library is beneficial to their users as Community Information Centre and we convert these public libraries as a Community Information Centres".[60]

"Rao, Chandrashekhar (2007) describes that the how the beneficial of Regional public libraries towards education, eradication of literacy in the state. It is also finding the present status of Regional Public Libraries, their services, user satisfaction towards services given by these libraries".[61]

"Sridevi, J. (2007) it is provided information about the rural libraries in state. It find that the provision and pattern of services of rural libraries and also gave some suggestion to further improvement to the public library system especially towards to rural Libraries of state".[62]

"Tankir, Ama (2007) it is describe the how the public library system works in state and further explain the role of public library as a Community Information Centre in state, further it was also explained the how public library is beneficial to their users as Community Information Centre and we convert these public libraries as a Community Information Centres".[63]

"Vijay Kumari (2007) these study revel that public libraries have been functioning as daily routine work to meet the information needs of the society. Public libraries are establishing for the social cultural and educational development of the society and its main purpose is to give and serve the society in their various development activities viz. education, economic, socio-cultural activities, health, employment etc. This is an accepted fact that public libraries play a vital role for socio-cultural and educational development of the society in which the government has a lot to do".[64]

"Vinayagamurthy, P. (2007) had finds the Digital Library initiative taken by the Engineering Educational Institution in Tamil Nadu, the present status of Library towards Digital Library, and latest services provided by these libraries to their user".[65]

"Dhiman and Goswami (2008) emphasized the need of traditional libraries in digital age. Today, libraries are moving towards digital age, but the importance of traditional libraries cannot be ignored. It highlights some of the problems of digital libraries in digital environment. They also stated that digital libraries, virtual libraries or electronic libraries may provide better services and quick information to their users, but this is the fact that still there is a need of traditional libraries due to our economic condition, literacy rate an un-acquaintance and unwillingness of readers in using the electronic resources, traditional libraries will remain be an essentially to play its social and cultural role in much better sense than digital, electronic or virtual libraries".[66]

"Jani, A. K. (2008) ascertain that the present status of public libraries where the public library act was passed and Implementating. The data shows that the condition of public libraries is better than the others stats where public libraries is not implanted, also working in good shap and supported by their governments".[67]

"Kala, C. K. (2008) it is describe the how the public library system works in state and further explain the role of public library as a Community Information Centre in state, further it was also explained how we implementing e-Governance with the help of public libraries and it is also benefit to the general community of society and convert these public libraries as a Community Information Centres".[68]

"Krishnamurthy, C.K. (2008) ascertain that present status of public library system in state, their services, user satisfaction towards services and gave some suggestion and future planned towards restructuring for public library system in state. It was also beneficial to the authorities to further development of public library system".[69]

"Nagartinkhama, R. K. (2008) find the role and present status of District Public Libraries, services provided by these libraries and also find how these libraries useful and gave the their contributions towards development of socio-cultural for the society".[70]

"Naik, A. K. (2008) the study about the public library act of Goa, where public library implementing. It is a critical study of Goa public library act and also gave the some suggestion to better function of public library in the state".[71]

"Upadhyay, M. M. (2008) the find present status of rural libraries in the state, services provided by these libraries, also gave some finding the further development and proposed plan for the Rural Information System for the state as well as the rest of India".[72]

"Ganesh, Y. (2009) it finds the present status of public library in Island, their services, role of libraries in eradication of illiteracy, future plan for the development of public libraries, how public libraries act as community information centre for their community and proposed plan for the further development of public library in the Island".[73]

"**Lalresiari (2009)** it is defined what is the village libraries and role of these libraries. It also defined role of village libraries in development of society. The village libraries play an important role in development of rural community".[74]

"**Pradhan, Debashish (2009)** it find that how public library systems work and also further discussing about services given by the public libraries in Darjeeling District of West Bengal state. But it is different study from the other studies; it is analysis the service of public library for information marketing point of view".[75]

"**Sharma, P. L. (2009)** the find the present status of public libraries in tribal areas, the services given to the users, find the role of rural libraries education in rural areas, discuss about the proposed plan for development rural libraries and proposed plan for public library system in Rajasthan".[76]

"**Wani (2009)** had finds the current structure public library system in the states of Haryana, Jammu and Kashmir and Punjab and also find the present status of Public Library, developmental plan, their structure, their services and future planning in the states".[77]

"**Kapse, Santosh (2010)** had finds the comparative study of public library act where state where public library acts is implementing and also gave comparative study of all public library acts. It is gave information about efforts to implementing public library acts in Madhya Pradesh".[78]

"**Nagartinkhuma, N. K. (2010)** these study revel that public libraries have been functioning as daily routine work to meet the information needs of the society. Public libraries are establishing for the social cultural and educational development of the society and its main purpose is to give and serve the society in their various development activities viz. education, economic, socio-cultural activities, health, employment

etc. This is an accepted fact that public libraries play a vital role for socio-cultural and educational development of the society in which the government has a lot to do".[79]

"**Kumar, Dhiran P. (2011)** had finds the role and important of community information for development to rural community and as well as information needs. It is further find that the rural libraries serve as community information centre".[80]

Conclusion

Analysis of all these literature reviewed above that, these studies concentrate on Public Library, Historical Development of Public Library, Public Library Act, Public Library System, Public Library as a Community Information Centre, State Central Libraries, District Public Libraries, Rural Public Libraries, Development of Rural Information System and Proposed Network for Rural Libraries. Thus none of studies seem to be comprehensive in their approach to the Public Libraries as an electronic library, as we assume that combination of Public Library and e-library is called as Public e-library for the people, by the people, of people and via electronic way. It is combination of traditional public library as well as electronic library it called Public e-library. This library to open for the people, to collect, storage and disseminated the information in traditional way via electronic form.

References:

1. Vyas, S. D. Pushkalaya Aur Samaj (New Delhi: Panchsheel Prakashan: 1998), 64.
2. Ibid., 65-66.
3. Ibid., 69.
4. Ibid., 70.
5. Mishra Jogesh., History of Libraries and Librarianship in Modern India (Delhi: Atma Ram and Sons: 1979), 19.
6. Ibid., 19.
7. Sadhu, S. N. and B. N.Saraf. Library Legislation in India: A Historical and Comparative Study (New Delhi: Sagar Publications, 1967), 4.
8. Ibid., 71.
9. V. S. Moghe, "'Public Libraries of Indore Souvenir': (paper presented at the annual meeting for the ILA XVIL All India Library Conference, Indore, December 27-30, 1968).
10. ibid., p. 68.
11. Mishra, "Library Movement in Bihar". Herald of Library Science 189, no.4 (1964).
12. Bhatt, R. K. Libraries in India: Collection to Connectivity (New Delhi: Ane Books, 2011), 58.

13. Kaula, P. N. "Library Schools in India". Herald of Library Science 308, no.4 (1966).

14. Ibid., p. 4.

15. http://www.jainmanuscripts.nic.in/arrah.aspx.

16. http://www.bori.ac.in/library.html

17. Mishra Jogesh., History of Libraries and Librarianship in Modern India (Delhi: Atma Ram and Sons: 1979), 45.

18. www.mhrd.nic.in

19. http://www.nlindia.org/history.html

20. http://kblibrary.bih.nic.in/default.htm

21. http://razalibrary.gov.in/index.asp

22. http://www.sarasvatimahallibrary.tn.nic.in/library/library.html

23. http://hkmsl.gov.in/glance.htm

24. *Advisory Committee for Libraries*, 1959, prepared by Department of the Education Youth Affairs, (New Delhi, 1959).

25. *Advisory Committee for Libraries*, 1970, prepared by the Ministry of Education (Delhi: 1970).

26. Gopal Rao Ekbote Committee, 1970, prepared by Ministry of Education (Hyderabad, 1970)

27. Subharayan, V N. Committee, 1974, prepared by Ministry of Edcuation, Madras, 1974.

28. Committee on National Policy on Library & Information Systems, 1986, prepared by Department of Culture, Report. (New Delhi, 1986).

29. www.knowledgecommission.gov.in/download/NKC_Library.pdf

30. www.rrrlf.nic.in

31. Berg, S. (2005)

32. Best, R. C. Research in Education (New Delhi: PHI.2005), 4.

33. West Dictionary. London: Oxford University Press, 1987. West, John.

34. Lalaresisami. "Role of Village Libraries in Development: A Case Study of Mizoram" (PhD diss. University of Mizoram, 1983).

35. Singh, Jagtar. "Rural Public Library Network in Punjab: A study". (PhD diss. Panjab University, 1986).

36. Pandhi and Panda. "Harekrushna Mahtab State Library: An Appraisal". CLIS Observe. (1988).

37. Konar, Satynnangsu Sekhar. "Impact of Public Library Legislation on the Socio-Economic Development of West Bengal: A Critical Study". (PhD diss. University of Burdwan, 1990).

38. Singh, Thaunojam Khomdon. "Public Library System in Manipur and How to Develope it by Library Legislation". (PhD diss. Manipur University, 1991).

39. Nigam, Bir Singh. "Mass Communication and Public Libraries: A Critical Study of Delhi Public Library System". (PhD. Diss. Sambalpur University, 1993).

40. Chandra, Harish. "Rural information System: Design and Development".(PhD diss. Jiwaji University, 1994).

41. Nandwana, H. V. "Public Library System in Madhya Pradesh". (PhD diss.Vikram University, 1994).

42. Ijari, S. R. and Khan, (1996). H. A. State Central Reference Library, In Gupta, B. M. (Ed), Handbook of Libraries, Achieves and Information Centers in India: Library Development in India. vol. 16 (pp. 293-301). New Delhi, India: Segment Books.

43. Ohedkar, A. K. (1996) State Central Library, West Bengal. In Gupta, B. M. (Ed). Handbook of Libraries, Achieves and Information Centres in India: Library Development in India. Vol.16 (pp. 331). New Delhi, India: Segment Books.

44. Khanna, S. N. (1996). Delhi Public Library: Past, Present and Future. In Gupta, B. M. (Ed). Handbook of Libraries, Achieves and Information Centres in India: Library Development in India. Vol. 16 (pp. 236-49) New Delhi, India: Segment Books.

45. Bajpai, R. P. "Bharatvarsh Me Gramin Pushtkalaya Sewa: A Critical Study with Special Reference to Madhya Pradesh". (PhD diss. Mahatma Gandhi Chitrakoot Grammoodaya Vishwavidyalaya, 1998).

46. Shukla, S. P. "Role of Libraries in Adult Education: A Study with Special Reference to Madhya Pradesh". (PhD diss. Mahatma Gandhi Chitrakoot Grammoodaya Vishwavidyalaya, 1998).

47. Sharma, Ramkant. "A Critical Study of Public Library Services in Madhya Pradesh: Model Plan for Resource Sharing and Networking". (PhD. Diss. Guru Ghasidas University, 1999).

48. Kumar, Sunil. "Rural Libraries and Community Information Centres in India with Special Reference to States having Library Legislation: Problems and Prospects". (PhD diss. Jiwaji University, 2004).

49. Majumdar, Swapna. "Public Library Acts in India: A Comparative Study". (PhD diss. University of Kolkatta, 2003).

50. Naik, A. K. "Public Library Legislation in Goa: A Critical Study". (PhD diss. Pune University, 2008).

51. K., Manjunatha and Shivalinaiah. "Electronic Resource Sharing in Academic Libraries". Annals of Library and Information Studies, no.50.

52. Tiwari, Ramakant. "Bharatiya Rajoyan Ke Pushtakalaya Adhiniyam Ka Adhayan: Madhya Pradesh Main Pushtakalaya Adhiniyam Ki Annuvarti Evam Bhavisha". (PhD diss. Guru Ghasidas University, 2008).

53. Umajee, Pandurmin Nalhe. "Working and Finance of Aided Public Libraries in Maharashtra with Special Reference to Nagpur District. (PhD diss. University of Nagpur, 2003).

54. Inamdar, S.A.N. "Digital and Electronic information handling in libraries". Indian Journal, Information library and Science. no.17 (1-2), 2004.

55. Pandey, Vinita. "Gram Viaks Me Sarvakanik Pushtkakalaya Avm Scuhana Kendra Ki Bhumika (Jabalpur Ka Gram). (PhD diss. Mahatma Gandhi Chitrakoot Grammoodaya Vishwavidyalaya, 2004).

56. Ghosh, Malabika, (2005). Need for the Conservation Activities in State Central Library, In Proceedings of the National Seminar on Public Library Movement, Chennai. Tamil Nadu, Directorate of Public Libraries, Chennai, pp. 236-249.

57. Mishra, J. K. "Madhya Pradesh Mai Granthalaya Adhiniyam Hatu Prayas: Eke Athiasik Sinhovalokan Evam Bhavi Sambhavniya". (Ph D diss. Vikram University, 2004).

58. Talakeer, A. "Role of Public Libraries and Community Centre and their Services to Society in Vidhrabha Region of Maharashtra State". (PhD diss. Sant Gadge Baba Amravati University, 2006).

59. Singh, Balwan, Kapila, and Pateria, Rajive. University Libraries in Digital Environment: vision 2020. ILA Bulletin, no. 43(3).

60. Kumar, Ashok. "Public Library System and Services in Tamil Nadu: A Case Study of Urban and Rural Libraries". (PhD diss. Madras University, 2007).

61. Imachen, A. T. "A Study of Public Libraries System as Community Information Centre in Nagaland: Reedits and Challenges". (PhD diss. University of Guhawati, 2007).
62. Chandrashekhar, Rao. "Functioning of Regional Public Libraries in Andhra Pradesh: A Study". (PhD diss. Andhra University, 2007).
63. Sridevi, J. "Provision and Pattern of Rural Libraries and Informal Services in Uttar Pradesh with Special Reference to Jhansi District". (PhD diss. University of Jhansi, 2007).
64. Tankir, Amit. "Role of Public Libraries as Community Centres and their Services of Society in Vidarbha Regional of Maharashtra State". (PhD diss. Augrandabad University, 2007).
65. Vijay Kumari. "Public Library System and Socio-cultural, Political Movement during Freedom Movement in Circar area of Andha Pradesh: A Study". (PhD diss. Andhra University, 2007).
66. Vinayagamurthy, P. "Public Library System and Socio-Cultural Political Movement during Freedam Movement in Circar areas of Andhra Pradesh: A Study". (PhD diss. Andhra University, 2007).
67. Dhiman, Anil Kumar and Goswami, Ravinder. "Conventional or traditional libraries in digital era". Library Progress (International), no 28 (1), 2008).
68. Jani, A. K. "Comparative Study of Public Library Acts of Various States of India". (PhD diss. 2008).
69. Kala, C. K. "Public Libraries as Community Information Centres in Relation to e-governance to Madhya Pradesh". (PhD diss. Vikram University, 2008).
70. Krishnamurhty, C. K. "Restructuring the Public Library System in Karnataka". (PhD diss. University of Karnataka, 2008).
71. Ngurthinkhuma, R. K. "An Assessment of Role of State and District Libraries in the Socio-Cultural in Educational Development of Mizoram". (PhD diss. University of Mozoram, 2008).
72. Upadhyay, M. M. "Design and Development of an Information System for Rural Development". (PhD diss. Mahatma Gandhi Chitrakoot Grammodaya Vishwavidyalaya, 2009).
73. Ganesh, P. "Public Library and community Information Centres: A Development Plan for Adman and Nicobaar Island". (PhD diss. Jiwaji University, 2008).

74. Lalaresisami. "Role of Village Libraries in Development: A Case Study of Mizoram". (PhD diss. University of Mizoram, 2009).

75. Pradhan, Debashish. "An Assessment of Public Library System and Services in Darjeeling District of West Bengal for Information Marketing Points of View". (PhD diss. University of Brudawan, 2009).

76. Sharma, P. L. "Role of Libraries in Upliftment of Education in the Rural Area: with Special Reference to the Tribal Areas of Rajasthan". (PhD diss. Mohanlal Sukhadia University, 2009).

77. Wani, A. "Public Library System in Haryana, Jammu and Kashmir and Punjab". (PhD diss. University of Kashmir, 2008).

78. Kapse, Santosh. "Bharat Ka Rajiyo Ka Pustakalaya Abiniyam ka anubhav Ke Aadhar Par Madhya Pradesh Le Liya Eke Aadrash Saarvajanik Pustakalaya Abdiniyam ka Nirman". (PhD diss. Makhanlal Chaturvedi National University of Journalism and Communication, 2010).

79. Nagartinkhuma, N. K. "An Assessment and Role of State and District Public Libraries in the Socio-Cultural and Educational Development in Mizoram". (PhD diss. University of Mizoram, 2010).

80. Dhiran, P. Kuamr. "Community Information Service: A study of Information Needs of Rural Community in Shivamoga District". (PhD diss. Kuvempuuvi University, 2011).

Chapter Three

Administrative Organization of Public Libraries in Madhya Pradesh

Introduction

The present chapter depicts the administrative organization of Public Libraries and e-Libraries under the Sarve Shiksha Mission in Madhya Pradesh. Present Status of Public Libraries in Madhya Pradesh

Public Libraries governed by two Different Departments Directorate of Public Instruction and e-libraries under Sarve Shiksha Mission.

No	Categories of Public Libraries	Number
1.	State Central Library	01
2.	Divisional Central Libraries	04
3.	District Public Libraries	50
4.	E-Libraries (Under the Sarve Shiksha Mission)	50
5.	Branch Libraries	381
6.	Delivery Station	13985
7.	Rural Libraries (Under the Panchayat and Social Welfare Department)	507
6.	Rural Libraries (Under the Sarve Shiksha Mission)	47100

Table 3.1 Present Status of Public Libraries in Madhya Pradesh

Table 3.1 reveals that the state has 01 State Central Library in State Capital of Bhopal, 04 Divisional Central Libraries, 36 District Public Libraries,

50 e-libraries established under the General Information Access Network (GIAN) project by the Sarve Shiksha Mission in Madhya Pradesh, 381 Branch Libraries, 13985 Delivery Stations, 507

Rural Libraries under the Panchayat & Social Welfare Department and 47,100 Rural Libraries (Under the Sarve Shiksha Mission).

At present in Madhya Pradesh 50 District is exist, but only 36 District Public Libraries are in working, so government should take a further step to establish remaining 14 District Public Libraries in state.

The total no of Tehasils in state is 272, but there is no Public Libraries are still established at Tehasils places, so government also opens the public libraries at Tehasils places, so required total no of public libraries at Tehasils place is 272, and also Development Blocks in state is 313, but there is no Public Libraries is exist, so government take initiate to opens public libraries at Blocks places, so required public libraries at Blocks is 313.

Name of Districts	No. of Libraries	Name of Districts	No of Libraries	Name of Districts	No of Libraries	Name of Districts	No of Libraries
Bhopal	496	Datia	572	Chhindwara	1652	Panna	767
Sehore	978	Hoshangabad	870	Seoni	1485	Chhatrpur	956
Raisen	1220	Harda	452	Mandla	973	Tikamgarh	870
Rajgarh	1496	Indore	9217	Dindori	603	Dewas	871
Vidisha	950	Dhar	1490	Balaghat	1102	Ratlam	1057
Betul	1320	Jhabua	1311	Rewa	1454	Shajapur	1065
Sheopur	486	Khargone	1323	Shahdol	780	Mandsour	899
Morena	698	Badwani	649	Anuppur	565	Neemuch	492
Bhind	883	Khandwa	649	Umaria	578	Ujjain	1088
Gwalior	604	Burhanpur	252	Sidhi	1822	Shivpuri	1300
Jabalpur	1245	Satna	1410	Guna	1005	Katni	829
Sagar	1777	Ashoknagar	700	Narsinghpur	990	Damoh	1994

Table 3.2 Rural Libraries under the Save Shiksha Mission

Table 3.2 shows the status 47,100 Rural Libraries under the Sarve Shiksha Mission in Madhya Pradesh, the rural libraries working in 42 district of state.

The total no of villages in state is 55,393, but populated villages are 52,143, but 47,100 rural libraries is established under the Sarve Shiksha Mission in Madhya Pradesh, these rural libraries are still working in 42 District, so further required of village libraries in 5043 in remaining Districts.

Authority of Public Library in State

In Madhya Pradesh Public Libraries (Divisional & District) governed by Directorate of Public Instructions, Rural Libraries governed by Panchayat and Social Welfare and e-libraries and Rural Libraries is governed by Sarve Shiksha Mission.

Working Hours and Holidays

The Public Libraries of Madhya Pradesh remains open all the day thought year excepting State and National Holidays.

Information about Working Hours and Holidays of Public Libraries:

No.	Place of District Public Library	01 April to 30 September		01 October to 31 March		Working Hours	Weekly Holidays
1.	Ashoknagar	NR	NR	NR	NR	NR	NR
2.	Damoh	07.30 A.M. 05.30 P.M.	10.30 A.M. 08.30 P.M.	08.00 AM 05.00 P.M.	11.00 A.M. 08.00 P.M.	06.00 Hours	Ever Third Saturday and Govt. Holidays
3.	Dewas	07.30 A.M. 05.30 P.M.	10.30 A.M. 08.30 P.M.	08.00 AM 05.00 P.M.	11.00 A.M. 08.00 P.M.	06.00 Hours	Ever Third Saturday and Govt. Holidays
4.	Gwalior	07.30 A.M. 05.30 P.M.	10.30 A.M. 08.30 P.M.	08.00 A.M 05.00 P.M.	11.00 A.M. 08.00 P.M.	06.00 Hours	Ever Third Saturday and Govt. Holidays
5.	Hoshangabad	07.30 A.M. 05.30 P.M.	10.30 A.M. 08.30 P.M.	08.00 AM 05.00 P.M.	11.00 A.M. 08.00 P.M.	06.00 Hours	Ever Third Saturday and Govt. Holidays
6.	Indore	NR	NR	NR	NR	NR	NR
7.	Jabalpur	07.30 A.M. 05.30 P.M.	10.30 A.M. 08.30 P.M.	08.00 A.M. 05.00 P.M.	11.00 A.M. 08.00 P.M.	06.00 Hours	Ever Third Saturday and Govt. Holidays
8.	Katni	NR	NR	NR	NR	NR	NR
9.	Khargone	07.30 A.M. 05.30 P.M.	10.30 A.M. 08.30 P.M.	08.00 A.M. 05.00 P.M.	11.00 A.M. 08.00 P.M.	06.00 Hours	Ever Third Saturday and Govt. Holidays

10.	Panna	07.30 A.M. 05.30 P.M.	10.30 A.M. 08.30 P.M.	08.00 A.M. 05.00 P.M.	11.00 A.M. 08.00 P.M.	06.00 Hours	Ever Third Saturday and Govt. Holidays
11.	Rajgarh	07.30 A.M. 05.30 P.M.	10.30 A.M. 08.30 P.M.	08.00 A.M. 05.00 P.M.	11.00 A.M. 08.00 P.M.	06.00 Hours	Ever Third Saturday and Govt. Holidays
12.	Ratlam	07.30 A.M. 05.30 P.M.	10.30 A.M. 08.30 P.M.	08.00 A.M. 05.00 P.M.	11.00 A.M. 08.00 P.M.	06.00 Hours	Ever Third Saturday and Govt. Holidays
13.	Reewa	NR	NR	NR	NR	NR	NR
14.	Sagar	07.30 A.M. 05.30 P.M.	10.30 A.M. 08.30 P.M.	08.00 A.M. 05.00 P.M.	11.00 A.M. 08.00 P.M.	06.00 Hours	Ever Third Saturday and Govt. Holidays
15.	Satna	07.30 A.M. 05.30 P.M.	10.30 A.M. 08.30 P.M.	08.00 A.M. 05.00 P.M.	11.00 A.M. 08.00 P.M.	06.00 Hours	Ever Third Saturday and Govt. Holidays
16.	Sidhi	07.30 A.M. 05.30 P.M.	10.30 A.M. 08.30 P.M.	08.00 A.M. 05.00 P.M.	11.00 A.M. 08.00 P.M.	06.00 Hours	Ever Third Saturday and Govt. Holidays
17.	Tikamgarh	07.30 A.M. 05.30 P.M.	10.30 A.M. 08.30 P.M.	08.00 A.M. 05.00 P.M.	11.00 A.M. 08.00 P.M.	06.00 Hours	Ever Third Saturday and Govt. Holidays
18.	Ujjain	07.30 A.M. 05.30 P.M.	10.30 A.M. 08.30 P.M.	08.00 A.M. 05.00 P.M.	11.00 A.M. 08.00 P.M.	06.00 Hours	Ever Third Saturday and Govt. Holidays
19.	Umaria	NR	NR	NR	NR	NR	NR
20.	Vidisha	07.30 A.M. 05.30 P.M.	10.30 A.M. 08.30 P.M.	08.00 A.M. 05.00 P.M.	11.00 A.M. 08.00 P.M.	06.00 Hours	Ever Third Saturday and Govt. Holidays
21.	Bhopal	07.30 A.M. 05.30 P.M.	10.30 A.M. 08.30 P.M.	08.00 A.M. 05.00 P.M.	11.00 A.M. 08.00 P.M.	06.00 Hours	Ever Third Saturday and Govt. Holidays
22.	Singrauli	NR	NR	NR	NR	NR	NR
23.	Khandwa	07.30 A.M. 05.30 P.M.	10.30 A.M. 08.30 P.M.	08.00 A.M. 05.00 P.M.	11.00 A.M. 08.00 P.M.	06.00 Hours	Ever Third Saturday and Govt. Holidays
24.	Burhanpur	NR	NR	NR	NR	NR	NR
25.	Neemuch	NR	NR	NR	NR	NR	NR
26.	Balaghat	NR	NR	NR	NR	NR	NR
27.	Shivpuri	07.30 A.M. 05.30 P.M.	10.30 A.M. 08.30 P.M.	07.30 A.M. 05.30 P.M.	10.30 A.M. 08.30 P.M.	06.00 Hours	Ever Third Saturday and Govt. Holidays
28.	Shajapur	07.30 A.M. 05.30 P.M.	10.30 A.M. 08.30 P.M.	07.30 A.M. 05.30 P.M.	10.30 A.M. 08.30 P.M.	06.00 Hours	Ever Third Saturday and Govt. Holidays
29.	Betul	07.30 A.M. 05.30 P.M.	10.30 A.M. 08.30 P.M.	07.30 A.M. 05.30 P.M.	10.30 A.M. 08.30 P.M.	06.00 Hours	Ever Third Saturday and Govt. Holidays

30.	Narsinghpur	07.30 A.M. 05.30 P.M.	10.30 A.M. 08.30 P.M.	07.30 A.M. 05.30 P.M.	10.30 A.M. 08.30 P.M.	06.00 Hours	Ever Third Saturday and Govt. Holidays
31.	Morena	07.30 A.M. 05.30 P.M.	10.30 A.M. 08.30 P.M.	07.30 A.M. 05.30 P.M.	10.30 A.M. 08.30 P.M.	06.00 Hours	Ever Third Saturday and Govt. Holidays
32.	Guna	07.30 A.M. 05.30 P.M.	10.30 A.M. 08.30 P.M.	07.30 A.M. 05.30 P.M.	10.30 A.M. 08.30 P.M.	06.00 Hours	Ever Third Saturday and Govt. Holidays
33.	Datia	07.30 A.M. 05.30 P.M.	10.30 A.M. 08.30 P.M.	07.30 A.M. 05.30 P.M.	10.30 A.M. 08.30 P.M.	06.00 Hours	Ever Third Saturday and Govt. Holidays
34.	Mandusar	07.30 A.M. 05.30 P.M.	10.30 A.M. 08.30 P.M.	07.30 A.M. 05.30 P.M.	10.30 A.M. 08.30 P.M.	06.00 Hours	Ever Third Saturday and Govt. Holidays
35.	Sehore	07.30 A.M. 05.30 P.M.	10.30 A.M. 08.30 P.M.	07.30 A.M. 05.30 P.M.	10.30 A.M. 08.30 P.M.	06.00 Hours	Ever Third Saturday and Govt. Holidays
36.	Raisen	07.30 A.M. 05.30 P.M.	10.30 A.M. 08.30 P.M.	07.30 A.M. 05.30 P.M.	10.30 A.M. 08.30 P.M.	06.00 Hours	Ever Third Saturday and Govt. Holidays
37	Harda	NR	NR	NR	NR	NR	NR
38.	Chhindwara	07.30 A.M. 05.30 P.M.	10.30 A.M. 08.30 P.M.	08.00 A.M. 05.00 P.M.	11.00 A.M. 08.00 P.M.	06.00 Hours	Ever Third Saturday and Govt. Holidays
39.	Seoni	NR	NR	NR	NR	NR	NR
40.	Bhind	NR	NR	NR	NR	NR	NR
41.	Chhatrpur	NR	NR	NR	NR	NR	NR
42.	Badwani	NR	NR	NR	NR	NR	NR
43.	Dhar	07.30 A.M. 05.30 P.M.	10.30 A.M. 08.30 P.M.	08.00 A.M. 05.00 P.M.	11.00 A.M. 08.00 P.M.	06.00 Hours	Ever Third Saturday and Govt. Holidays
44.	Jhabua	07.30 A.M. 05.30 P.M.	10.30 A.M. 08.30 P.M.	08.00 A.M. 05.00 P.M.	11.00 A.M. 08.00 P.M.	06.00 Hours	Ever Third Saturday and Govt. Holidays
45.	Shahdol	07.30 A.M. 05.30 P.M.	10.30 A.M. 08.30 P.M.	08.00 A.M. 05.00 P.M.	11.00 A.M. 08.00 P.M.	06.00 Hours	Ever Third Saturday and Govt. Holidays
46.	Mandla	07.30 A.M. 05.30 P.M.	10.30 A.M. 08.30 P.M.	08.00 A.M. 05.00 P.M.	11.00 A.M. 08.00 P.M.	06.00 Hours	Ever Third Saturday and Govt. Holidays
47.	Anuppur	NR	NR	NR	NR	NR	NR
48.	Dindori	NR	NR	NR	NR	NR	NR
49.	Sheopur	NR	NR	NR	NR	NR	NR
50.	Alirajpur	NR	NR	NR	NR	NR	NR

Table 3.3 Working Hours and Holidays of Public Libraries

From the Table No 3.3 is reveals about the working hours and holidays of Public Libraries under Directorate of Public Instructions. It shows that the working hours of the libraries is different, from 01 April to 30 September is opening hours in the morning 7.30 AM to 10.30 AM and in evening 5.30 PM to 8.30 PM and from 01 October to 31 March is opening hours in the morning 08.00 AM to 11.00 AM and en evening 05.00 PM to 08.00 PM. The libraries are closed all Government holidays.

Chapter Four

Status of Collection of Reading Materials

"A particular service and reading materials should be provided those users who cannot, use the service and reading materials.

All the readers, who belongs any age groups must find reading materials which fulfill their needs. Reading collection and services, which provided by appropriate media and latest technologies as well as traditional materials. The reading material is fulfilling local needs and condition is fundamental need and it is also latest and helps in the evolution of society, which belongs to human endeavor and imagination.

The collection and services should be neither unfair on from the ideological, political or religious censorship, nor commercial pressures."[1]

Categories of Library Materials:

The public library should provide a wide range of materials which available in different formats and in sufficient quantity to meet the needs and interests of the community. The following categories of library materials must be available in any public library;

"Fiction and non-fiction for adults and children, reference works, access to databases, periodicals, local, regional and national newspapers, information related to community, government it including local, administrations, business, local history resources, genealogical resources and thesis resources is available in local language of any community, resources in other languages, and minority languages in the community, music scores, computer games, toys, games, puzzles and study materials."[2]

Format of Library Materials in Public Library

"The following formats may be included in a public library collection and new formats are continually appearing: books, e-books, pamphlets and ephemera, newspapers and periodicals including cuttings files, digital information through the Internet, online databases, CD-ROM databases, software programmes, microforms, tapes and CDs, DVDs, videocassettes, laser discs, large print materials, braille materials, audio video books and posters."[3]

"Standards for Book Collections"[4]

The following proposed standards relate to book collections.

> *In a general rule to established book collection should be between 1.5 to 2.5 books per capita.*
> - *The minimum stock should not be less than 2500 books.*
> - *If a new library should be established with a minimum stock of 1.0 book per capita.*

In the smallest collections materials for children, adult fiction and adult nonfiction may be provided in equal proportions and in large library the percentage of non-fiction titles will tend to increase. These ratios can vary according to the needs of the local community and the role of the public library.

The following examples suggest the size of book stock for communities of different sizes."[5]

Scenario 1
- Should established library service serving for 100 000 population;
- Median book stock of 200 000 volumes;
- Annual acquisition of 20 000 volumes

Scenario 2

- Should established library service serving for 50 000 population;
- Median book stock of 100 000 volumes;
- Annual acquisition of 11 250 volumes

Scenario 3

- Should established library service serving for 20 000 population;
- Median book stock of 40 000 volumes;
- Annual acquisition of 5000 volumes.

Collection of Reading Materials of Divisional Public Libraries:

No.	Place of Divisional Public Library	Books	Newspapers	Magazines	Average Availability Of Reading Material for Per Person	Total Collection	Non Book Material
1.	Gwalior	1,14,000	15	23	0.69%	1,14,000	-
2.	Indore	60,000	12	19	0.024%	60,000	60
3.	Jabalpur	30,000	05	07	0.013%	30,000	-
4.	Rewa	30,000	04	06	0.152%	30,000	-
5.	Bhopal	65,000	12	08	0.035%	65,000	300
Grand Total		**299000**	**48**	**63**	**0.18 %**	**299000**	**360**

Table 4.1 Collection of Reading Materials of Divisional Public Libraries

From the Table No 4.1 the collection finds out of *05 Divisional Public Libraries in Madhya Pradesh.* Posses a total book stock of **2, 99, 000,** The total number of collection of Divisional Public Libraries ranges from **30000 at Jabalpur to 1, 140,00 at Gwalior.** The ascending order of number of books stocked in Divisional Public Libraries proceeds as follows: **Gwalior (1,14,000), Bhopal (65,000) and Indore (60,00).** The descending order of number of books stocked in Divisional Public Libraries proceeds as follows: **Jabalpur (30,000) and Rewa (30000).**

The average available of reading materials for every person is calculate here, where reading materials is available i.e Gwalior (0.69%), Indore(0.024%), Jabalpur (0.013%), Rewa (0.0152%) and Bhopal (0.035%).

It revealed that the availability of reading materials to every person is average mere about 0.18 % and it is not satisfactory.

From the Table No 4.1 Divisional Public Libraries also have *48* titles of *News papers* and *63* titles of *Magazines.*

From the Table No 4.1 Divisional Libraries also have non book materials, but it is available only *02 libraries i. e. Bhopal (300) and Indore (60).* The percentage of non-book materials compared to the total collection of Divisional Public Libraries in insignificant is *0.12 %.*

Collection of Reading Materials of District Public Libraries:

No.	Place of District Public Library	Books	Newspapers	Magazine	Non Book Material	Average Availability Of Reading Material for Per Person	Total Collection
1.	Damoh	7000	05	04	NA	0.0064 %	7000
2.	Dewas	7466	06	-	NA	0.005%	7466
3.	Gwalior	9845	15	23	NA	0.60%	9845
4.	Hoshangabad	1740	05	10	NA	0.001%	1740
5.	Jabalpur	12345	05	07	NA	0.57%	12345
6.	Khargone	5000	11	03	NA	0.003%	5000
7.	Panna	11500	24	-	20	0.013%	11500
8.	Rajgarh	12000	10	15	NA	0.009%	12000
9.	Ratlam	17930	14	18	NA	0.145%	17930
10.	Sagar	8950	09	06	NA	0.001%	8950
11.	Satna	8953	15	09	NA	0.004%	8953
12.	Sidhi	15000	08	08	NA	0.008%	15000

No.	Place of District Public Library	Books	Newspapers	Magazine	Non Book Material	Average Availability Of Reading Material for Per Person	Total Collection
13.	Tikamgarh	22506	13	-	NA	0.018%	22506
14.	Ujjain	14500	10	10	NA	0.08%	14500
15.	Vidisha	24780	24	30	NA	0.02%	24780
16.	Bhopal	13000	04	-	NA	0.007%	13000
17.	Khandwa	15000	04	09	NA	1.99%	15000
18.	Shivpuri	12000	06	16	NA	0.083%	12000
19.	Shajapur	22000	04	09	NA	0.017%	22000
20.	Betul	21000	15	06	NA	0.015%	21000
21.	Narsinghpur	3000	10	02	NA	0.0025%	3000
22.	Morena	5056	12	11	NA	0.0031%	5056
23.	Guna	17644	18	23	230	0.010%	17644
24.	Datia	10250	04	03	NA	0.016%	10250
25.	Mandusar	17000	23	30	NA	0.014%	17000
26.	Sehore	10500	05	07	NA	0.009%	10500
27.	Raisen	8740	04	05	NA	0.007%	8740
28.	Chhindwara	25000	04	11	NA	1.35%	25000
29.	Dhar	8050	13	17	80	0.004%	8050
30.	Jhabua	8943	17	-	NA	0.006%	8943
31.	Shahdol	10,278	22	09	NA	0.006%	10278
32.	Mandla	9000	05	06	NA	0.010%	9000
33.	Ashoknagar	NR	NR	NR	NR	NR	NR
34.	Indore	NR	NR	NR	NR	NR	NR
35.	Katni	NR	NR	NR	NR	NR	NR
36.	Rewa	NR	NR	NR	NR	NR	NR
37.	Umaria	NR	NR	NR	NR	NR	NR
38.	Burhanpur	NR	NR	NR	NR	NR	NR
39.	Neemuch	NR	NR	NR	NR	NR	NR
40.	Balaghat	NR	NR	NR	NR	NR	NR
41.	Harda	NR	NR	NR	NR	NR	NR

No.	Place of District Public Library	Books	Newspapers	Magazine	Non Book Material	Average Availability Of Reading Material for Per Person	Total Collection
42.	Seoni	NR	NR	NR	NR	NR	NR
43.	Bhind	NR	NR	NR	NR	NR	NR
44.	Chhatrpur	NR	NR	NR	NR	NR	NR
45.	Badwani	NR	NR	NR	NR	NR	NR
46.	Anuppur	NR	NR	NR	NR	NR	NR
47.	Dindori	NR	NR	NR	NR	NR	NR
48.	Sheopur	NR	NR	NR	NR	NR	NR
49.	Alirajpur	NR	NR	NR	NR	NR	NR
50.	Singrauli	NR	NR	NR	NR	NR	NR
Grand Total		3,95,976	344	307	330	0.16%	3,95,976

Table 4.2 Collection of Reading Materials of District Public Libraries

From the Table No 4.2 the collection finds out of *32 out of 36* District *Public Libraries.* Posses a total book stock of 3,95,976. The collection of District Public Libraries ranges from **1740 at Hoshangabad to 25,000 at Chindwara.** The ascending order of number of books stocked in District Public Libraries proceeds as follows: *Chindwara (25,000), Vidisha (24780) and Tikamgarh (22506).* The descending order of number of books stocked in District Public Libraries proceeds as follows: *Khargone (5000), Narsinghpur (3000) and Hoshangabad (1740).*

The average available of reading materials for every person is calculate here, where reading material is available i.e Damoh 0.0064%, Dewas 0.005%, Gwalior o.60%, Hoshangabad 0.001 %, Jabalpur 0.013%, Khargone 0.003%, Panna 0.013%, Rajgarh 0.009%, Ratlam 0.145%, Sagar 0.001%, Satna 0.004%, Sidhi 0.008%, Tikamgarh 0.018%, Ujjain 0.08%, Vidisha 0.02%, Bhopal 0.007%., Khandwa 1,99%, Shivpuri 0.0083 %, Shajapur 0.017%, Betul 0.015%, Narsinghpur 0.0025%, Morena 0.0031 %, Guna 0.010%, Datia 0.016%, Mandusar 0.014%, Sehore 0.009%,

Raisen 0.007%, Chindwara 1.3 %, Dhar 0.004%, Jhabua 0.006%, Shahdol 0.006% and Mandla 0.010 %.

It revealed that the availability of reading materials to every person is average mere about 0.16 % and it is not satisfactory.

From the Table No 4.2 District Public Libraries also have *344 titles of News papers and 307 titles of Magazines. Newspaper* subscribed by *32* libraries and *Magazine* subscribed by *27* libraries.

From the Table No 4.2 District Public Libraries also have non book materials, but it is available only *03 District Public Libraries i. e. Panna (20), Guna (230) and Dhar (80).*The percentage of non-book materials compared to total collection of District Public Libraries in insignificant is mere about *0.08 %.*

Collection of Reading Materials of e-Libraries under the Sarve Shiksha Mission:

After the analyzed and interpretation data of Divisional Public Libraries and District Public Libraries, here we analysis and interpretation collection of reading material of e-Libraries under the Sarve Shiksha Mission.

No.	Place of e-Library	Books	Newspaper	Magazines	Average Availability Of Reading Material for Per Person	Total Collection
1	Bhopal	4969	04	05	0.0027 %	4969
2	Gwalior	3540	15	23	0.0021%	3540
3	Indore	3495	12	19	0.0014%	3495
4	Jabalpur	3109	05	07	0.001%	3109
5	Sagar	2540	09	06	0.001%	2540
6	Umaria	2475	08	NA	0.004%	2475
7	Betul	2456	15	06	0.001%	2456
8	Vidisha	2310	24	30	0.001%	2310

9	Shivpuri	2220	06	16	0.001%	2220
10	Ratlam	2029	14	18	0.001%	2029
11	Ujjain	2021	10	10	0.001%	2021
12	Rewa	1990	04	06	0.001%	1990
13	Guna	1950	18	23	0.001%	1950
14	Tikamgarh	1895	13	NA	0.001%	1895
15	Panna	1850	24	NA	0.002%	1850
16	Jhabua	1790	17	NA	0.001%	1790
17	Hoshangabad	1750	05	10	0.001%	1750
18	Mandla	1690	05	06	0.001%	1690
19	Dhar	1656	13	17	0.001%	1656
20	Sidhi	1456	08	08	0.008%	1456
21	Harda	1452	05	06	0.001%	1452
22	Neemuch	1290	12	09	0.001%	1290
23	Khargone	1245	11	03	0.001%	1245
24	Satna	1245	15	09	0.001%	1245
25	Damoh	1235	22	04	0.008%	1235
26	Dewas	1056	06	NA	0.001%	1056
27	Morena	1056	12	11	0.001%	1056
28	Ashoknagar	NR	NR	NR	NR	NR
29	Katni	NR	NR	NR	NR	NR
30	Rajgarh	NR	NR	NR	NR	NR
31	Narsinghpur	NR	NR	NR	NR	NR
32	Datia	NR	NR	NR	NR	NR
33	Badwani	NR	NR	NR	NR	NR
34	Shahdol	NR	NR	NR	NR	NR
35	Anuppur	NR	NR	NR	NR	NR
36	Dindori	NR	NR	NR	NR	NR
37	Sheopur	NR	NR	NR	NR	NR
38	Alirajpur	NR	NR	NR	NR	NR
39	Khandwa	NR	NR	NR	NR	NR
40	Burhanpur	NR	NR	NR	NR	NR
41	Balaghat	NR	NR	NR	NR	NR
42	Singrauli	NR	NR	NR	NR	NR
43	Chhindwara	NR	NR	NR	NR	NR

44	Seoni	NR	NR	NR	NR	NR
45	Bhind	NR	NR	NR	NR	NR
46	Chhatrpur	NR	NR	NR	NR	NR
47	Mandusar	NR	NR	NR	NR	NR
48	Sehore	NR	NR	NR	NR	NR
49	Raisen	NR	NR	NR	NR	NR
50	Shajapur	NR	NR	NR	NR	NR
Grand Total		**57,770**	**312**	**252**	**0.0149%**	**57,770**

Table 4.3 Collection of Reading Materials of e-Libraries under Sarve Shiksha Mission

From the Table No. 4.3 it shows that collection of *27 out of 50 e-libraries;* it poses a total book stock of 57,770. The total number of collection of e-Libraries ranges from *4969 at Bhopal to 1056 at Morena.* The ascending order of number of books stocked in e-libraries proceeds as follows: *Bhopal (4969), Gwalior (3540) and Indore (3495).* The descending order of number of books stocked in e-libraries proceeds as follows: *Damoh (1235), Dewas (1056), and Morena (1056).*

The average available of reading materials for every person is calculate here, where reading material is available i.e Bhopal 0.0027 %, Gwalior 0.0021%, Indore 0.0014%, Jabalpur 0.001%, Sagar 0.001 %, Umaria 0.004%, Betual 0.001 %, Vidisha 0.001 %, Shivpuri 0.001 %, Ratlam 0.001 %, Ujjain 0.001 %, Rewa 0.001 %, Guna 0.001 %, Tikamgarh 0.001 %, Panna 0.002 %, Jhabua 0.001 %, Hoshangabad 0.001 %, Mandla 0.001 %, Dhar 0.000 %, Sidhi 0.008 %, Harda 0.003 %, Neemuch 0.001 %, Khargone 0.000 %, Satna 0.001 %, Damoh 0.008 % and Dewas 0.000 %.

It reveals that availability of reading materials to every person is average mere about 0.0149 % and it is not satisfactory.

From the Table No. 5.3 The e-libraries have *312 titles of Newspaper and 252 titles of Magazines. Newspaper* subscribe by *27* e-libraries and *Magazines* subscribed by *22* e-libraries.

No.	Availability of reading material	Availability of reading Material (Average Per Person)	Availability of reading material
1.	Divisional Public Library	0.18%	
2.	District Public Library under	0.16%	**0.17%**
3.	E-Libraries under the Sarve Shiksha Mission	0.0149%	

Table 4.4 Propose Availability of reading material

From the Table No 4.4 reveals the availability of *reading material (Average per Person)* in *Divisional Public Library 0.18% District Public Library 0.16% and e-libraries under Sarve Shiksha Mission is 0.0149 %* and If the merge these libraries in under *Integrated Public Library System for Madhya Pradesh or GIAN Network* than *availability average reading materials to every person* would be increased and it is may be *0.17%*.

After the analysis and interpretation of available collection of reading materials and non-books materials of Public Libraries and e-libraries, none of Public Libraries and e-libraries is satisfying the standard.

References:

1. International Federation of Library Associations and United Nations Educational, Scientific and Cultural Organization. The Public Library Service: IFLA/UNESCO Guidelines for Development. Munchen: K. G. Saur Verlag. 2001. 49.
2. Ibid, p. 52
3. Ibid, p. 53
4. Ibid, p. 57
5. Ibid, p. 59

Chapter Five

Status of Manpower

*"The operation of any public library should be organized,
effectively and as per professional standards.*

*The librarian is work as a bridge between users and resources.
Professional and continuous education of the librarian is indispensable
to ensure adequate services."*[1]

Professionally trained manpower is essential for effective and efficient functioning of any library. The success of a library should depend on the quality, expertise, experiences and aptitude of the manpower. The management of manpower involves-arriving at a decision of manpower required, selecting those who are the best suitable candidates for requirement, preparing them for efficient service in the organization and keeping them in the service of the organization as long as their services are mutually beneficial and obligatory. The size of manpower of a public library depends on the variety of reading materials and the services to the users.

New Skills Required for Library Professional

The fundamental qualities and skills required of public library staff can be defined as:

To communicate with users, to understand the needs of users, to co-operate with individuals and groups in the community, knowledge and understanding of cultural diversity, material that forms the library's collection and how to access it, an understanding of and sympathy with the principles of public service, the ability to work with others to providing effective library service, organizational skills, flexibility to identify and implement changes as for time to time, imagination, vision and openness to new ideas and practice, to ready change methods of working to meet new situations and uses the knowledge of ICT's.

New Skills Required for Library Professional in ICT Environment

The library professional is changing time to time to perform each task associated with the job. It is not always possible every time to recruit the staff for new skills, so, what is possible is to provide in-service training, refreshers courses to development opportunities that prepare them for the new roles and also to meet the demands, changing environment by the society. Library and Information professionals need to continue to learn and update their knowledge to upgrade their performance and adopt the culture and change prevalent in a new information environment (Odini,103).

The rapid change in ICT's, so it is essential to library professional to adopt and required new hybrid skills because all the services is become customer-sensitive and customer-centered. The hybrid skills is combination of generic, traditional and ICT skills like digital archiving, content development, develop metadata for their local needs, electronic database searcher, network and consortia access. (Singh, 520).

Categories of Skills Required

"The various skills are required it is depend on role and context of the any institute/organization. The skills under three broad categories of skills, i. e. generic skills, managerial skills and professional skills; (Fisher 2004), (Fouire 62-74) (Oldroyd 30:45-49:69:78:99; Sridhar 141-149); TFPL Skills Set: '2-7".

Sr. No.	Generic skills	Managerial skills	Professional skills
1.	Communication skill	Local and global thinking	**Information technology skills**: Hardware/software & Networking skill • MS-Office suite • Presentation software's • Library automation • Database creation • Internet e.g. E-Mail management • Intricacies of internet search tool • Scanning techniques • Networking skills • On-line search engines • On-line databases search • Desktop publishing • Content development • Digitization • Web based services • Virtual learning
2.	Flexibility	Planning and organizational skills	Information literacy:
3.	Adaptability	Finance management skills: • Fund raising • Skillful use of financial resources • Accounting and auditing skill	Technical professional skills: Information resource management • E-serial management • Metadata1 standards e.g. Dublin core, MARC, TEI2, XML3, etc • Standards e.g.Z39.504
4.	Assertiveness	Managing change	
5.	Self-confidence	Team building	
6.	Creativity	Decision making	
7.	Innovation	Leadership	
8.	Analytical skills	Negotiation skills	
9.	Problem solving	Consumer management skills User need analysis Information seeking Behavior analysis	
10.	Decision making	Project management	

11.	Service attitude	People management	
12.	Customer relationship	Stress management	
13.	Improving one's learning's Experience	Time management	
14.	Presentation skills	Resource management	
15.	Stress management		
16.	Time management		
17.	Interpersonal		
18.	Group skills		
19.	Working with difficult people		

Table 5.1 New Skills Requirement for Staff in ICT's Environment

- **Metadata:** It is essentials part of digital environment and it data that describe the content and attributes of any particular item. It is a catalogue card for web document and also prints it.

- **Text Encoding Initiative (TEI):** It is concerned with two things: one is what textual feature should be encoded in electronic environment to make it more explicit and how encoding should be represented for loss-free, platform independent interchange.

- **Extensible markup language:** It allows designers to customize formatting (tags), to greater definition, achieves transmission, validation, and interpretation of data between applications and organizations.

- **Z 39.50:** It is a standard developed by National Information Standard Organization for information retrieval and also compatible automated library system to access remote library collection via client and server environment.

- **Knowledge management:** It is managing organizational knowledge to solve the organizational problems. It includes managing tacit as well as explicit knowledge.

Staff Formula for Library

The number of staff members required for a public library should also be limited to the total user population of the library.

"1996 American Library Association standard (for USA) recommended one staff member per 2000 population;[8]

The Roberts Committee (UK) suggested that the staff for urban libraries excluding the Chief Librarian and at least **1 Assistant per 3000 population in the community served";**[9]

S. R. Rangathan suggested (It is Indian standards for staff formula for public libraries):

- **Book Section:** 1 person for every 6,000 volumes added in a year.
- **Periodical Publication Section:** 1 person for every 1,000 periodicals.
- **Classification and Cataloguing Section:** 1 person for every 2,000 volumes added in a year.
- **Maintenance Section:** 1 person for every 2,000 volumes added in a year and 1 person for every 50,000 volumes in the library.
- **Publicity Section:** Minimum 1 artist.
- **Administrative Section:** Minimum 1 each of Library Accountant, Steno typist and Correspondent Clerk.
- **Reference Section:** 1 person for every 50 readers using the library in a day;
- **Circulation Section:** 1 person for every 1,500 hours for which one wicket get of the library has to be kept open in a year.
- **Supervising Section:** Librarian and 1 Deputy Librarian;"[10]

"IFLA standards recommended that between 33% and 40% of the staff should be professionally qualified".[11]

The guidelines evolved by Raja Rammohun Roy Library Foundation (RRRLF) stipulated that "The (State) Central Libraries, the proportion of professional staff to the total staff should be **40% against 33% in other public libraries.**"[12]

National Knowledge Commission 2006 is also some recommendations to recruit manpower for Public Libraries and recommendations are: library and information handling skills; ICT knowledge skills; communication and training skills; marketing and presentation skills; understanding of cultural diversity; knowledge mapping skills.[13]

Present Status of Manpower in Divisional Public Libraries:

No	Name of Library	Designation	Year	Qualifications			Total Experience
				Academic	Professional	Computers (ICT's)	
1.	Govt. Regional Public Library, Gwalior	Librarian	1928	B. A.	M. Lib. Sc.	Yes	Around 20 Years
2.	Devi Ahiliya Regional Public Library, Indore	Librarian	1854	B. Sc.	M. Lib. Sc.	Yes	Around 20 Years
3.	Govt. Regional Public Library, Jabalpur	Librarian	1956	B. A.	M. Lib. Sc.	Yes	Around 05 Years
4.	Govt. Regional Public Library, Rewa	Librarian	1939	M. A.	C. Lib. Sc.	Yes	Around 20 Years
5.	Govt Regional Public Library, Bhopal	Librarian	1965	M. Com	M. Lib. Sc.	Yes	Around 24 Years

Table 5.2 Qualification and Experience of Library Incharge of Divisional Public Libraries

From the Table no 5.2 reveal information about the Library In-charge of Divisional Public Libraries by their designation. It shows that In-charge of Divisional Public Libraries is 05 Librarian.

From the Table no 5.2 it seen that of In-charge of Divisional Public Libraries have qualification is 02 B. A., Incharge of Divisional Public Library is 01 B. Sc., Incharge of Divisional Public Library is 01 M. A., and Incharge of Divisional Public Library is 01 M. Com.

From the Table no 5.2 it seen In-charge of Divisional Public Library are qualified persons i.e. 01 have C. Lib. & Inf. Sc. and 03 have M. Lib. & Inf. Sci,

From the Table no 5.2 it seen that Incharge of Divisional Public Library have experience up to 5 years is 01, have experience up to-20 years is 03 and have experience 21-25 years is 01.

From the Table no 5.2 all the in-charge of Divisional Public Library has aware about Computer (ICT's).

Status of Manpower in term of Professional and Non-Professional

No.	Place of Divisional Public Library	Professional	Non Professional	Total
1.	Gwalior	02	19	21
2.	Indore	01	12	13
3.	Jabalpur	01	15	16
4.	Reewa	01	12	13
5.	Bhopal	03	11	14
	Grand Total	**09**	**69**	**78**

Table 5.3 Manpower in Divisional Public Libraries

From the Table no. 5.3 Among the total number of **78** staff members in Divisional Public Libraries under Directorate of Public Instructions, **09** is professional staff and **69** is non-professional staff.

Divisional Library has only 7% professional manpower and it is needless to emphasis that un-adequate professional manpower available for Divisional Public Libraries and not fulfilling the standard for manpower in Public Libraries:

Present Status of Manpower in District Public Libraries:

No	Place of D. P. L.	Designation	Year	Qualifications			Total Experience
				Academic	Professional	Computers (ICT's)	
1	Damoh	Deputy Librarian	1980	B. Com.	B. Lib. Sc.	No	Around 15 Years
2	Dewas	Librarian	-	-	-	Yes	Around 20 Years
3	Gwalior	Librarian	1954	B. A.	M. Lib. Sc.	Yes	Around 20 Years
4	Hoshangabad	Librarian	1995	B. A.	C. Lib. Sc.	Yes	Around 05 Years
5	Jabalpur	Librarian	1956	B. A.	M. Lib. Sc.	No	Around 05 Years
6	Khargone	Assistant Librarian	1982	B. A.	-	No	Around 15 Years
7	Panna	Librarian	1928	B. A.	B. Lib. Sc.	Yes	Around 15 Years
8	Rajgarh	Assistant Librarian	1980	M. Com.	M. Lib. Sc.	No	Around 15 Years
9	Ratlam	Deputy Librarian	1980	M. Com.	M. Lib. Sc.	No	Around 15 Years
10	Sagar	Librarian	-	M. A.	-	No	Around 05 Years
11	Satna	Librarian	1985	B. A.	B. Lib. Sc.	No	Around 15 Years
12	Sidhi	Librarian	1931	B. Com.	M. Lib. Sc.	No	Around 20 Years
13	Tikamgarh	Librarian	1955	B. A.	B. Lib. Sc.	No	Around 05 Years
14	Ujjain	Deputy Librarian	1980	M. Sc.	M. Lib. Sc.	No	Around 05 Years
15	Vidisha	Deputy Librarian	1980	M. Com.	M. Lib. Sc.	Yes	Around 10 Years
16	Bhopal	Deputy Librarian	1965	B. A.	B. Lib. Sc.	No	Around 10 Years
17	Khandwa	Librarian	1967	B. Com.	B. Lib. Sc.	No	Around 05 Years
18	Shivpuri	Deputy Librarian	1981	M. A.	M. Lib. Sc.	Yes	Around 20 Years
19	Shajapur	Librarian	1981	B. A.	B. Lib. Sc.	No	Around 10 Years
20	Betul	Librarian	1955	B. A.	-	No	Around 15 Years
21	Narsinghpur	Librarian	1995	B. A.	M. Lib. Sc.	No	Around 10 Years
22	Morena	Librarian	1998	M. A.	M. Lib. Sc.	No	Around 20 Years
23	Guna	Librarian	1980	B. A.	B. Lib. Sc.	Yes	Around 20 Years
24	Datia	Librarian	1977	B. A.	B. Lib. Sc.	No	Around 20 Years
25	Mandusar	Librarian	1981	B. A.	B. Lib. Sc.	No	Around 20 Years
26	Sehore	Librarian	1980	B. Com.	-	No	Around 10 Years

27.	Raisen	Librarian	1980	B. A.	B. Lib. Sc.	No	Around 10 Years
28.	Chhindwara	Librarian	1978	B. A.	M. Lib. Sc.	No	Around 05 Years
29.	Dhar	Deputy Librarian	1956	B. Com.	B. Lib. Sc.	Yes	Around 05 Years
30.	Jhabua	Deputy Librarian	1980	B. Com.	B. Lib. Sc.	No	Around 20 Years
31.	Shahdol	Deputy Librarian	1955	M. Com.	B. Lib. Sc.	No	Around 05 Years
32.	Mandla	Librarian	1935	M. A.	M Lib. Sc.	No	Around 20 Years
33.	Ashoknagar	NR	NR	NR	NR	NR	NR
34.	Indore	NR	NR	NR	NR	NR	NR
35.	Katni	NR	NR	NR	NR	NR	NR
36.	Rewa	NR	NR	NR	NR	NR	NR
37.	Umaria	NR	NR	NR	NR	NR	NR
38.	Burhanpur	NR	NR	NR	NR	NR	NR
39.	Neemuch	NR	NR	NR	NR	NR	NR
40.	Balaghat	NR	NR	NR	NR	NR	NR
41.	Harda	NR	NR	NR	NR	NR	NR
42.	Seoni	NR	NR	NR	NR	NR	NR
43.	Bhind	NR	NR	NR	NR	NR	NR
44.	Chhatrpur	NR	NR	NR	NR	NR	NR
45.	Badwani	NR	NR	NR	NR	NR	NR
46.	Anuppur	NR	NR	NR	NR	NR	NR
47.	Dindori	NR	NR	NR	NR	NR	NR
48.	Sheopur	NR	NR	NR	NR	NR	NR
49.	Alirajpur	NR	NR	NR	NR	NR	NR
50.	Singrauli	NR	NR	NR	NR	NR	NR

Table 5.4 Qualification and Experience of Library Incharge of District Public Libraries

From the Table no 5.4 it reveal information about the Library In-charge of District Public Libraries by their designation. It shows that In-charge of District Public Libraries is *21 Librarian;* Incharge of District Public Library is *09 Deputy Librarian*, Incharge of District Public Library *02 Assistant Librarian.* The data available of 32 District Public Library out of 50, but present status of Manpower is not satisfactory. So further required of 29 *Librarian, 41 Deputy Librarian* and *48 Assistant Librarian* should be recruiting to smooth running of District Public Libraries.

From the **Table no 5.4** it reveal that In-charge of District Public Libraries have qualification is **16 B. A.**, Incharge of District Public Library is **06 B. Com,** Incharge of District Public Library **01 M. Sc,** Incharge of District Public Library is **04 M.A.** Incharge of District Public Library is **M.Com 04** and no data is available **for 01.**

From the **Table no 5.4** it revel that In-charge of District Public Library are qualified persons i.e. **01** have **C. Lib. & Inf. Sc.**, **14** have **B. Lib. & Inf. Sci,** **23** have **M. Lib. & Inf. Sci** and no information of **05.**

From the **Table no 5.4** it reveal that Incharge of District Public Library have experience **up to 5 years is 09**, have experience between **06-10 years is 06,** have experience between **11-16 years is 07,** have experience above **21 years is 10.**

From the **Table no 5.4** In-charge of District Public Library has aware about the **ICT are 08** and **24 don't know about ICT.**

Status of Manpower in term of Professional and Non-Professional:

No.	Place of D. P. L.	Professional	Non Professional	Total
1.	Damoh	01	04	04
2.	Dewas	01	-	01
3.	Gwalior	01	04	05
4.	Jabalpur	01	02	03
5.	Hoshangabad	01	01	02
6.	Khargone	01	02	03
7.	Panna	02	02	04
8.	Rajgarh	01	03	04
9.	Ratlam	04	-	04
10.	Sagar	01	01	02
11.	Satna	01	02	03
12.	Sidhi	01	03	04
13.	Tikamgarh	01	03	04

14.	Ujjain	02	01	03
15.	Vidisha	01	03	04
16.	Bhopal	01	03	04
17.	Khandwa	01	02	03
18.	Shivpuri	01	03	04
19.	Shajapur	00	04	04
20.	Betul	01	03	04
21.	Narsinghpur	01	03	04
22.	Morena	01	02	03
23.	Guna	01	03	04
24.	Datia	02	00	02
25.	Mandusar	01	03	04
26.	Sehore	01	01	02
27.	Raisen	01	01	02
28.	Chhindwara	01	01	02
29.	Dhar	01	05	06
30.	Jhabua	01	02	03
31.	Shahdol	01	03	04
32.	Mandla	01	02	03
33.	Ashoknagar	NR	NR	NR
34.	Indore	NR	NR	NR
35.	Katni	NR	NR	NR
36.	Rewa	NR	NR	NR
37.	Umaria	NR	NR	NR
38.	Burhanpur	NR	NR	NR
39.	Neemuch	NR	NR	NR
40.	Balaghat	NR	NR	NR
41.	Harda	NR	NR	NR
42.	Seoni	NR	NR	NR
43.	Bhind	NR	NR	NR
44.	Chhatrpur	NR	NR	NR
45.	Badwani	NR	NR	NR
46.	Anuppur	NR	NR	NR
47.	Dindori	NR	NR	NR
48.	Sheopur	NR	NR	NR

49.	Alirajpur	NR	NR	NR
50.	Singrauli	NR	NR	NR
	Grand Total	**37**	**72**	**109**

Table 5.5 Manpower in District Public Libraries

From the Table no. 5.5 It reveal the Among the total number of *109* staff members in District Public Libraries under Directorate of Public Instructions, *37 is professional staff and 72 is non professional staff.* It is needless to emphasis that adequate professional manpower should available.

Public Library has 33% professional manpower and it is needless to emphasis that adequate professional manpower available for District Public Libraries and fulfilling the standard for manpower in Public Libraries:

Present Status of Manpower in e-Libraries under Sarve Shiksha Mission:

No	Place of e-Library	Designation	Year	Qualifications			Total Experience
				Academic	Professional	Computers	
1	Bhopal	Assistant Librarian	2002	B. A.	B. Lib. Sc.	Yes	Around 04 Years
2	Gwalior	Assistant Librarian	2002	B. A.	B. Lib. Sc.	Yes	Around 02Years
3	Indore	Assistant Librarian	2002	B. A.	B. Lib. Sc.	Yes	Around 05 Years
4	Jabalpur	Assistant Librarian	2002	B. A.	B. Lib. Sc.	Yes	Around 03 Years
5	Sagar	Assistant Librarian	2002	B. A.	B. Lib. Sc.	No	Around 05 Years
6	Umaria	Assistant Librarian	2002	B. A.	B. Lib. Sc.	Yes	Around 10 Years
7	Betul	Assistant Librarian	2002	B. A.	B. Lib. Sc.	No	Around 10 Years
8	Vidisha	Assistant Librarian	2002	B. A.	B. Lib. Sc.	Yes	Around 10 Years

9	Shivpuri	Assistant Librarian	2002	B. A.	B. Lib. Sc.	Yes	Around 10 Years
10	Ratlam	Assistant Librarian	2002	B. A.	B. Lib. Sc.	Yes	Around 10 Years
11	Ujjain	Assistant Librarian	2002	B. A.	B. Lib. Sc.	Yes	Around 10Years
12	Reewa	Assistant Librarian	2002	B. A.	B. Lib. Sc.	Yes	Around 10 Years
13	Guna	Assistant Librarian	2002	B. A.	B. Lib. Sc.	Yes	Around 10 Years
14	Tikamgarh	Assistant Librarian	2002	B. A.	B. Lib. Sc.	Yes	Around 10 Years
15	Panna	Assistant Librarian	2002	B. A.	B. Lib. Sc.	Yes	Around 10 Years
16	Jhabua	Assistant Librarian	2002	B. A.	B. Lib. Sc.	Yes	Around 10 Years
17	Hoshangabad	Assistant Librarian	2002	B. A.	B. Lib. Sc.	Yes	Around 10 Years
18	Mandla	Assistant Librarian	2002	B. A.	B. Lib. Sc.	Yes	Around 10 Years
19	Dhar	Assistant Librarian	2002	B. Com.	C. Lib. Sc.	Yes	Around 10 Years
20	Sidhi	Assistant Librarian	2002	B. Com.	M. Lib. Sc.	Yes	Around 10 Years
21	Harda	Assistant Librarian	2002	B. Com.	M. Lib. Sc.	Yes	Around 12 Years
22	Neemuch	Assistant Librarian	2002	B. Com.	C Lib. Sc.	Yes	Around 13 Years
23	Khargone	Others	2002	B. Com.	M. Lib Sc.	Yes	Around 12 Years
24	Satna	Others	2002	B. Com.	C Lib Sc.	Yes	Around 11 Years
25	Damoh	Others	2002	B. Com.	C Lib. Sc.	Yes	Around 11 Years
26	Dewas	Others	2002	B. Com.	C. Lib. Sc.	Yes	Around 11 Years
27	Morena	Others	2002	B. Com.	M. Lib Sc.	Yes	Around 11 Years

Table 5.6 Qualification and Experience of Library Incharge of e-Libraries under Sarve Shiksha Mission

From the Table 5.6 The 50 e-Library under the Sarve Shiksha Mission, but information available is 27 e-libraries. It reveals that Incharge of e-libraries is 22 Assistant Librarian and 05 are others.

From the Table 5.6 it reveals that In-charge of e-Libraries have qualification *18 is B. A.,* Incharge of e-Libraries have qualification *09 is B. Com.*

From the Table 5.6 it reveals that In-charge of e-Libraries *05 have C. Lib. & Inf. Sci, Incharge of e-Libraries 18 have B. Lib. & Inf. Sci, Incharge of e-Libraries is 04 have M. Lib. & Inf. Sci;*

From the Table 5.6 it reveals that Incharge of e-Libraries has experience in between *0 to 5 Year is 05,* Incharge of e-Libraries has experience in between *06 to 10 is 15,* Incharge of e-Libraries has experience in between *11-15 years is 07.*

From the Table 5.6 it reveals that In-charge of e-Libraries have aware about the *ICT is 25* and In-charge of e-Libraries have no about *ICT are 02.*

Status of Manpower in term of Professional and Non-Professional:

No.	Name of e-Library	Professional	Non Professional
1.	Alirajpur	NA	NA
2.	Anuppur	NA	NA
3.	Ashoknagar	NA	NA
4.	Badwani	NA	NA
5.	Balaghat	NA	NA
6.	Betul	1	NA
7.	Bhind	NA	NA
8.	Bhopal	1	NA
9.	Burhanpur	NA	NA
10.	Chhatrpur	NA	NA
11.	Chhindwara	NA	NA
12.	Damoh	1	NA
13.	Datia	NA	NA
14.	Dewas	1	NA
15.	Dhar	1	NA
16.	Dindori	NA	NA
17.	Guna	1	NA

18.	Gwalior	1	NA
19.	Harda	1	NA
20.	Hoshangabad	1	NA
21.	Indore	1	NA
22.	Jabalpur	1	NA
23.	Jhabua	1	NA
24.	Katni	NA	NA
25.	Khandwa	NA	NA
26.	Khargone	1	NA
27.	Mandla	1	NA
28.	Mandsour	-	NA
29.	Morena	1	NA
30.	Narsinghpur	NA	NA
31.	Neemuch	1	NA
32.	Panna	1	NA
33.	Raisen	NA	NA
34.	Rajgarh	NA	NA
35.	Ratlam	1	NA
36.	Reewa	1	NA
37.	Sagar	1	NA
38.	Satna	1	NA
39.	Sehore	NA	NA
40.	Seoni	NA	NA
41.	Sheopur	NA	NA
42.	Shahdol	NA	NA
43.	Shajapur	NA	NA
44.	Shivpuri	1	NA
45.	Sidhi	1	NA
46.	Singrauli	NA	NA
47.	Tikamgarh	1	NA
48.	Ujjain	1	NA
49.	Umaria	1	NA
50.	Vidisha	1	NA
	Total	27	

Table 5.7 Status of Manpower in e-libraries under the Sarve Shiksha Mission

From the Table No 5.7 it reveals that total number of 27 staff members in e-Libraries under Sarve Shiksha Mission in Madhya Pradesh.

E-Library has only 27% professional manpower and it is needless to emphasis that un-adequate professional manpower available for e-Libraries and not fulfilling the standard for manpower in Public Libraries.

No.	Name of Department	Staff		Total
		Professional	Non-Professional	
1.	Divisional Public Library	09	69	78
2.	District Public Library	37	72	109
3.	e-libraries under the Sarve Shiksha Mission	27	-	27
Grand Total		73	141	214

Table 5.8 Availability of Manpower

From the Table No 5.8 reveals that availability of manpower in Divisional Public Libraries, District Public Library and e-libraries. Among staff members the professional staff is *73* and non professional staff is *141*. If the merge the above manpower under the proposed ***Integrated Public Library System for Madhya Pradesh or GIAN Network***, than available manpower is increase and also solved the problem to related ICT knowledge among the manpower.

Human Resources

The most important part of any system is the manpower to run the library services effectively and to cater various kinds of information needs of the any community, so following human resource in needed.

Category of Staff

The various categories of the staff is defined as per recommendations of ***National Knowledge Commission 2006. (Detailed are given in Annexure III).***

I. Managerial Staff (Group A)

a. State Librarian
b. Deputy Library Director
c. Assistant Library Director (presently designated as Information Officer)
d. Divisional Librarian
e. District Librarian
f. Town Librarian

II. Professional/ Technical Staff (Group B)

a. Information Assistant
b. Junior Information Assistant
c. Data Entry Operator

III. Para-professional/ Support Staff (Group C)

a. Library Attendant
b. Village Level Volunteers (only Rural/Village Libraries)

IV. Administrative Staff

a. Administrative Officer
b. Stenographer
c. Cashier

V. Administrative Support Staff

Night Watchman; Cleaner; Mali; Driver; Book Binder; Sweeper (*to be Outsourced*).

Requirement of Total Staff for the Proposed Integrated Public Library System for Madhya Pradesh

To operate the State Library System and to serve the people of the state there shall be requirement of professional trained manpower. The total proposed requirement of the staff shall be as under. *Detailed given in Table No 5.9*

Category of Libraries	Total No. in the State	Staff Required	Total No. of Staff Required
State Central Library & Knowledge Centre	1	State Librarian = 1 Deputy Library Director = 6 Assistant Library Director = 8 Information Assistant = 12 Junior Information Assistant = 8 Data Entry Operator = 4 Library Attendant = 10 Administrative Officer = 1 UDC = 4 LDC = 2 Stenographer = 1 Cashier (Accountant) = 2 Peon = 10	State Librarian = 1 Deputy Library Director = 6 Assistant Library Director = 8 Information Assistant = 12 Junior Information Assistant = 8 Data Entry Operator = 4 Library Attendant = 10 Administrative Officer = 1 UDC = 4 LDC = 2 Stenographer = 1 Cashier (Accountant) = 2 Peon = 10
Divisional Library & Knowledge Centre	4	Divisional Librarian = 1 Assistant Librarian= 2 Information Assistant = 6 Junior Information Assistant = 2 Data Entry Operator = 1 Library Attendant = 4 Peon = 5	Divisional Librarian = 4 Assistant Librarian= 8 Information Assistant = 24 Junior Information Assistant = 8 Data Entry Operator = 4 Library Attendant = 16 Peon = 20
District Library & Knowledge Centre	50	District Librarian = 1 Information Assistant = 2 Junior Information Assistant = 1 Data Entry Operator = 1 Library Attendant = 1 Peon = 1	District Librarian = 50 Information Assistant = 100 Junior Information Assistant = 50 Data Entry Operator = 50 Library Attendant = 50 Peon = 50
Tehsil Library & Knowledge Centre	272	Tehsil Librarian = 1 Information Assistant = 1 Library Attendant = 2 Peon = 1	Tehsil Librarian = 272 Information Assistant = 272 Data Entry Operator = 272 Library Attendant = 272 Peon = 272
Block Library & Knowledge Centre	313	Block Librarian = 1 Junior Information Assistant = 1 Library Attendant = 1 Peon = 1	Block Librarian = 313 Junior Information Assistant = 313 Library Attendant =313 Peon = 313
Panchayat & Community Information Centre	23051	Panchayat Librarian = 1 Library Attendant = 1	Panchayat Librarian = 23051 Library Attendant = 23051
Village & Community Information Centre	52143	Information Assistant = 1 Village Level Volunteers = 1	Information Assistant = 52143 Village Level Volunteers = 52143
Branch Libraries	381	Information Assistant = 1 Library Attendant = 1 Peon = 1	Information Assistant = 381 Library Attendant = 381 Peon = 381

Delivery Station	13985	Information Assistant = 1	Information Assistant = 13985
Mobile Library	313	Junior Information Assistant =1 Peon = 1	Junior Information Assistant = 313 Peon = 313
			State Librarian = 1 Deputy Library Director = 6 Assistant Library Director = 8 Divisional Librarian = 4 District Librarian = 50 Tehsil Librarian =272 Block Librarian = 313 Panchayat Librarian = 23051 Assistant Librarian = 8 Information Assistant = 66917 Junior Information Assistant = 692 Data Entry Operator = 330 Library Attendant = 24093 Administrative Officer = 1 UDC = 4 LDC = 2 Stenographer = 1 Cashier (Accountant) = 2 Peon = 1359
Total	90513		115745 (Only Library Professional Required) & 117114 (with administrative Staff)

Table 5.9 Total Requirements of Human Resources

Table 5.9 revealed that the total requirement of human resources for proposed *Integrated Public Library System for Madhya Pradesh of GIAN Network,* it shows that the proposed total no of library 90513 and it will be required 1,17,637 human resource to smoothly functioning public library in state.

Category of Library Staff	Total No. of Staff Required	
	Existing	Balance
State Librarian	1	-
Deputy Library Director	6	6
Assistant Library Director	8	8
Divisional Librarian	4	-
District Librarian	50	29
Tehsil Librarian	272	272

Block Librarian	313	313
Panchayat Librarian	23051	23051
Assistant Librarian	8	8
Information Assistant	66917	66917
Junior Information Assistant	692	692
Library Attendant	2409324093	23704
Administrative Officer	1	1
UDC	4	4
LDC	2	2
Stenographer	1	1
Cashier (Accountant)	2	2
Data Entry Operator	330	330
Peon	1359	1359
Total	**117114**	**117114**

Table 5.10 Proposed Required Manpower

Table 5.10 9 revealed that the total requirement of human resources for proposed *Integrated Public Library System for Madhya Pradesh of GIAN Network*, it shows that the proposed total no of library 90513 and it will be required 1,17,114 human resource to smoothly functioning public library in state.

References:

1. International Federation of Library Associations and United Nations Educational, Scientific and Cultural Organization. The Public Library Service: IFLA/UNESCO Guidelines for Development. Munchen: K. G. Saur Verlag. 2001. 61.

2. "Fisher Workforce Skills Development: The Professional Imperative for Information Services in the United Kingdom". http://conference.alia.au/alia2004/pdfs/fisher.paper.pdf.

3. "Odini. Training and Development ok Skills in a Changing Information Environment". Library Management 20.2(1999): 100-104. Delhi U Lib., Delhi, IN 28 August 2006

4. "Oldroyd, ed. Developing Academic Library Staff for Future Success. http://www.emeralddinsight.com

5. "Singh, Special Libraries in India: Some Current Tends". Library Review 55.8(2006): 520-53. Delhi U Lib., Delhi, IN 28 August 7 http://www.emeralddinsight.com

6. "Sridhar Skills Requirements of LIS Professionals in the New E-World". Library Science with a Slant to Documentation and Information Studies 36.3 (Sept.2000):141-149. 30 November 2006 http://eprints.rclis.org/archive/00009637/01/J42_itskills.pdf

7. "TEFL Skills Set: Knowledge and Information Management Skills Toolkit. 16 August 2006. http://skillskit.tfpl.com.

8. www.ala.org

9. Mookerjee, S. K. and B. Sengupta, "Library Organization and Administration". (Calcutta: The World Press, 1977), 408.

10. Ranganthan, S. R. "Library Manual: For Library Authorities, Librarians and Library Workers". (Bangalore: Sarda Ranganthan Endowment for Library Science, 1988), 414.

11. Ibid, 66.

12. Kalia, D. R. "Guidelines for the Public Library Systems and Services". Granthana: Indian Journal of Library Studies. No. 2(1) (1999): 31-84.

13. www.knowledgecommission2005.nic.in.

Chapter Six

Status of Financial Organization

Public Libraries is by nature a spending institutions and do not have any self-supporting on financial base. A public library should have regular and guaranteed sources of income. Finance is required for to purchase of reading materials, furniture, equipments, staff salary, construction and maintenance of buildings and to meet the emerging contingent expenditure for day to day functioning. The availability of adequate financial resources is required to effective functioning of any public library. The motto of public library service, "The best reading material for the largest number at the least cost", can't be implemented It is the life blood for the functioning of any type of Public Libraries. The budget for the Public Libraries is normally sanctioned by the concern authority.

Resources of Finance for Public Libraries

The finance of public library primarily deals with the allotment and management of the finance, so as to secure maximum social, economic, cultural and educational gains for the community. Therefore, provision of finance to public libraries is made by taking into consideration the following factors;

- **Libraries are expenditure institute:** Libraries are not revenue earning entities, provision for finance should be compulsory;
- **Libraries are growing organizations:** According to the First Law of Library and Information Science, the demand for books, staff, etc will be constantly increasing, thereby, implying need for a constant flow f money;

- **Financial demands are recurring:** To provision for permanent source of income is a perquisite for rendering library service.

The Resources of Finance for the Public Libraries is given below points:

Government Sources
Local Bodies, Co-Operative Societies and endowments, State Government Central Government;

Library Cess and Library Fund
Cess with matching and without grant from the state government, but state government meeting establishment charges in lieu of it.

Self Generated Income
Overdue charges, cost collected for loss of books, xerox copies, rents on space/accommodation, interest on investments and fee from users

Savings
Savings generated through Networking of Libraries, Library Co-Operation, Resource Sharing and Inter Library Loan.

Other Sources
Gifts, Fund raising, Philanthropic and Voluntary Sources

Government Sources

Local Bodies
The Government of India in 1992 enacted two amendments to the Constitution namely the 73rd amendments pertaining to Panchayat for the rural areas and 74th amendments relating to Municipalities for the urban areas. Now public administration in India become three tiered under the Constitution namely the Central Government, State Government and Local Self Government both in rural and urban areas.

Panchayats

The subjected as listed in the 11th Schedule for Panchayats include also *'Libraries' (Item No. 20)* which obviously means 'Public Libraries'. The state governments have been empowered to decide whether Public Libraries will be placed under the Village Panchayat, Samiti Panchayat or the Parishad Panchayat.

After X Schedule in the Constitution, Schedule XI (Article 243 G) shall be treated as included: Agriculture. Including agricultural extension; Land improvement, implementation of land reforms, land consolidation and soil conservation; Minor irrigation, water management and watershed development; Animal husbandry, dairy and poultry; Fisheries; Social forestry and farm forestry; Minor forest produce; Small-scale industries, including the food processing industries; Khadi, village and cottage industries; Rural housing; Drinking water; Fuel and fodder; Roads, culverts, bridges, ferries, waterways and other means of communications; Rural electrification, including distribution of electricity; Non-conventional energy sources; Poverty alleviation programme; Education, including primary and secondary schools; Technical training and vocational education; Adult and non-formal education; **Libraries;** Cultural activities; Markets and fairs; Health and sanitation, including hospitals, primary health centres and dispensaries; Family welfare; Women and child development; Social welfare, including welfare of handicapped and mentally retarded; Welfare of weaker section and in particular of the SC/STs; Public distribution system; Maintenance of community assets.

Municipalities

The 25th schedule of the Consistitution for municipalities does not specifically mention the word 'Libraries' as is the case with the 11 schedule for Panchayat but under item '13' Promotion of cultural, educational and aesthetic is provided for.

State Government

In India 'Libraries' are included under the State list in the 7th schedule of the Constitution. Under the Constitution, 'Libraries', museums and other similar institutions controlled and financed by the States, ancient and historical monuments and records and other than those declared by or under law made by Parliament to be 'national importance' are state subject. With the transfer of 'Education' from the State List to the Concurrent List by the 42nd amendment;

Central Government

In India 'Library' being included in item 12th of the State List in the Seventh schedule of Constitution, the Central Governments restrict itself to limited activities in the field of public libraries. The Raja Rammohun Roy Library Foundation is responsible for the overall development of public libraries in India.

Central Government Agencies

The Raja Rammohun Roy Library Foundation-Kolkatta, it is an autonomous body fully financed by the Department of Culture, Ministry of Human Resource Development by Government of India.

Library Cess Library Fund

The provision for levying cess as prevalent in India today is as follows is comparative study about the public library finance is different public library acts in India in **Table No 5.18**

Self Generated Income

Overdue charges, cost collected for loss of books, xerox copies, rents on space/accommodation, interest on investments and fee from users

Savings

Savings generated through resource sharing, networking of libraries and library cooperation.

Resource Sharing

Resource Sharing means the sharing of the information resources available in one library by the clientele to other libraries, co-operative acquisition of books/equipment, cooperative processing of document

Networking

Networking of libraries is one way of achieving maximum results with minimum inputs. No library would be financially strong enough to be self sufficient as far as information resources are concerned. Hence the concept of resources sharing becomes the central theme of any networking system. The rise in the cost of publications, lack of adequate manpower to organize the same and the location of the libraries at distant and remote area have necessitated the need of networking. **The Chattopadhyay Committee on National Policy on Library and Information System** which submitted its report in 1986 had underlined the urgent need for networking of Public Libraries. All the libraries within a state should form part of a network extending from the community library of the village through the district and state central library. The state network should eventually connect with the national level.

Name of Library Act	Library Cess	Library Fund
Madras Public Libraries Act (1948)	Every Local Library Authority collects Library Cess at the rate of 6 paise per rupee as surcharge for taxable property or house tax from its area.	To this Library Fund will be contributed the amount collected as source grants from Government or any others sources and it maintained by Local Library Authority.
Andhra Pradesh Public Libraries Act (1960)	Every District Grandhalaya Sanstha collects library cess at the rate of 8 paise per rupees as surcharge from taxable property and house tax from its area.	Library Fund which will receive the amount under the different provision of Act or Grants by the Government and it maintain by Zilla Grandhalaya Sanstha.
Mysore Public Libraries Act (1965)	Every Local Library Authority collects Library Cess at the rate of 3 paise per rupee as surcharge for taxable property and revenue, sale tax, commercial and professional tax	Each District and City Library Authority maintains a Library Fund which will receive the amount under the provisions of the Act in addition there is provision for State Library Fund also
Maharashtra Public Libraries Act (1967)	No provision for library cess and State Govt. provides the necessary grant from time to time	State Government maintains a Library Fund which will be made up of amounts received from Government and other sources.

West Bengal Public Libraries Act (1979)	No provision for library cess and State Govt. provides the necessary grant from time to time	Library Funds which will be run by the grant received from the Government and it maintained by Local Library Authority.
Manipur Public Libraries Act (1988)	No provision for library cess or tax	Library fund is maintained by District Library Authority. To this State Government will contribute annually, besides other sources
The Kerala Pradesh Public Libraries Act (1989)	State Library Council may levy cess in the form of surcharge on the building tax or property tax at the rate of 5 paise per whole rupee	State Library Council maintains a Library Fund from which expenses of SLC, DLC's and Taulak Library Union will be met
The Haryana Pradesh Public Libraries Act (1989)	Local body in district may levy cess in the form of surcharge on the property tax or house tax at the Govt. may decide.	Provision for 3 types of Fund viz. State Funds, District Library Fund at City or Village Library Fund
Rajasthan Pradesh Public Libraries Act (2006)	Dr The State Govt. shall provide annually equal of 3% of State Education Budget or levy Library cess @ 3% on sales tax as surcharge or 8% on State excise on surcharge; plus matching grant equal to the cess collected will be provided by the Government, as state Share.	It shall consist of the following budgetary Provisions made by State Govt, Any grant given by the State Govt for specific purposes, Grant given by the Central Govt, Amount received as gift, contribution or endowment for development of public libraries; Library Cess, Amount received as levy on publications of various Academics, Boards etc., Assistance received from Raja Rammohan Roy Library Foundation, Income from any other Sources.

Gujarat Pradesh Public Libraries Act (2000)		There shall be a fund to be called the State Library Development Fund For modernization and development of public libraries in the State, The State Library Development fund shall consist of, (a)Grant received from the State Government other than grant Specified In sub-section (2) of section 17; (b) Any contributions or special grants from the Central Government for Modernization and development of public libraries; (c) All money received by way of contributions or gifts made by the Public or any other agency for modernization and development of Public libraries; the money in the State Library Development Fund shall be utilized by the Director in consultation with the Council to defray the expenditure for the following purposes, namely; (a) Modernization and development of public libraries in the State; (b) Payment of allowance to the members of the Council under Section 10; (c)Such other purposes as may be prescribed.

Table 6.1 Comparative Study for finance for Public Library in Difference Public Library Acts

Other Sources

Others Sources of finance include gifts, resources gained through fund raising and assistance from philanthropic and voluntary sources.

Gift/Donations

Gifts may vary from books, periodicals to land and building emanating from individuals, organization or local bodies.

Fund Raising

Library fund raising is critical, and it demands increased professional and skillful volunteer efforts to meet the increasing needs of library users in a time of increased competition for public and private resources.

Philanthropic and Voluntary Sources:

The early history of public library development is the history of philanthropy and voluntary efforts. Public libraries created out of legislation were the result of generosity of individuals and organizations. As regards the role played by voluntary organizations in India, it is observed that in socially advanced states like Kerala, Maharashtra, West Bengal they have played a significant role in the development of public libraries.

"Sources of funding as per IFLA Guidelines:

A number of sources of funding are used to finance public libraries but it will depend on local factors in each country and primary sources are:

- Taxes by local, regional or central level;
- Grants from local, regional or central level;
- Secondary sources of different income;
- Donations from bodies, private or individuals;
- Revenue from commercial activities, e.g., publishing, book sales, sale of works of art and handicrafts;
- Charges from user fees,
- Charges individual services, e.g., photocopying, printing facilities;
- Sponsorship from external organizations;[1]

"Committee on National Policy on Library and Information System:

The CONPOLIS was set up in 1985 by the Department of Culture under the Chairmanship of Prof D. P. Chattopadhyay, *it recommended enactment of library legislation by state and allocation of a larger role to the Central Government as under . . . It is vital that each state enacts its own library legislation. The Central Government should revise the model library bill, which it has already prepared, in the light of experience gained in recent years and urge upon the states the importance of enacting such legislation. Finances for library development should be found by each state from its general resources or local taxation.* It recommended allocation of 6-10 percent of education budget for libraries. Public Libraries, especially at the rural level, should draw resources from all official agencies working at the level (e.g. national adult education programme, agricultural extension programmes etc). It also recommends that coordinating, monitoring and developing of public libraries be entrusted to the Raja Rammohun Roy Library Foundation. The committee has not indicated specifically what proportion of the recommended 6-10 per cent of the education budget is spent on the public libraries. It was however, emphatic on creation of linkages between public libraries, rural primary schools and official agencies involved in rural development."[2].

6th Five Year Plan

"In the 6th Five Year Plan, a National Commission on Library and Information Science and a National Policy on Public Library System was proposed. It was recommended that 5 per cent of education budget should be spent on public libraries and for modernizing their services."[3]

8th Five Year Plan

"The Planning Commission set up a Working Group for Libraries and Information for formulation of the 8th Five Year Plan. The Working Group, on its part, set up several sub-groups including one for Public Libraries. It recommended should spend Rs. 1 per capita on public libraries in place of 70 paise (average) at present. The states and union territories spending at present less than Rs. 1 per capita should reach that level during the current plan."[4]

Per Capita Method: Public library services in the states are achieved by applying the following formula: **L * S** where L is Literate population, S= average unit cost of library service for each literate person.

> *As far as concern Per Capita Method used in Madhya Pradesh for budget allocation for Public Libraries, so average cost is 0.77*

Budget Allocation in Divisional Public Libraries:

No.	Place of District Public Library	2002-03	2003-04	2004-05	2005-06	2006-07	2007-08	2008-09	2009-10	Grand Total
1.	Gwalior	-	-	-	1723316	3557500	1420425	1270875	617900	8590016
2.	Indore	55000	31000	11600	-	-	-	-	-	97600
3.	Jabalpur	-	-	-	-	-	7000	10000	21000	38000
4.	Reewa	-	-	-	-	-	-	-	-	-
5.	Bhopal									
	Grand Total									11185002

Table 6.2 Budget Provision for Divisional Public Libraries

From the Table 6.2 reveals about the budget allocation of Divisional Public Libraries. We can get information only 03 Divisional Public Libraries out of 05. The information revel that budget allocation is very poor of Divisional Public Libraries and it is further reveals that budget allocation for libraries in not equal basis. It is very unbalance budget allocation for libraries.

The Grand total of budget allocation is 1, 11, 85,002 of Divisional Public Libraries and average budget allocation is 22, 37,000.

Budget Allocation in District Public Libraries:

No.	Place of D. P. L.	2002-03	2003-04	2004-05	2005-06	2006-07	2007-08	2008-09	2009-10	Grand Total
1.	Ashoknagar	NR	NR	NR	NR	NR	NR	NR	NR	NR
2.	Damoh	-	19970	6500	8800	3200	139591	12525	7000	197586
3.	Dewas	5000	10000	5000	10000	5000	10000	5000	10000	60000
4.	Gwalior	NR	NR	NR	NR	NR	NR	NR	NR	NR
5.	Hoshangabad	5000	5000	7000	7000	8000	8500	9000	11000	60500
6.	Indore	NR	NR	NR	NR	NR	NR	NR	NR	NR
7.	Jabalpur	NR	NR	NR	NR	NR	7000	10000	21000	38000
8.	Katni	NR	NR	NR	NR	NR	NR	NR	NR	NR
9.	Khargone	NR	NR	NR	NR	NR	NR	NR	NR	NR
10.	Panna	NR	NR	NR	NR	NR	NR	NR	NR	NR
11.	Rajgarh	19000	36000	4300	8000	16000	NA	26400	6900	116600
12.	Ratlam	NR	NR	NR	NR	NR	NR	NR	NR	NR
13.	Reewa	NR	NR	NR	NR	NR	NR	NR	NR	NR
14.	Sagar	NR	NR	NR	NR	NR	NR	NR	NR	NR
15.	Satna	NR	NR	NR	NR	NR	NR	NR	NR	NR
16.	Sidhi	NR	NR	NR	NR	NR	NR	NR	NR	NR
17.	Tikamgarh	NR	NR	NR	NR	275300	231000	370000	301900	1178200
18.	Ujjain	NR	NR	NR	NR	NR	NR	NR	NR	NR
19.	Umaria	NR	NR	NR	NR	NR	NR	NR	NR	NR
20.	Vidisha	NR	NR	NR	NR	NR	NR	NR	NR	NR
21.	Bhopal	NR	NR	NR	NR	NR	NR	NR	NR	NR
22.	Singrauli	NR	NR	NR	NR	NR	NR	NR	NR	NR
23.	Khandwa	NR	NR	NR	NR	NR	NR	NR	NR	NR
24.	Burhanpur	NR	NR	NR	NR	NR	NR	NR	NR	NR
25.	Neemuch	NR	NR	NR	NR	NR	NR	NR	NR	NR
26.	Balaghat	NR	NR	NR	NR	NR	NR	NR	NR	NR
27.	Shivpuri	326000	246000	60386	252200	216000	247000	251000	NA	1598586
28.	Shajapur	NR	NR	NR	NR	NR	NR	NR	NR	NR
29.	Betul	6500	7000	7000	6700	6800	7000	6500	7000	54500
30.	Narsinghpur	NR	NR	NR	NR	NR	NR	NR	NR	NR
31.	Morena	19000	17000	16000	16500	13000	15000	18000	14000	128500
32.	Guna	29000	26000	38000	6000	13800	13000	25500	6900	158200
33.	Datia	NR	NR	NR	NR	NR	NR	NR	NR	NR
34.	Mandusar	NR	NR	NR	NR	NR	NR	NR	NR	NR
35.	Sehore	NR	NR	NR	NR	NR	NR	NR	NR	NR

36.	Raisen	NR	NR	NR	NR	NR	NR	NR	NR	NR
37.	Harda	NR	NR	NR	NR	NR	NR	NR	NR	NR
38.	Chhindwara	NR	NR	NR	NR	NR	NR	NR	NR	NR
39.	Seoni	NR	NR	NR	NR	NR	NR	NR	NR	NR
40.	Bhind	NR	NR	NR	NR	NR	NR	NR	NR	NR
41.	Chhatrpur	NR	NR	NR	NR	NR	NR	NR	NR	NR
42.	Badwani	NR	NR	NR	NR	NR	NR	NR	NR	NR
43.	Dhar	NR	NR	NR	NR	NR	NR	NR	NR	NR
44.	Jhabua	NR	NR	NR	NR	NR	NR	NR	NR	NR
45.	Shahdol	NR	NR	NR	NR	NR	NR	NR	NR	NR
46.	Mandla	NR	NR	NR	NR	NR	NR	NR	NR	NR
47.	Anuppur	NR	NR	NR	NR	NR	NR	NR	NR	NR
48.	Dindori	NR	NR	NR	NR	NR	NR	NR	NR	NR
49.	Sheopur	NR	NR	NR	NR	NR	NR	NR	NR	NR
50.	Alirajpur	NR	NR	NR	NR	NR	NR	NR	NR	NR
	G Total									3590672

Table 6.3 Budget Provision for District Public Libraries

From the Table 6.3 reveals about the budget allocation of District Public Libraries. We can get information only 09 District Public Libraries out of 36. The information revel that budget allocation is very poor of District Public Libraries and it is further reveals that budget allocation for libraries in not equal basis, one library got budget in lakh and one another library got budget in thousand, so it is very unbalance budget allocation for libraries.

The Grand total of budget allocation is 3590672.00 of 16 District Public Libraries and average budget allocation is 99740.00.

Budget Allocation in e-libraries under the Sarve Shiksha Mission:

GIAN (General Information Access Network) is the project upgrading the Public Libraries of Madhya Pradesh and promote information in electronic content with the help of 11th Finance Commission and budget provision of 50 Lakhs is available for Upgrading State Central Library and 20 Lakhs for the District Public Libraries on one time grant.

No.	Budget Allocation in District Public Library(Department Wise)	Availability of Budget Allocation (Average)	Availability of Budget Allocation
1.	Divisional Public Library under Directorate of Public Instructions	22,37,000	As per capita method, average cost of is **Rs. 0.77.**
1.	District Public Library under Directorate of Public Instructions	99740.00	
2.	e-Libraries under Sarve Shiksha Mission, Madhya Pradesh	**20 Lakh for one time grant**	
	Grand Total	**2286870.00**	

Table 6.4 Proposed Availability of Budget allocation

From the Table No 6.4 reveals that, the Average Budget allocation for Divisional Public Libraries is 22, 37,000, District Public Library **3590672.00** and e-libraries under Sarve Shiksha Mission **20 Lakh for one time grant**. If merge the existing libraries in under the proposed *Integrated Public Library System for Madhya Pradesh or GIAN Network*, than available budget is increase.

How to meet out our library financial Requirement Finance?
Various standards have been suggested by various authorities for the allocation of funds amongst various heads of expenditure

Dr Ranganthan has suggested at least 50% should be spent on salaries so that qualified and adequate staff may be recruited in order to transform the money spent for books into books service, otherwise the amount spent on books will be a sheer wastage.

Allocation of Funds
The various activities are decided on priority basis and accordingly funds are distributed and expenditures were met in two heads i. e. Current Expenditure (establishment, acquisition of books and periodicals), conservation, training, publications. Capital Expenditure (land and building, machinery and equipment, furniture and fittings etc, since capital expenditure is temporary in nature and exclusively meant for specific purposes for a specific period, the distribution of current expenditure on different items were followed in the following manner.

No.	Budget Heads	Allocation
1.	Salaries and wages	50%
2.	Books	20%
3.	Periodicals and other materials viz Newspaper	5%
4.	Binding	5%
5.	Heating and Lightning	2%
6.	Rent & Loans	5%
7.	Library supplies, equipments and other Miscellaneous	13%
	Total	**100%**

Table No 6.5 Budget Heads for Public Library

New areas of services like Bibliographic service, Documentation service, indexing, abstracting, reprographic service, Library automation (computerization of house-keeping operation, creation of database, resource sharing through local-national-international networks), SDI, CAS, document delivery service are essentials to provide library service to the users and adequate funds should to provide these purpose.

Sample Budget for Public Libraries of Madhya Pradesh

The sample budget of a public library of a town with a population of 6,00,0000 is given below. If assume that one rupee per capita will be tax for financial arrangement for library, then total revenue would be collect 1,00,000,00. The allocation to various heads would be done on the basis of the standards laid town previously.

No.	Head of Accounts 1	Estimate for 2
1.	Local rates @50 nP per capita	50,000,00
2.	State Govt. contribution @37 nP per capita	37,000,00
3.	Central Govt (through RRRLF). contribution @ 13 nP per capita	13,000,00
4.	Gifts	5,000,00
5.	Fines and Fees	2,000,00
6.	Sale of Library Publications	3,000,00
Total Rs.		**1,010,000,0**

Expenditure in Rupees:

No.	Head of Demand 5	Estimate for 6
1.	Salaries and Wages	50,000,00
2.	Books	20,000,00
3.	Periodicals and other reading materials	50,000,0
4.	Binding	50,000,0
5.	Lighting and Heating etc.	20,000,0
6.	Rents and Loans etc.	50,000,0
7	Misllen. (postage, stationery, library supplies, repairs of building and equipment)	130,000,0
	Total	1,00,000,00
	b. Non-Recurring	
7.	Cost of Publications	20,000,0
8.	Furniture, Stings and Equipment	80,0000
	Total	**10,000,0**
	Grand Total (A+B)=	**18100000**

Table No 6.6 Specimen Budget estimate of Public Library 'A'

Category of Library Staff	No of Staff Required	Pay Scale	Approx Salary	Total Salary	Grand Total
State Librarian	-	37500-59600 with Grade Pay 10,000	1,10000	1320000	
Deputy Library Director	6	15600-39000 with Grade Pay 9000	95000	1140000	6840000
Assistant Library Director	8	15600-39000 with Grade Pay 8000	85000	1020000	8160000
Divisional Librarian	-	15600-39600 with Grade Pay 5400	35000	-	-
District Librarian	29	9300-34800 with Grade Pay 4800	30000	360000	10440000

Tehsil Librarian	272	9300-34800 with grade pay 4200	26000	312000	84864000
Block Librarian	313	5200-20200 with grade pay 2800	17000	204000	63852000
Panchayat Librarian	23051	5200-20200 With grade pay 2400	15000	180000	4149180000
Assistant Librarian	8	15600-39600 with Grade Pay 5400	35000	4200000	3360000
Information Assistant	66917	9300-34800 with grade pay 4200	26000	312000	20878104000
Junior Information Assistant	692	5200-20200 With grade pay 2800	17000	204000	14116800
Library Attendant	23093	5200-20200 With grade pay 1800	14000	204000	471097200
Data Entry Operator	330	5200- With grade pay 2800	17000	204000	6732000
Grand Total	**115745**				**25696746000.00**

Table No 6.7 Finance Requirements for Proposed Human Resource

Table No. 6.7 revealed about the finance requirements under the proposed *Integrated Public Library System for Madhya Pradesh or GIAN Network,* 25696746000.00 for 115745 proposed human resources, but it is huge amount for State Government to allocation for Public Libraries, but it is possible if it should be implement in four to six different phases.

Reference:

1. www.knowledgecommission2005.nic.in.
2. Ibid,. 19
3. Committee on National Policy on Library & Information Systems, 1986, prepared by Department of Culture (New Delhi, 1986).
4. Development of Public Libraries in Orissa: Analytical Aspects. Ed. Panda., B. D. 2 vols. (Delhi: Pratibha Prakashan, 1992), 54.
5. Sub-Group on Public Library System of the Working Group on Libraries and Informatics India, 1988, prepared by Planning Commission of India (New Delhi, 1988).

Chapter Seven

Status of Infrastructure Physical (Building) and ICT's

The most of significant principle among the five Laws of Library Science, enunciated by *"Dr. S. R. Ranganthan is the fifth law which state that "Library is a growing organism". He says, "The building of storage library— say a State Central Library or National Central Library-should be capable of indefinite growth. The site chosen for it should be very large indeed. Its building— particularly the stack room-will has to extend in a number of successive phases".* 1 To satisfy that fifth law of library science, the building of every library should be planned to accommodate materials with a provision for the future expansion for perform the library services efficiently and effectively to the satisfaction for the readers. The design of building should be open access, provision of reading rooms around the stack room, it allowing natural light and air and it should be located in its own building at the central part of town.

Standard for Library Buildings
"The following methods are used by Ontario Public Libraries to determine floor-space requirements.

1. **Average square feet per capita.** For a community under 100000 populations the appropriate standard is 56 sq. m. (600 sq. ft.) per 1000 capita.

2. **Building size determined by major components.**
   2.1 **Collection space:** The average standard of 110 volumes per sq. m. (10.8 sq. ft.), it allows for low shelving and wider aisles areas for children's and reference collections and allocations in the larger non-fiction area.
   Space required = 1 sq. m. (10.8 sq. ft.) for every 110 volumes.
   2.2 **User space:** For user space in a library is 5 user spaces per 1000 capita. It allows to user to informal seating, reference tables, A/V stations, public Internet stations. A space of 2.8 sq. m. (30 sq. ft.) for each reader.
   2.3 **Staff space:** For staff is 1 staff member per 2000 population. Staff space should be per staff member of 16.3 sq. m. (175 sq. ft.) and the space used for work-stations, reader services desks, circulation areas, lounge, locker facilities, etc.
   2.4 **Multi-purpose rooms:** Should assign space for these rooms which based on community service and programme objectives.
   2.5 **Non-assignable space:** It includes washrooms, janitorial space, mechanical, elevators, staircases, etc. Space required = 20% of net space (i.e. 20% of the total of items (1) to (4).
   2.6 **Minimum overall size:** Minimum should not be less than 370 sq. m. (4000 sq. ft.).

If library construct on floor basis then branch should have not less than 230 sq. m. (2500 sq. ft.) of floor space plus 14 sq. m. (150 sq. ft.) for each additional 1000 volumes over 3000 volumes in its collection."[2]

(2) "RRRLF Guidelines for Public Library: "The State Reference Libraries in State and Union Territories having a population of over 20 lakhs (I Category) will have a gross area of 50,000 sq. ft (4,645 sq. mt). The State Reference Library in States and Union Territories having a population of less than 20 lakhs (II Category) will have an area of 25,000 sq. ft. (2,324 sq. ft)."[3]

"In 2003 a joint publication between Resource and the Center for Architecture and the Environment (CABE) recommend in their publication better Public Libraries to be the differences between traditional architecture and modern library architecture."[4]

Traditional Library Architecture	Modern Library Architecture
Neo classical pattern book	Modern free style
Imposing steps and entrance halls	Street level, retail entrances
Needs of disabled people	Good disability access
Domes and rotunda	Atriums and top-floor cafes
Galleries and mezzanines	Escalators and lifts
Clerestory light	Atrium light
Restricted access to books	Open access to books and other materials
Bookshelves requiring ladders	Bookshelves at human scale
Temple of knowledge	The 'living in the city'
Institutional furniture	Domestic or club furniture
Stand alone building	Shared space with other services
Hierarchical design and circulation	Open-plan design and circulation
Canonical stock-holding	Contemporary cultural market-place
Individual study carrels	Seminar rooms and computer suites
Defensive space	Networked space
Librarians as knowledge custodians	Librarians as knowledge navigators
The rule of silence	The culture of mutual respect
Child free	Child friendly

**Table 7.1 Better Public Libraries Comparison between
Old and New Library Architecture**

Because of its special place in the community, a number of ideas are important to keep in mind when planning library buildings.

Status of Physical Infrastructure (Building) in Divisional Public Libraries:

No.	Place of Divisional Public Library	Status of Physical Infrastructure	Approx Available Area (in Sq ft)
1.	Gwalior	Own	2100
2.	Indore	Own	2200
3.	Jabalpur	Own	2200
4.	Reewa	Own	1800
5.	Bhopal	Own	3900

Table 7.2 Status of Physical Infrastructure (Buildings) of Divisional Public Libraries

From the Table 7.2 reveals the information about Physical Infrastructure (Building) of Divisional Public Libraries under the Directorate of Public Instructions. It seen that all Divisional libraries have their own building and approx available area 1800 sq ft up to 3900 sq ft libraries. All Divisional Public Libraries located in central part of city and extension possibility is available for future prospects as far as services concern, but is possible on floor basis.

Only 20% or one Divisional Public Library-Bhopal is not fulfilling the standard, but it is same to extent fulfill the standard for requirement accommodation for public library.

Status of Physical Infrastructure (Building) District Public Libraries:

No.	Place of D. P. L.	Status of Physical Infrastructure	Available Area (in Sq ft)
1.	Damoh	Own	NA
2.	Dewas	Own	1200
3.	Gwalior	Own	1800
4.	Hoshangabad	Own	1200
5.	Jabalpur	Own	1800

6.	Khargone	Own	NR
7.	Panna	Own	1600
8.	Rajgarh	Own	NR
9.	Ratlam	Own	1800
10.	Sagar	Own	NR
11.	Satna	Own	NR
12.	Sidhi	Own	1500
13.	Tikamgarh	Own	1500
14.	Ujjain	Rented	NR
15.	Vidisha	Rented	NR
16.	Bhopal	Rented	NR
17.	Khandwa	Rented	NR
18.	Shivpuri	Own	NR
19.	Shajapur	Own	NR
20.	Betul	Own	1200
21.	Narsinghpur	Own	NR
22.	Morena	Rented	NR
23.	Guna	Own	1900
24.	Datia	Own	NR
25.	Mandusar	Own	NR
26.	Sehore	Own	NR
27.	Raisen	Own	NR
28.	Chhindwara	Rented	NR
29.	Dhar	Own	1500
30.	Jhabua	Own	NR
31.	Shahdol	Own	NR
32.	Mandla	Own	NR
33.	Ashoknagar	NA	NR
34.	Indore	NA	NR
35.	Katni	NA	NR
36.	Rewa	NA	NR
37.	Umaria	NA	NR
38.	Burhanpur	NA	NR
39.	Neemuch	NA	NR

40.	Balaghat	NA	NR
41.	Harda	NA	NR
42.	Seoni	NA	NR
43.	Bhind	NA	NR
44.	Chhatrpur	NA	NR
45.	Badwani	NA	NR
46.	Anuppur	NA	NR
47.	Dindori	NA	NR
48.	Sheopur	NA	NR
49.	Alirajpur	NA	NR
50.	Singrauli	NA	NR

**Table 7.3 Status of Physical Infrastructure (Buildings)
of District Public Libraries**

From the Table 7.3 reveals that *26* of Library have their own building and *only 06* Libraries have not own their building, only 11 libraries has available area 1200 sq ft up to 1900 sq ft libraries. All libraries located in central part of city and extension possibility is available for future prospects as far as services concern and it is possible on floor basis.

Only 30% District Public Library is fulfilling the standard for requirement accommodation for public library.

**Status of Physical Infrastructure (Building)
e-libraries under the Sarve Shiksha Mission:**

No.	Place of e-Library	Status of Physical Infrastructure (Building)
1	Bhopal	Own
2	Gwalior	Own
3	Indore	Own
4	Jabalpur	Own
5	Sagar	Own
6	Umaria	Own
7	Betul	Own

8	Vidisha	Own
9	Shivpuri	Own
10	Ratlam	Own
11	Ujjain	Own
12	Reewa	Own
13	Guna	Own
14	Tikamgarh	Own
15	Panna	Own
16	Jhabua	Own
17	Hoshangabad	Own
18	Mandla	Rented
19	Dhar	Rented
20	Sidhi	Rented
21	Harda	Rented
22	Neemuch	Own
23	Khargone	Own
24	Satna	Rented
25	Damoh	Own
26	Dewas	Own
27	Morena	Own
28	Ashoknagar	NA
29	Katni	NA
30	Rajgarh	NA
31	Narsinghpur	NA
32	Datia	NA
33	Badwani	NA
34	Shahdol	NA
35	Anuppur	NA
36	Dindori	NA
37	Sheopur	NA
38	Alirajpur	NA
39	Khandwa	NA

40	Burhanpur	NA	
41	Balaghat	NA	
42	Singrauli	NA	
43	Chhindwara	NA	
44	Seoni	NA	
45	Bhind	NA	
46	Chhatrpur	NA	
47	Mandusar	NA	
48	Sehore	NA	
49	Raisen	NA	
50	Shajapur	NA	

Table 7.4 Physical Infrastructure (Building) of e-Libraries under the Sarve Shiksha Mission

From the Table 7.4 reveals the Physical Infrastructure (Building) of e-libraries under the Sarve Shiksha Mission in Madhya Pradesh and it seen that **22** of Library have their own building and **05** libraries have not own their building.

No	Public Library	Physical Infrastructure (Building)	
		Own	Rented
1.	Public Library	05	-
2.	District Public	26	06
3.	e-Libraries under Sarve Shiksha Mission	22	07
	Grand Total	**53**	**13**

Table 7.5 Availability of Physical Infrastructure (Building) for Public Library

From the Table No 7.5 reveals that all *Divisional Public Libraries* have their own Physical Infrastructure (Building), 26 *District Public Library* have their own building and *06* rented building, and *e-libraries 22* have own and *05* rented building. If merge the existing libraries in under the

134

proposed Integrated Public Library System for Madhya Pradesh, then available Physical Infrastructure (Building) is increase.

How to meet out our Library Building Requirement?

To established (or repairing. Modification and alteration of existing library building) various types of libraries as per discuss in previous chapter. The total requirement of buildings (physical infrastructure) requires shall be as under given below table.

Types of Library	No of Building	No of Building	
		Existing	Requirement
State Central Library and Knowledge Centre	1	1	-
Divisional Public Library and Knowledge Centre	4	4	-
District Public Library and Knowledge Centre	50	26	24
Tehsil Public Library and Knowledge Centre	272	-	272
Block Public Library and Knowledge Centre	313	-	313
Panchayat Library and Community Information Centre	23051	-	23051
Village Library and Community Information Centre	52143	47,100	5043
Branch Libraries	381	381	-
Delivery Station	13985	13985	-
Mobile Library	313	-	313
Total	**90513**	**61497**	**29016**

Table 7.6 Requirement of Physical Infrastructure (Building) Public Library

Table 7.6 revealed that total no of requirement of library building for proposed IPLS-MP. The total no of library building is available is 61497 and required is 90513, so it is further required is 29016 buildings for future prospects.

Information and Communication Technology Infrastructure

Every library needs the equipment to completions of daily routine work, it gave the proper information and serving their clientele, to latest equipment is very essential part. In equipment should be add the PC's printers, scanners, photocopier machines, LCD, TV, OHP and internet facility. Major equipment is essential for any public library".[5]

"A list is furnished as per guidelines of IFLA **in Table No 7.7**

No	Major Equipments for Public Libraries as per IFLA Guidelines
1.	Drop Boxes to Returning materials after and before library hours
2.	Self-service issue and return kiosks
3.	Answering machines for communicating with the library
4.	Catalogues
5.	Atlas Cases
6.	Newspaper Stands
7.	Dictionaries
8.	Wall-mounted display racks
9.	Displays and Stands
10.	PC's with Internet Access
11.	OPAC
12.	Microform and Tap Readers
13.	Slide Projectors
14.	Special equipment and reading materials for those with physical and sensory disabilities and Speech synthesizers for the visually impaired
15.	Special materials for people with learning difficulties easy-to-read materials and cassettes

Table No. 7.7 Major Equipments is required for Public Library

Current standards for electronic information facilities is the following:"[6]

- *In Canda—One computer access point per 5000 population;*
- *In England – The total number of workstations, including those for online catalogues, that are available for public use, should not be less than 6 per 10 000 population;*
- *In* Queensland, Australia:
- *For populations up to 50 000 – one PC per 5000 population.*
- *For populations over 50 000 – one PC per 5000 population for 50 000 population and one PC per each additional 10 000 population.*
- *These standards recommend that at least half the public PCs should have access to the Internet and all should have access to a printer.*

Equipments in Divisional Public Libraries:

No.	Place of Divisional Public Library	Computers	Printers	Photo Copier	Scanners	External CD Writers	TV	OHP	LCD	Others
1.	Gwalior	10	01	01	01	01	-	-	01	-
2.	Indore	12	04	01	01	01	-	-	01	-
3.	Jabalpur	10	01	01	01	01	-	-	01	-
4.	Reewa	10	01	01	01	01	-	-	01	-
5.	Bhopal	17	04	-	01	01	01	-	01	01
	Grand Total	**49**	**11**	**04**	**05**	**05**	**01**	-	**05**	**01**

Table 7.8 Equipments in Divisional Public Libraries

From the Table No 7.8 reveals that the data show the present status of library equipments in Divisional Public Libraries. It shows that Divisional Public Libraries have the equipments like Computers (49), Printers (11), Photo Copier (04), Scanners (05), External-CD Writers (05), TV (01), LCD (05) and others (01).

The Divisional Public Libraries fulfill the Major Equipments for Public Libraries as per IFLA Guidelines.

Equipment of District Public Libraries:

No.	Place of D. P. L.	Computers	Printers	Photo Copier	Scanners	External CD Writers	TV	OHP	LDC	Total
1.	Damoh	NA	NA	NA	NA	NA	NA	NA	NA	NA
2.	Dewas	NA	NA	NA	NA	NA	NA	NA	NA	NA
3.	Gwalior	NA	NA	NA	NA	NA	NA	NA	NA	NA
4.	Hoshangabad	02	01	NA	NA	NA	NA	NA	NA	NA
5.	Jabalpur	NA	NA	NA	NA	NA	NA	NA	NA	NA
6.	Khargone	NA	NA	NA	NA	NA	NA	NA	NA	NA
7.	Panna	04	02	-	-	-	-	-	-	-
8.	Rajgarh	NA	NA	NA	NA	NA	NA	NA	NA	NA
9.	Ratlam	NA	NA	NA	NA	NA	NA	NA	NA	NA
10.	Sagar	NA	NA	NA	NA	NA	NA	NA	NA	NA
11.	Satna	NA	NA	NA	NA	NA	NA	NA	NA	NA
12.	Sidhi	NA	NA	NA	NA	NA	NA	NA	NA	NA
13.	Tikamgarh	NA	NA	NA	NA	NA	NA	NA	NA	NA
14.	Ujjain	NA	NA	NA	NA	NA	NA	NA	NA	NA
15.	Vidisha	04	02	NA	NA	NA	NA	NA	NA	NA
16.	Bhopal	NA	NA	NA	NA	NA	NA	NA	NA	NA
17.	Khandwa	NA	NA	NA	NA	NA	NA	NA	NA	NA
18.	Shivpuri	NA	NA	NA	NA	NA	NA	NA	NA	NA
19.	Shajapur	NA	NA	NA	NA	NA	NA	NA	NA	NA
20.	Betul	NA	NA	NA	NA	NA	NA	NA	NA	NA
21.	Narsinghpur	NA	NA	NA	NA	NA	NA	NA	NA	NA
22.	Morena	NA	NA	NA	NA	NA	NA	NA	NA	NA
23.	Guna	04	02	NA	NA	NA	NA	NA	NA	NA
24.	Datia	NA	NA	NA	NA	NA	NA	NA	NA	NA
25.	Mandusar	NA	NA	NA	NA	NA	NA	NA	NA	NA
26.	Sehore	NA	NA	NA	NA	NA	NA	NA	NA	NA
27	Raisen	NA	NA	NA	NA	NA	NA	NA	NA	NA
28	Chhindwara	NA	NA	NA	NA	NA	NA	NA	NA	Total
29	Dhar	06	02	NA	NA	NA	NA	NA	NA	NA
30	Jhabua	NA	NA	NA	NA	NA	NA	NA	NA	NA
31	Shahdol	NA	NA	NA	NA	NA	NA	NA	NA	NA
32	Mandla	NA	NA	NA	NA	NA	NA	NA	NA	NA

33	Ashoknagar	NA	NA	NA	NA	NA	NA	NA	NA	NA
34	Indore	NA	NA	NA	NA	NA	NA	NA	NA	NA
35	Katni	NA	NA	NA	NA	NA	NA	NA	NA	NA
36	Rewa	NA	NA	NA	NA	NA	NA	NA	NA	NA
37	Umaria	NA	NA	NA	NA	NA	NA	NA	NA	NA
38	Burhanpur	NA	NA	NA	NA	NA	NA	NA	NA	NA
39	Neemuch	NA	NA	NA	NA	NA	NA	NA	NA	NA
40	Balaghat	NA	NA	NA	NA	NA	NA	NA	NA	NA
41	Harda	NA	NA	NA	NA	NA	NA	NA	NA	NA
42	Seoni	NA	NA	NA	NA	NA	NA	NA	NA	NA
43	Bhind	NA	NA	NA	NA	NA	NA	NA	NA	NA
44	Chhatrpur	NA	NA	NA	NA	NA	NA	NA	NA	NA
45	Badwani	NA	NA	NA	NA	NA	NA	NA	NA	NA
46	Anuppur	NA	NA	NA	NA	NA	NA	NA	NA	NA
47	Dindori	NA	NA	NA	NA	NA	NA	NA	NA	NA
48	Sheopur	NA	NA	NA	NA	NA	NA	NA	NA	NA
49	Alirajpur	NA	NA	NA	NA	NA	NA	NA	NA	NA
50	Singrauli	NA	NA	NA	NA	NA	NA	NA	NA	NA
Grand Total		20	09	-	-	-	-	-	-	-

Table 7.9 Equipments Details of District Public Libraries

From the Table No 7.9 reveals that the data show the present status of equipments in District Public Libraries. It shows that the only **05** Libraries have the **Computers and Printers** and **33** Libraries have not the library equipments.

None of them District Public Libraries fulfill the Major Equipments for Public Libraries as per IFLA Guidelines.

Equipment in e-Libraries under Sarve Shiksha Mission:

No.	Place of e-Library	Server	Computers	Laser Printers	Scanners	UPS	Modem	Photo Copier	DVD Writer	TV	OHP	LDC
1.	Ashoknagar	NA	NA	NA	NA	NA	NA	NA	NA	NA	NA	NA
2.	Bhopal	01	09	01	01	02	01	NA	01	NA	NA	02
3.	Damoh	01	09	01	01	02	01	01	01	NA	NA	01
4.	Dewas	01	09	01	01	02	01	01	NA	NA	NA	NA
5.	Gwalior	01	09	01	NA	02	01	01	NA	1	NA	NA
6.	Hoshangabad	01	09	01	NA	02	01	NA	NA	NA	NA	NA
7.	Indore	01	11	01	NA	02	01	01	NA	1	NA	01
8.	Jabalpur	01	09	01	NA	02	01	01	01	1	NA	01
9.	Katni	NA	NA	NA	NA	NA	NA	NA	NA	NA	NA	NA
10.	Khargone	01	09	01	NA	02	01	NA	NA	NA	NA	NA
11.	Panna	01	09	01	NA	02	01	01	01	01	NA	NA
12.	Rajgarh	NA	NA	NA	NA	NA	NA	NA	NA	NA	NA	NA
13.	Ratlam	01	08	01	NA	02	01	01	NA	NA	NA	01
14.	Reewa	01	09	01	NA	02	01	NA	NA	NA	NA	NA
15.	Sagar	01	09	01	NA	02	01	NA	NA	NA	NA	NA
16.	Satna	01	09	01	NA	02	01	NA	NA	NA	NA	NA
17.	Sidhi	01	05	01	NA	02	01	NA	NA	NA	NA	NA
18.	Tikamgarh	01	09	01	NA	02	01	NA	NA	NA	NA	NA
19.	Ujjain	1	09	01	01	02	01	01	NA	NA	NA	NA
20.	Umaria	01	08	01	NA	02	01	NA	NA	NA	NA	NA
21.	Vidisha	01	09	01	NA	02	01	01	NA	01	NA	NA
22.	Shivpuri	01	09	01	NA	02	01	NA	NA	NA	NA	01
23.	Betul	01	09	01	NA	02	01	NA	NA	NA	NA	NA
24.	Narsinghpur	NA	NA	NA	NA	NA	NA	NA	NA	NA	NA	NA
25.	Morena	01	09	01		02	01	01	NA	NA	NA	NA
26.	Guna	01	09	01	01	02	01	01	01	NA	NA	01
27.	Datia	NA	NA	NA	NA	NA	NA	NA	NA	NA	NA	NA
28.	Harda	01	09	01	NA	02	01	NA	NA	NA	NA	NA
29.	Badwani	NA	NA	NA	NA	NA	NA	NA	NA	NA	NA	NA
30.	Dhar	01	01	01	NA	02	01	NA	NVA	NA	NA	NA
31.	Jhabua	01	09	01	NA	02	01	NA	NA	NA	NA	NA
32.	Shahdol	NA	NA	NA	NA	NA	NA	NA	NA	NA	NA	NA
33.	Mandla	01	09	01	NA	02	01	01	NA	NA	NA	NA
34.	Anuppur	NA	NA	NA	NA	NA	NA	NA	NA	NA	NA	NA
35.	Dindori	NA	NA	NA	NA	NA	NA	NA	NA	NA	NA	NA

36.	Sheopur	NA	NA	NA	NA	NA	NA	NA	NA	NA	NA	NA
37.	Alirajpur	NA	NA	NA	NA	NA	NA	NA	NA	NA	NA	NA
38.	Khandwa	NA	NA	NA	NA	NA	NA	NA	NA	NA	NA	NA
39.	Burhanpur	NA	NA	NA	NA	NA	NA	NA	NA	NA	NA	NA
40.	Neemuch	01	09	01	NA	02	01	NA	NA	NA	NA	01
41.	Balaghat	NA	NA	NA	NA	NA	NA	NA	NA	NA	NA	NA
42.	Singruli	NA	NA	NA	NA	NA	NA	NA	NA	NA	NA	NA
43.	Chhindwara	NA	NA	NA	NA	NA	NA	NA	NA	NA	NA	NA
44.	Seoni	NA	NA	NA	NA	NA	NA	NA	NA	NA	NA	NA
45.	Bhind	NA	NA	NA	NA	NA	NA	NA	NA	NA	NA	NA
46.	Chhatrpur	NA	NA	NA	NA	NA	NA	NA	NA	NA	NA	NA
47.	Mandusar	NA	NA	NA	NA	NA	NA	NA	NA	NA	NA	NA
48.	Sehore	NA	NA	NA	NA	NA	NA	NA	NA	NA	NA	NA
49	Raisen	NA	NA	NA	NA	NA	NA	NA	NA	NA	NA	NA
50.	Shajapur	NA	NA	NA	NA	NA	NA	NA	NA	NA	NA	NA
	Grand Total	27	231	27	05	54	27	12	05	05		09

Table 7.10 Equipments in e-libraries under the Sarve Shiksha Mission

No	Name of Library Equipments	Respondent
1.	Server	27
2.	Desktop System	231
3.	Laser Printers	27
4.	Modem	27
5.	UPS	54
6.	Scanner	05
7.	Photo Copier	12
8.	DVD Writer	05
9.	TV	05
10.	LCD	09

Table 7.11 Equipments Detailed of e-libraries
under the Sarve Shiksha Mission

Table 7.11 reveals the Library Equipments-Server, Desktop System (Computers), Laser Printers, Modem, UPS, Scanner, Photocopier, DVD

141

Writer, TV and LCD. It seen that 27 Libraries have Server, Desktop System (Computers), Laser Printers, Modem and UPS.

The e-Libraries fulfill the IFLA guidelines for essential equipments for public library.

No.	Name of Library	Server	Computers	Laser Printers	Scanners	UPS	Modem	Photo Copier	DVD Writer	LCD	TV
1.	Divisional Public Library	-	49	11	05	-	-	04	05	05	01
1.	District Public Library	-	20	09	-	-	-	-	-	-	-
2.	e-Libraries under Sarve Shiksha Mission	27	237	27	05	27	27	12	05	08	05
	Grand Total	**27**	**306**	**47**	**10**	**27**	**27**	**16**	**10**	**13**	**06**

Table 7.12 Proposed Availability of Equipment for Public Library

From the Table No 7.12 reveals that the available equipments for Public Libraries and e-Libraries under the Sarve Shiksha Mission i.e. *Servers 27, Computers 306, Laser Printers 47, Scanners 10, UPS 27, Modem 27, Photo Copier 16, DVD Writer 10 LCD13 and TV 06.* If merge the existing libraries in proposed under the *Integrated Public Library System for Madhya Pradesh or GIAN Network,* than availability of equipment is automatically increase.

How to meet out our Library Equipment Requirement?

The sample requirement of a public library of a town with a population of 1, 00,000 is given below. The requirement of Public PC with access Internet with printer would be done on the basis of the standards laid town previously.

Assume Population	Requirement of Equipments	Quantity	Rate (Rs)	Total (Rs)
1,00,000	Public PCs	8	20,000	1,60,000
	Laser Printer	8	6,000	48,000
	Internet Connection			
	UPS	2	9,000	18,000
Grand Total				2,26,000

Table No. 7.13 Requirements of ICT's for Public Library

Table No 7.13 is revealed that requirement of electronic infrastructure for population around 1,00,000 and also gave information about 8 Public PC's with Printer and Internet connection is required, so if we follow the *IFLA Guidelines for Public Library Service*, so required finance about 2,26000.

Uses of Computer in Public Libraries and e-libraries:

No.	Public Library	Purposes of Uses of Computer				
		For Office Use	Data Entry	OPAC Search	For Internet	For All Purpose
1.	Divisional Public	-	-	-	-	05
1.	District Public Library	05	04	-	-	01
2.	e-Libraries under Sarve Shiksha Mission	-	-	-	27	-
	Grand Total	05	04	-	27	06

Table 7.14 Uses of Computers in Public and E-Libraries

From the Table No. 7.14 reveals the uses of Computer in all Divisional Public Library is uses the computers for all purpose, *05* District Public Libraries to use *Computer* for *office purpose, 04 libraries uses for Data entry and only 01 library uses the computer for all purpose* and e-Libraries under Sarve Shiksha Mission uses the *Computers* for *Internet.*

Internet Availability of Divisional Public Libraries:

No.	Place of Divisional Public Library	Internet Connection	Broadband	Telephony	Leases Line	Wireless
1.	Bhopal	Y	Y	NA	NA	NA
2.	Gwalior	Y	Y	NA	NA	NA
3.	Jabalpur	Y	Y	NA	NA	NA
4.	Rewa	Y	Y	NA	NA	NA
5.	Indore	Y	N	NA	NA	NA

Table 7.15 Availability of Internet connection in Divisional Public Libraries

From the Table No. 7.15 reveals that the all Divisional Public Libraries have Internet connection in the form of Broadband.

All Divisional Public Libraries is fulfilling the standards for electronic information facilities for public libraries.

Internet Availability of District Public Libraries:

No.	Place of D. P. L.	Internet Connection	Broadband	Telephony	Leases Line	Wireless
1.	Ashoknagar	NA	NA	NA	NA	NA
2.	Bhopal	NA	NA	NA	NA	NA
3.	Damoh	NA	NA	NA	NA	NA
4.	Dewas	NA	NA	NA	NA	NA
5.	Gwalior	NA	NA	NA	NA	NA
6.	Hoshangabad	NA	NA	NA	NA	NA
7.	Indore	NA	NA	NA	NA	NA
8.	Jabalpur	NA	NA	NA	NA	NA
9.	Katni	NA	NA	NA	NA	NA
10.	Khargone	NA	NA	NA	NA	NA
11.	Panna	NA	NA	NA	NA	NA
12.	Rajgarh	NA	NA	NA	NA	NA
13.	Ratlam	NA	NA	NA	NA	NA
14.	Reewa	NA	NA	NA	NA	NA
15.	Sagar	NA	NA	NA	NA	NA
16.	Satna	NA	NA	NA	NA	NA

17.	Sidhi	NA	NA	NA	NA	NA
18.	Tikamgarh	NA	NA	NA	NA	NA
19.	Ujjain	NA	NA	NA	NA	NA
20.	Umaria	NA	NA	NA	NA	NA
21.	Vidisha	NA	NA	NA	NA	NA
22.	Shivpuri	NA	NA	NA	NA	NA
23.	Betul	NA	NA	NA	NA	NA
24.	Narsinghpur	NA	NA	NA	NA	NA
25.	Morena	NA	NA	NA	NA	NA
26.	Guna	NA	NA	NA	NA	NA
27.	Datia	NA	NA	NA	NA	NA
28.	Harda	NA	NA	NA	NA	NA
29.	Badwani	NA	NA	NA	NA	NA
30.	Dhar	NA	NA	NA	NA	NA
31.	Jhabua	NA	NA	NA	NA	NA
32.	Shahdol	NA	NA	NA	NA	NA
33.	Mandla	NA	NA	NA	NA	NA
34.	Anuppur	NA	NA	NA	NA	NA
35.	Dindori	NA	NA	NA	NA	NA
36.	Sheopur	NA	NA	NA	NA	NA
37.	Alirajpur	NA	NA	NA	NA	NA
38.	Khandwa	NA	NA	NA	NA	NA
39.	Burhanpur	NA	NA	NA	NA	NA
40.	Neemuch	NA	NA	NA	NA	NA
41.	Balaghat	NA	NA	NA	NA	NA
42.	Singrauli	NA	NA	NA	NA	NA
43.	Chhindwara	NA	NA	NA	NA	NA
44.	Seoni	NA	NA	NA	NA	NA
45.	Bhind	NA	NA	NA	NA	NA
46.	Chhatrpur	NA	NA	NA	NA	NA
47.	Mandusar	NA	NA	NA	NA	NA
48.	Sehore	NA	NA	NA	NA	NA
49	Raisen	NA	NA	NA	NA	NA
50.	Shajapur	NA	NA	NA	NA	NA
	Grand Total	-	-	-	-	-

**Table 7.16 Availability of Intern connection
in District Public Libraries**

From the Table No. 7.16 reveals that the not a single District Public Libraries have Internet connection in the form of Broadband;

None of District Public Libraries is fulfilling the standards for electronic information facilities for public libraries.

Internet Availability of e-Libraries under Sarve Shiksha Mission

No.	Place of e-Library	Internet Connection	Broadband	Telephony	Leases Line	Wireless
1.	Ashoknagar	NA	NA	NA	NA	NA
2.	Bhopal	Y	Y	NA	NA	NA
3.	Damoh	Y	Y	NA	NA	NA
4.	Dewas	Y	Y	NA	NA	NA
5.	Gwalior	Y	Y	NA	NA	NA
6.	Hoshangabad	Y	Y	NA	NA	NA
7.	Indore	Y	Y	NA	NA	NA
8.	Jabalpur	NA	NA	NA	NA	NA
9.	Katni	NA	NA	NA	NA	NA
10.	Khargone	Y	Y	NA	NA	NA
11.	Panna	Y	Y	NA	NA	NA
12.	Rajgarh	NA	NA	NA	NA	NA
13.	Ratlam	Y	Y	NA	NA	NA
14.	Reewa	NA	NA	NA	NA	NA
15.	Sagar	NA	NA	NA	NA	NA
16.	Satna	NA	NA	NA	NA	NA
17.	Sidhi	Y	Y	NA	NA	NA
18.	Tikamgarh	NA	NA	NA	NA	NA
19.	Ujjain	NA	NA	NA	NA	NA
20.	Umaria	Y	Y	NA	NA	NA
21.	Vidisha	Y	Y	NA	NA	NA
22.	Shivpuri	Y	Y	NA	NA	NA
23.	Betul	Y	Y	NA	NA	NA
24.	Narsinghpur	NA	NA	NA	NA	NA
25.	Morena	Y	Y	NA	NA	NA

26.	Guna	Y	Y	NA	NA	NA
27.	Datia	NA	NA	NA	NA	NA
28.	Harda	Y	Y	NA	NA	NA
29.	Badwani	NA	NA	NA	NA	NA
30.	Dhar	Y	Y	NA	NA	NA
31.	Jhabua	Y	Y	NA	NA	NA
32.	Shahdol	NA	NA	NA	NA	NA
33.	Mandla	NA	NA	NA	NA	NA
34.	Anuppur	NA	NA	NA	NA	NA
35.	Dindori	NA	NA	NA	NA	NA
36.	Sheopur	NA	NA	NA	NA	NA
37.	Alirajpur	NA	NA	NA	NA	NA
38.	Khandwa	NA	NA	NA	NA	NA
39.	Burhanpur	NA	NA	NA	NA	NA
40.	Neemuch	Y	Y	NA	NA	NA
41.	Balaghat	NA	NA	NA	NA	NA
42.	Singrauli	NA	NA	NA	NA	NA
43.	Chhindwara	NA	NA	NA	NA	NA
44.	Seoni	NA	NA	NA	NA	NA
45.	Bhind	NA	NA	NA	NA	NA
46.	Chhatrpur	NA	NA	NA	NA	NA
47.	Mandusar	Y	Y	NA	NA	NA
48.	Sehore	Y	Y	NA	NA	NA
49	Raisen	Y	Y	NA	NA	NA
50.	Shajapur	Y	Y	NA	NA	NA
	Grand Total	27	27	-	-	-

Table 7.17 Availability of Internet connection in e-Libraries under the Sarve Shiksha Mission

From the Table No. 7.17 reveals that the 27 e-libraries have Internet connection in the form of Broadband.

All e-libraries are fulfills the standards for electronic information facilities for public libraries.

147

No.	Public Library	Availability of Internet Connection
1.	Divisional Public Library	05
2.	District Public Library	-
3.	e-Libraries under Sarve Shiksha Mission	27
	Grand Total	**32**

Table 7.18 Proposed Availability of Internet Connection

From the Table No. 7.18 reveals that all Divisional Public Libraries have internet. *Not a Single* District Public Libraries have't Internet Connection and 27 e-Libraries under Sarve Shiksha Mission have Internet Connection. If merge these libraries proposed under the *Intergrated Public Library System for Madhya Pradesh or GIAN Network* then solve the problem of public libraries of Internet connevitiy.

Library Automation
Present Status of Library Automation of Divisional Public Libraries: Considering the need for application of Information and Communication Technologies in Public Libraries, a survey has been conducted to find out the status of application of Information and Communication Technologies in the form of library automation in Public Libraries.

Library Automation Status of Divisional Public Libraries:

No.	Place of Divisional Public Library	Status of Library Automation
1.	Gwalior	Under Process
2.	Indore	Under Process
3.	Jabalpur	Under Process
4.	Reewa	Under Process
5.	Bhopal	Under Process

Table 7.19 Status of Library Automation in Divisional Public Libraries

From the Table No 7.19 it reveals that all Divisional Public Libraries have e-Lib library software for the library automation purpose and under process of library automation.

Library Automation Status of District Public Libraries:

No.	Place of D. P. L.	Status of Library Automation
1.	Damoh	NA
2.	Dewas	NA
3.	Gwalior	NA
4.	Hoshangabad	Under Process
5.	Jabalpur	NA
6.	Khargone	NA
7.	Panna	NA
8.	Rajgarh	NA
9.	Ratlam	NA
10.	Sagar	NA
11.	Satna	NA
12.	Sidhi	NA
13.	Tikamgarh	NA
14.	Ujjain	NA
15.	Vidisha	Under Process
16.	Bhopal	NA
17.	Khandwa	NA
18.	Shivpuri	NA
19.	Shajapur	NA
20.	Betul	NA
21.	Narsinghpur	NA
22.	Morena	NA
23.	Guna	Under Process
24.	Datia	NA
25.	Mandusar	NA
26.	Sehore	NA
27.	Raisen	NA
28.	Chhindwara	NA
29.	Dhar	Under Process

30.	Jhabua	NA
31.	Shahdol	NA
32.	Mandla	NA
33.	Ashoknagar	NA
34.	Indore	NA
35.	Katni	NA
36.	Rewa	NA
37.	Umaria	NA
38.	Burhanpur	NA
39.	Neemuch	NA
40.	Balaghat	NA
41.	Harda	NA
42.	Seoni	NA
43.	Bhind	NA
44.	Chhatrpur	NA
45.	Badwani	NA
46.	Anuppur	NA
47.	Dindori	NA
48.	Sheopur	NA
49	Alirajpur	NA
50.	Singrauli	NA
	Grand Total	**04**

**Table 7.20 Status of Library Automation in
District Public Libraries**

From the Table No. 7.20 it reveals that only 04 District Public Library Vidisha, Guna, Hoshangabad and Dhar have e-Lib library software for this purpose.

No.	Public Library	Status of Library Automation
1.	Divisional Public Library	05
2.	District Public Library	04
Grand Total		**09**

Table 7.21 Status of Library Automation

From the Table No. 7.21 reveals the all Divisional Public Libraries have under process of library automation, only *04* District Public Libraries is in process of library automation.

References:

1. Ranganthan, S. R. "Library Manual: For Library Authorities, Librarians and Library Workers". (Bangalore: Sarda Ranganthan Endowment for Library Science, 1988), 88.
2. Ibid, 101-103.
3. 12. Kalia, D. R. "Guidelines for the Public Library Systems and Services". Granthana: Indian Journal of Library Studies. No. 2(1) (1999): 31-84.
4. Vincent, J. (2007) Welcome to Your Library: connecting public libraries and refugee communities, Good Practice Guide. www.welcometoyourlibrary.org.uk/content_files/ WTYLGoodPracticeGuideNov07.pdf
5. (ibid. p. 54-55)
6. (ibid. p. 56-57)

Chapter Eight

Services Offered
By the Public Libraries

"Public library service provide on equal basis without discrimination of age, race, sex, religion, nationality languages or social status.

It is responsible for coordination and cooperation, legislation among the library and also defines and promotes a national library network which based on required common service. The public library network on national, regional basis and it should be included research special university, college and school libraries also.

The physical accessible to all members of the community, where public library is, The design of building should be open access, reading and study facilities, provision of latest ICT equipment and proper opening and closing hours to the users and special service is to be available for those whose unable visit the library.

The library services should be provides to community of rural and urban areas."[1]

Services to users

The public library must provide services based on analysis of the needs of the local community. Services should be available for identified target groups to such groups exist in local community. Services must be able to adjust and develop to reflect changes in society, for example, variations in family structures, employment patterns, demographic changes, cultural diversity and methods of communication. They should take account of traditional cultures as well as new technologies, for example, support for oral methods of communication and uses of ICT'.

Service provision for Public Libraries

Public libraries provide a wide range of services within the library and community to satisfy users' needs. The library should facilitate access to its services for all on equal basis. "The following services, which should be easily accessible to the user in a variety of formats and media, should be provided:

- Loan of books and other media;
- To provide books and reading other materials in the library;
- Information services using print and electronic media;
- Readers education services including reservation services;
- Community information services;
- User education which support literacy programmes;
- Programming and events."[2]

It is not an ideal guideline for the public library on the service basis, but the range and depth of service will depend on the size of the library, community, readers and reading materials. The library services provide withinand out side the library; use should be of ICT's and traditional reading materials. The user of any public library is children, young adults, adults, lifelong learning, leisure time interests, information services, service to community groups, services to special user groups and reading promotion and literacy.

The Divisional Public Libraries and District Public Libraries is offered different *fundamental services* like lending document for home reading, lending within the libraries, reference service, searching through catalogue cards and referral services to their users, but it can't offered *applied services like or IT based information services like* Current Awareness Service (CAS), Selective Dissemination of Information (SDI), Bibliography, Inter Library Loan, Online Searching, Indexing Service, Abstracting Service, Document Delivery Service, Translation Service, Online Services, Bibliography information of document, Blogs, feedback of library and Resourcing Sharing due to library automation. Extension services like reading to illiterates, reading to manuscripts, reading circle, intellectual centre, library talk, story hours, lantern talks, festivals and fairs.

Services Offered By the Divisional Public Libraries:

No.	Place of Divisional Public Library	Lending Document for Home	Lending Within the Libraries	Reference Service	Searching Through Catalogue Cards
1.	Gwalior	Yes	Yes	Yes	Yes
2.	Indore	Yes	Yes	Yes	Yes
3.	Jabalpur	Yes	Yes	Yes	Yes
4.	Reewa	Yes	Yes	Yes	-
5.	Bhopal	Yes	Yes	Yes	Yes
	Grand Total	05	05	05	04

Table 8.1 Service Providing by Divisional Public Libraries

From the Table No 8.1 reveals that existing Divisional Public Libraries is provided only fundamental library services to their users *reading materials to lending document for home and lending within the libraries, reference service* to their users and **only 04** Divisional Public Libraries have facility the search the library materials with the help of *catalogue card*.

Services Offered By the District Public Libraries:

No.	Place of D. P. L.	Lending Document for Home	Lending Within the Libraries	Reference Service	Searching Through Catalogue Cards
1.	Damoh	Yes	Yes	-	-
2.	Dewas	Yes	Yes	Yes	Yes
3.	Gwalior	Yes	Yes	Yes	Yes
4.	Hoshangabad	Yes	Yes	Yes	-
5.	Jabalpur	Yes	Yes	Yes	-
6.	Khargone	Yes	Yes	Yes	-
7.	Panna	Yes	Yes	Yes	Yes
8.	Rajgarh	Yes	Yes	Yes	-
9.	Ratlam	Yes	Yes	Yes	-
10.	Sagar	Yes	Yes	-	-
11.	Satna	Yes	Yes	Yes	-
12.	Sidhi	Yes	Yes	Yes	-
13.	Tikamgarh	Yes	Yes	Yes	-
14.	Ujjain	Yes	Yes	Yes	Yes

15.	Vidisha	Yes	Yes	Yes	Yes
16.	Bhopal	Yes	Yes	Yes	-
17.	Khandwa	Yes	Yes	-	-
18.	Shivpuri	Yes	Yes	Yes	Yes
19.	Shajapur	Yes	Yes	-	-
20.	Betul	Yes	Yes	-	-
21.	Narsinghpur	Yes	Yes	-	-
22.	Morena	Yes	Yes	-	-
23.	Guna	Yes	Yes	Yes	Yes
24.	Datia	Yes	Ye	-	-
25.	Mandusar	Yes	Yes	-	-
26.	Sehore	Yes	Yes	-	-
27.	Raisen	Yes	Yes	-	-
28.	Chhindwara	Yes	Yes	-	-
29.	Dhar	Yes	Yes	Yes	Yes
30.	Jhabua	Yes	Yes	-	-
31.	Shahdol	Yes	Yes	-	-
32	Mandla	Yes	Yes	Yes	-
33.	Ashoknagar	-	-	-	-
34.	Indore	-	-	-	-
35.	Katni	-	-	-	-
36.	Rewa	-	-	-	-
37.	Umaria	-	-	-	-
38.	Burhanpur	-	-	-	-
39.	Neemuch	-	-	-	-
40.	Balaghat	-	-	-	-
41.	Harda	-	-	-	-
42.	Seoni	-	-	-	-
43.	Bhind	-	-	-	-
44.	Chhatrpur	-	-	-	-
45.	Badwani	-	-	-	-
46.	Anuppur	-	-	-	-
47.	Dindori	-	-	-	-
48.	Sheopur	-	-	-	-
49	Alirajpur	-	-	-	-
50.	Singrauli	-	-	-	-
	Grand Total	32	32	18	08

Table 8.2 Service Providing District Public Libraries

From the Table No 8.2 reveals that *32* District Public Libraries is provided the only fundamental library services to their users like *reading materials to lending document for home and lending within the libraries,* while *18* District Public Libraries gave the *reference service* to their users and *08* District Public Libraries have facility the search the library materials with the help of *catalogue card.*

No.	Public Library	Servicing offered by Public Libraries			
		Lending Document for Home	Lending Within the Libraries	Reference Service	Searching Through Catalogue Cards
1.	Divisional Public Library	05	05	05	04
2.	District Public Library	32	32	18	08
3.	e-Libraries under Sarve Shiksha Mission	-	-	-	-
	Grand Total	37	37	23	12

Table 8.3 Service offered

From the Table No. 8.3 reveals that Divisional Public Libraries and District Public Libraries offered only fundamental library services to their users due to lake of library automation and e-libraries under the Sarve Shiksha Mission is providing only Internet services to their users. If merge both libraries proposed under the *Integrated Public Library System for Madhya Pradesh or GIAN Network* then solve this problem.

Existing Status of Member

The real strength of a library is depending on the usage by users. The main purpose of functioning of any library is to used by the members both the registered and unregistered. The basic data required from a library to measure its social significance to the society is the number of volumes circulated or consulted and the number of borrowers served by the library. The District Public Libraries normally enrolls members from the city which the library is located.

Existing Library Member of Divisional Public Libraries:

No.	Place of Divisional Public Library	No of Existing Members
1.	Gwalior	1300
2.	Indore	5482
3.	Jabalpur	2000
4.	Reewa	4000
5.	Bhopal	2200
Grand Total		**14982**

Table 8.4 Status of Members Divisional Public Libraries

From the Table No 8.4 The data on exist library member of Divisional Public Libraries under Directorate of Public Instruction. The total no of library members are *14982.*

Existing Library Member of District Public Libraries:

No.	Place of D. P. L.	No of Existing Members
1.	Damoh	300
2.	Dewas	280
3.	Gwalior	1300
4.	Hoshangabad	105
5.	Jabalpur	1256
6.	Khargone	60
7.	Panna	250
8.	Rajgarh	157
9.	Ratlam	2390
10.	Sagar	245
11.	Satna	550
12.	Sidhi	110
13.	Tikamgarh	1250
14.	Ujjain	1997
15.	Vidisha	375
16.	Bhopal	121
17.	Khandwa	225

18.	Shivpuri	80
19.	Shajapur	150
20.	Betul	1034
21.	Narsinghpur	785
22.	Morena	90
23.	Guna	380
24.	Datia	70
25.	Mandusar	90
26.	Sehore	145
27.	Raisen	47
28.	Chhindwara	80
29.	Dhar	525
30.	Jhabua	378
31.	Shahdol	477
32.	Mandla	60
33.	Ashoknagar	NA
34.	Indore	NA
35.	Katni	NA
36.	Rewa	NA
37.	Umaria	NA
38.	Burhanpur	NA
39.	Neemuch	NA
40.	Balaghat	NA
41.	Harda	NA
42.	Seoni	NA
43.	Bhind	NA
44.	Chhatrpur	NA
45.	Badwani	NA
46.	Anuppur	NA
47.	Dindori	NA
48.	Sheopur	NA
49	Alirajpur	NA
50.	Singrauli	NA
	Grand Total	**15326**

Table 8.5 Status of Members District Public Libraries

From the Table No 8.5 The data on exist library member of District Public Library under Directorate of Public Instruction. The total no of library members are *15326.*

No.	Public Library	Existing Library Member
1.	Divisional Public Library	14982
2.	District Public Library	15326
3.	e-Libraries under Sarve Shiksha Mission	-
	Grand Total	*30308*

Table 8.6 Proposed Existing Library Member

From the Table No. 8.6 reveals the existing library member of Divisional Public Library, District Public Libraries and e-libraries. Divisional Public Libraries have 14982 library members, District Public Libraries have 15326 *library members and* e-library *under Sarve Shiksha Mission* **data not available** of library members. The *30308 persons are uses library services* in Madhya Pradesh.

Only 0.00502% persons are used the services of public library of current population of state.

Reference:

1. Vincent, J. ed. Welcome to Your Library: connecting public libraries and refugee communities, Good Practice Guide.
    http://www.welcometoyourlibrary.org.uk/content_files/
    WTYLGoodPracticeGuideNov07.pdf
2. (ibid. p. 54-55)

Chapter Nine

Resource Sharing and Network

Introduction

Electronic library as a manifestation of changes in the information media will not be a thing of the distant future. The electronic/digital library having digital environment in which digital information may be substitute to the print-based information in near future. Library has an mission, which ease the barriers of space, time and physical form of document. Their missions is link between the past and the present and shapes the future of society by preserving the records of human culture, as well as, enhance access to global information with the help of ICT's. This mission of libraries is unlikely to chance in the future. The focus of libraries should be acquisition, organization and dissemination of knowledge and information which available in any medium. The latest development in digital technology so it is possibility overall growth, development and integration of knowledge and information has increased significantly and it is affect on digitization of knowledge and information, so it can change the entire scenario of libraries.

We conceptualize as digital libraries today began with Vannener Bush's memex machine (Bush.1945) and have continued to evolve with each advance in information technology. With the arrival of computer, the concept centered on large bibliographic databases, the now familiar online retrieval and public access systems that are part of any library. When computers were connected into large networks forming the internet, the concept evolved again, and research turned to creating libraries of digital information that could be accessed by any from anywhere in the world, Phrases like "Virtual

Library"," Electronic Library", "Library Without Walls", and most recently "Digital Library".

The Michigan Electronic Library was the first "real" virtual library. The library went on line on February 1st 1993. It was established by the University Of Michigan to serve the citizens of the state. This has been organized through the Mlink program, which is a community and information partnership between Michigan Public libraries and University Of Michigan Library. The Michigan School Of information and Library Studies also runs an on line library called the Internet Public Library. The focal objective is to "provide services and information which enhances the value of the Internet" and it is also available for guests, patrons and staff to interact with one another, which is called MOO Multi User Object Oriented Service. The digital libraries were first made popular by the NSF/DARPA/NASA. The Digital Libraries initiative was in1994. The older names electronic library or virtual libraries were also used.

Genesis of Electronic Library

Today the world is witnessing quite a large number of digital libraries, though the concept of a digital library is rooted in the age old dream of creating a virtual library. Among early efforts, one can quote the efforts made by Paul Otlet and his colleagues in 1930s in order to design to complete of organization that function similarly to today's hypertext and hypermedia system. In 1945, Vannevar Bush made some efforts to give an idea of connecting the entire human knowledge. He gave a concept of Memex machine, which used a microfilm reading process to retrieve stored information. However, the interest in digital libraries, both scholarly and professional, grew very rapidly only in the 1990s. The digital library developments in the USA took place mainly in the course of research led primarily by the computer science community that concentrated on designing and developing technologies for various digital library systems. In the UK library professionals took initiatives in the direction of developing digital libraries and enhancing the information collection and services.

Electronic Library Information online Retrieval (ELINOR) was the first electronic library project in the UK started in 1992, which was funded by Dr. Montfort University, the British Library and IBM UK.

The Gutenberg project was started in 1971 at the Materials Research Lab at the University of Illinois. The Associations of Computing Machinery (ACM) developed a digital library called ACM Portal (www.portal.acm.org). The IEEE/IEE Electronic Library, known as IEL Online (www.ieee.org/products/onlinepubs/iel/iel.html), is a digital library of publications from the Institute of Electrical and Electronic Engineers (IEEE) and the Institution of Electrical Engineers (IEE). The Library of Congress developed in January 1995 a digital library called "THOMAS" (http:/Thomas.loc.goc/). The National Library of Canada (NLC) developed its digital library, which is accessible through the web page that allows a user to move to the specific digital library's page showing the list of resources accessible under each collection (www.nlc-bnc.ca/index-e/html). Likewise a number of universities have also launched several projects in order to develop their digital libraries. For example, the Bodleian Library started Digital Library Projects (www.bodley.ix.ac.uk/); the California Digital Library (www.cdlib.org/about/overview) was developed in 1997 at the University of California. The Department of Architecture and the University Library, University of Queensland, Australia developed a digital library called DIGILIB (www.architect.uq.edu.au/digitlib/). The Scholarly Electronic text and Image Service (SETIS) formed in 1995 at the University of Sydney Library established a digital library known as SETIS (http://setis.library.Used.edu.au/ozlit). Digital libraries are also created for special materials. The Alexandria Digital Library (www.alexendria.ucsb.edu/frame.Ihtml) was created in 1995 to provide access to large information Digital Video Library. (www.informed.ia.cs.cmu.edu), Grainger Engineering Library Information Centre (www.libra.ru.uiuc.edu/grainger), NDLTD (Networked Digital Library of Theses and Dissertations) (www.ndltd.org), Greenstone Digital Library (www.nzdl.org/cgi-bin/library).

Concept of Electronic Library

The library community has used several different phrases over the years for electronic library, virtual library, library without walls, digital library and it never was quite clear.

Digital library is not only a collection of electronic information, but also it is an organized digitized system of data that can serve for its community.

A digital Library is a library in which collection are stored in digital forms and accessible by computers via network, the digital content may be stored locally, or accessed remotely via computer networks. Digital library is also called electronic library on early days other developments. Digital library or electronic library may not necessarily be networked, but it contains digitized information and print-based publications. Digital information can be stored on any medium which able to represent binary digits 0 and 1. Every computer stores numbers, letters, and other special characters in the binary form. Digital Library is most popular electronic way to replacing the traditional collection, archive and print media to inclusive of greater information exchange.

Definitions of Electronic Library

To gain knowledge what constitutes digital library let us have a look into few definitions of electronic library;

Met Collier: "managed environment of multimedia materials in digital forms, designed for the benefit of its user population, structured to facilities access to its content, and equipped with aids to navigate the global networks . . . with users and holdings totally distributed, but managed as a coherent whole".[1]

"Sun Microsystems: It is an electronic extension of functions for the users, by the uses of resources which they access in a traditional library. It is an electronic way functioning of any library. The information resources in digital library are available in digital form, stored in multimedia system, distributed via network and available on web-based services".[2]

"Berkeley Digital Library Project, University Of California: It is a collection of distributed information resources; producers of information will make it available, and consumers will find help of automated agents";[3]

"The Information Infrastructure Technology and Applications (IITA) working group: "Digital libraries are systems providing users with coherent access to a very large, organized repository of information and knowledge".[4]

Digital library is an electronic version of of any library, to replacing paper with electronic storage but it have three major differences; Storage in digital form, direct communication to obtain material and copying form a master version or server.

Digital libraries may be treated as repository of information in digital forms, store in different servers, to diverse formats to access over networks in a distributed environment. The Digital Library is a virtual library. This is a network of thousands of online libraries and it has valuable resource for students, researchers, academicians, businessman, industrialists etc.

Traditional libraries budgets mainly focus on increasing share of their funds to electronic services, whether in the form of CD-ROM's, OPAC or online databases, digital storage costs go down relatives to cost of library shelf space, and as electronic services become more useful, affordable, available. In the digital library, users use multiple information sources which they differ in content, form and sources. Which sources is useful for theym to use and they also need to manipulate the access results and incorporate the information into larger tasks in short "the digital library will require effective means for amplification of information intensive work.

Goals of Electronic Library

"Here discuss some goals of electronic library.[5]

- Communication Revaluations and Information Explosion;
- Information Storage and Transmission;
- Storage of Information;
- Economic Feasibility;
- Information in Machine Readable form;
- Increase in Users.
- **Communication Revaluations and Information Explosion:** The accessing and sharing of information contributes to its further growth and its multiplier affects results in the information explosion. Thus the communication and telecommunication revolution that contributes to a reliable and easily affordable mode of information exchange. The ease of communication has made a significant shift in

the information use paradigm from the need to know basis to that of information being available when and where you need it. This is also avoids duplication of information and has convert world in a global village. A typical digital library is a media server connected to high-speed networks. The information revolution is affected on the Internet, networks and telecommunication. The advance search engines available on the net allow one to navigate effectively through trillions of bytes of data store on diverse computers located across continents. The global network of telecommunication provides a very cost effective global library.

- **Information Storage and Transmission:** Traditionally, transmission and storage of information have been by paper. In the recent past few years there have been developments in storage and transmission of information. First, the advent of low cost computers and they easy-to-use word processing software has results in increasingly larger share of documents originating on the computer, paving the way for "digitized information". The emergence of the machine-readable bolographic database is distinctly different from the current developments. The storage and transmission of library information thus shifted from papers form to a multimedia digital form.

  Storage of Information: In traditional library it required a large space to establish of a library. It is very costly for an organization, but digital library is not required a large space to store the information, because the information is stored in digital form, some of the common digitized storage media that are presently used world like that: CD-ROM, Internet, Blue Ray Disk Multimedia, etc.

- **Economic Feasibility:** Sharing the resources become inevitable due to increase prices in publishing and distributing of information among the librarian, to make it economically in sharing the resources, utilization of computers in libraries now a day becomes mandatory.

- **Information in Machine Readable Form:** Today most of the information is available in machine readable from; because of the recent of development of telecommunication system it has become possible to access such data from any part of the world.

- **Increase in Users:** The increase in information users and need of specialization of information by these users necessitates implementations of new methods such CAS/SDI. The methods can be used in a better and faster way by using computers.

Characteristics of Electronic Library

"Here we discuss characteristics of electronic library".[6]
- Collections;
- Technology;
- Work;
- Transbordering of Information;
- Perform all function of Traditional Library;
- Accessible from the outside of the Library;
- Cheaper than Traditional Library
- **Collections**
  Digital library collections contain fixed, permanent documents not only those current libraries has more dynamic collections, but also digital environment will enable of quick handling and or ephemeral information.

- **Technology**
  Digital libraries are based on digital technologies. The underlying assumption is that the digital libraries will contain only digital materials, may be wrong. It is likely that both digital and non-digital information material will have to coexist.

- **Work**
  Digital libraries are to be used by individuals working alone. There is work-oriented perspective focusing on group of information analysis, work being done and the documents and technologies that support it.

- **Transbordering of Information**
  Breaking the physical boundaries of data transfer within and outside the countries, It is viewed that the support for communications and collaboration is as important seeking activities.

- **Performa all the function of Traditional Library**
  Digital library just equals to traditional library. It is performing all the functions of traditional library, like that acquisition, circulation, membership resource sharing etc. But the main difference is that digital library is totally based on the latest devices. These are basic requirement for digital library. But in the traditional library perform all the function without latest devices, which are used in digital library.

- **Accessible From the outside of the Library**
  Digital library is accessible from the outside of the library, when we required using it.

- **Cheaper than Traditional Library**
  A common assumption among technology reporters about the costs of "digital libraries" is that digital is cheaper than paper. Although many libraries project savings, especially when substitution strategies are used which replace selected serials titles with document delivery services, the cost analysis of making this switch remains unclear. The expenses will increase new hardware will be required, more licenses to software, increased infrastructure administration and training and costs are borne by libraries that only be acquiring digital materials and services can expect all of the above plus extensive design, digitization and implementations costs.

Advantages of Electronic Library

Traditional libraries are limited by storage space; digital libraries have the potential to store much more information, simply because digital information requires very little space to contain it. The cost of maintaining a digital library is much lowers than a traditional library. A traditional library must spend large sums of money paying for staff, reading materials and maintenance. Digital libraries do away with these fees. Digital libraries can immediately adopt innovations in technology providing users with improvements in electronic and audio book technology as well as presenting new forms of communication.

There are many advantages of digital libraries".[7]

- No Physical Boundaries;
- Round the Clock availability;
- Multiple Access;
- Structured Approach;
- Information Retrieval;
- Preservation and Conservation;
- Space;
- Networking;
- Cost.

- **No Physical Boundaries**

   The users of a digital library need to go the library physically; people from all over the world can access to the same information, as long as Internet connections are available at same time with different places.

- **Round the Clock Availability**

   The digital library is that people can gain access the information at any time, night or day.

- **Multiple Accesses**

   The same resources can be used at the same time by a number of users.

- **Structured Approach**

   Digital libraries provide access to much richer content in a more structured manner, i.e. we can easily move from the catalog to the particular book then to a particular chapter and so on.

- **Information Retrieval**

The user is able to use any search term (word, phrase, title, name, and subject) to search the entire collection. Digital libraries can provide very user-friendly interfaces, giving clickable access to its resources.

- **Preservation and Conservation**
  An exact copy of the original can be made any number of times without any degradation in quality.

- **Space**
  Whereas traditional libraries are limited by storage space, digital libraries have the potential to store much more information, simply because digital information requires very little physical space to contain them. When a library has not space for extension digitization is only solution.

- **Networking**
  A particular digital library can provide a link to any other resources of other digital libraries very easily; thus a seamlessly integrated resource sharing can be achieved.

- **Cost**
  A traditional library must spend large sums of money paying for staff, reading materials and maintenance. Digital libraries do away from these things; it has since been found that digital libraries can be no less expensive in their own way to operate. Digital Libraries can occur a large amount for the conversion of print materials into digital form, for technical skills of staff, maintain and online access.

Resource Sharing

The fact that no library can be self sufficient to have all reading materials which may be in demand by its clientele, nor is it possible to meet all the information queries by the users by purchase of such reference materials that would meet the information needs of them. Resource sharing has been considered as a powerful instrument for information source in the context of 'distributed environment' and 'digital environment'. It is also an indispensable tool in the context of 'information for all' and it is an effort of collaborative, coordinated and cooperative endeavor. Resource sharing is an effective medium of library cooperation through a number of libraries join together to form a network of libraries. Resource sharing is the cooperative endeavor that aims at extending access to all the resources and services of member libraries to a wider category of users in the region. It is reciprocal in nature not only sharing of reading materials but also of the functions, service and expertise of the professional and non-professional staff the cooperative utilization of all resources.

Economic pressures, shrinking budget, enormous growth of publications and emergence of subject specialization have compelled the libraries to think of sharing the information resources and optimizing the use of existing resource, infrastructure. Present time have witnessed knowledge and information explosion all over the world and inadequate financial resources. Under these circumstances, resource sharing and cooperative functioning of libraries through networking becomes vital. Efficient resource sharing can be achieved by networking of libraries through local area networks, metropolitan library network and wide area network. The goal of resource sharing is to maximize the availability of materials and services at the minimum expense."**8** "Library resources comprise manpower material, function, method and services. Resource sharing encompasses information, bibliographical and textual database, cooperative acquisition, cataloguing, manpower, equipment, expertise and services. Resource sharing via network implies automation, data communication and effective co-operations."**9**

Need for Resource Sharing

The following are the main reasons need for resource sharing:

- Information explosion and scattering of literature in both form i. e. published and unpublished;
- To face difficulties handling of different types data by library staff;
- Complexity and diversity of user's demands;
- To lack of resources and facilities in libraries;
- ICT's and its impact on Library and information Science and services;

- Emergence of e-resources, interdisciplinary research and subjects;
- Bibliographic data storage;
- Increasing cost of information materials, uses of existing resources and eliminating duplication;
- Development of new subjects and subject specialization;
- Increase and diversity of reading community, user groupd and their information needs;
- Access to existing information and service at less cost;
- Libraries face the problem of adequate space and hence think of cooperative storage;
- It ease pressure among the libraries on budget allocation;

Objectives of Resource Sharing

"The following are the noteworthy objectives of resource sharing".[10]
- To optimize the utilization of information resources through shared cataloguing, inter library loan, cooperative catalogue, collection development and it will be avoiding duplication in acquisition;
- To encourage cooperation among libraries, documentation centres and information centres;
- Assist member libraries in selection of reading material, purchase, catalogue;
- To promote maximum use of library resources;
- Improvement of library facilities and services;
- To provide cooperative in different areas among voluntary organization, materials beyond the reach of individual libraries.

Feasible Areas for Resource Sharing

Here we discuss feasible area for resource sharing in given below;.[11]

Inter Library Loan
In the network environment inter library loan possible through electronic mail facility. The person at the other end reads the mail and locates the relevant document. If the document is available in machine readable from, it will be sent through e-mail; otherwise the hard copy will be sent through

courier service. In online environment one can search the holding of the other library. If the documents are available message can also be sending it on loan.

Acquisition

The acquisition system can be easily possible with the help of online ordering facility. It enables the publisher and book supplier to connect via networks. The libraries thus have access to latest information and can decide whether they should acquire a particular book and it is also possible in serial control;

Library Automation and Network

Library automation and networks are growing the need for trained and skilled manpower also grows. It is essentials that the expertise of the skilled personnel is shared.

Union Catalogue

Union catalogue of all participating libraries of network should be compiled and updated regularly;

Information Services

Information is an important resource of the library, it can be shared through e-mail and networking if available in machine readable form.

Development of Special Collection

To make information available through resource sharing, each library in the network should develop collection specializing in the areas of their interest.

Cooperative Storage

It is achieved by arranging the deposit of publications at local and regional levels. It reduces duplication of material and provides more space for new books to the particular library.

Importance of Resource Sharing

The important of library resource sharing are:
- Bibliographic controlling of the explosion of literature and knowledge;
- Avoiding duplication in purchase of costly reading materials;
- Facilitating the adoption of new areas in every field of knowledge;
- For improving the mobility of data;
- Developing the flow of information among special information Centres/libraries;

Methods of Resource Sharing

Resource sharing was done through inter library lone with the help of union catalogue and union list of periodicals. Resource Sharing is operated in two ways:

Library resource sharing through telecommunication networks: Exchange of information through electronic mail, online facility or a terminal is possible if a database is created. Databases are collections or records in machine readable form that is made available for searching from remote computer terminals. Bibliographic details of a document are needed for identification storage and retrieval purpose:

Library resource sharing through database in optical media: The information is stored in computers, the cooperation and sharing of resources that was prevalent on a manual Scale in the past got introduced on an automated scale through Networking, Modern technology can now provides us with main ways in which Library networks can store, process economically, effectively and on a Scale that would be near impossible with traditional manual operation.

Definitions of Network
"A library network bodily described as a group of libraries coming Together with some agreement of understanding to help each other to satisfy the information needs of their clientele."[12]

"UNISIST II working document defines Information Networks as: ".[13]
"A set of inter-related information systems associated with communication facilities, which are cooperating through more or less formal agreements in order to implement information-handling operations to offer services to the users".

"The National Commission on Libraries and Information Science (NCLIS) (1975) defines a network as"[14]
"Two or more libraries and or/other organization engaged in a common pattern of information exchange through communications, for some functional purpose. A network usually consists of a formal arrangement whereby materials, information, and services provided by a variety of libraries and other organizations are available to all potential users. Libraries may be in different jurisdiction but agree to serve one another on the same basis as each serves it own constituent. Computer and Telecommunications may be among the tools used for facilitating communication among them.

"Alphones F. Trezza defines it as: ". . . . a formal organization among libraries for cooperation and sharing of resources, in which the group as a whole is organized into subgroups with the exception that most of the needs of a library will be satisfied within the subgroups of which it is a member".[15]

"Raynard C. Swank defines library networks as a "concept that includes the development of cooperative systems of libraries on geographical, subject or other lines, each with some kind of centre that not only coordinates the internal activities of the system but also serves as the system outlet to, and inlet from, the centres of other systems. The concept is also hierarchical . . . .".[16]

"Harold, M in Librarian's Glossary has defined collaborators as one who is associated with another or others . . . . Hence, collaboration can viewed as having association with another or other libraries. In other words this association can be explained as co-operation with other libraries or in modern context as resource sharing or library consortia".[17]

"According to Miller "it is a cooperative system established by libraries and information centres, which are brought by common subject, geographical proximity to share informational resources, human resources and all other elements for providing effective information service".[18]

"The ALA Seminar on 'Networking and Multiple Library Co-operations (1977) defined 'library networking as follows "The cooperative structures, which cross jurisdictional, institutional, and often political boundaries to join in a common enterprises, several types of libraries academic, special and public".[19].

A library network means more than two libraries or information centers inter-related in support of a common goal. The main thrust area of library networking is library co-operation and resource sharing and it is working in a particular city/area, subject like science, technology or research based institute networks. The network is a set of technologies (including hardware, software and cabling or some other means) that can be used to connect computers together, enabling them to communicate, exchange information and share resources in real time. Networks allow many users to access shared data and programs. Some organizations, institutions, use a centralized system. When data and program are stored on a network and can be shared,

The following advantages of any network;
- It allow users to share printers and scanners;
- It make personal communication easier;
- It make easy for users and administrators to back up important data file;
- It allow to users access to larger collection of materials from different libraries and location,
- Maximum use of library resources at minimum cost;
- Service to more number of users;
- Save the time as well as finance.

Advantages of Network

Library network provide several advantages;

- A network facilitates data communication amongst geographical dispersed nodes;
- The networking of computers permits the sharing of computing resources available at geographically dispersed locations;
- Networking also provides stand by backup options to it nodes;
- The use of networking allows a very flexible working environment;
- Concerted use of computer and communication technology provides for rapid exchange of information.

Network offer the following services:

ICT's based services; catalogue based services, Database services, bibliographical based services, Selective Information of Dissemination, Current Awareness Services, Abstracting Services and other related services to the library.

Requirements to Establish a Network

Standardization: The problem with different classification schemes, cataloguing codes and subject headings for libraries have to solve for smooth functioning of any network and network can adopt the CCF, AACR-2 and LCSH for standardization in information heading.

Network Architecture: The network centre will linked all member libraries with the network host system through telephone line or V-SAT links. The member libraries need to pay STD charges as the State Centre or another way to wireless telephone and libraries also can establish their own LAN.

Data Base: Should be installed to creating a union catalogue, for all member libraries and main centre handled bibliographic record, system software, communication software and application software will be used. The all data will be stored in Main Server and database is made available to all "Authenticate" users logging in through their respective state centres. The data base is 24 hours online and is updated periodically.

Network Components: The network centre at State Central Library, Bhopal will have essentially these components. Routers usually provides by the V-SAT service provider.

LAN Switch: The LAN switch interfaces all the terminal points in the network centre. It configured depending on the number of nodes required.

Remote Access Server (RAS): The RAS should have a minimum 6 ports, enabling a minimum of 6 logins simultaneously. Depending on the traffic the capacity of RAS could be increased in future.

Telephone Lines: The network centre should have adequate number of telephone lines to enable the remote server to login any time

V-SAT Connectivity: Very small apparatus terminal usually provided by the telephone company but it provide by rivate service providers.

Hardware Requirements: Dual-processor 500 MHz server class machine, 500 and above MB RAM, Minimum of 120 GB Hard disk space, 10/100 NIC (Network Interface Card), Database Backup solution, UPS with at least 6 hours battery backup time with about 10 computers, CD/DVD-ROM, OCR Scanner and Printer with network compatibility.

Software Requirements: Windows 2007 service pack 2+ security holes up, Internet Explorer 7.0 or higher version, Terminal service pact 2.

Internet Information Server (IIS) included with windows: MS SQL Server 7 or higher or Linux, library software packages, Visual Studio packages, Ms Office 2007, Coral Draw 11.00 or higher graphic software such as Photoshop 7.0, Fractal Painter, Illustrator, Multi Media software such as 3D Studio Max or Maya or any other software and Oracle 8.1 or higher.

Web Portal: Web site can be developed uses for this network. Access can be restricted by login or password systems. Users with different levels of permission can access/contributions articles. This type of system helps in sharing practices, experiments, innovations, failure stories etc. Web portal are developed with database supporters to keep the records of authors, members, visitors and many other things.

Discussion Board or Forum: A virtual community can be created using Web-based discussion boards. Different sections or areas can be created for discussions. This is an ideal solution for different locations, different areas, different geographical areas, but have a common area of interest. They can share their problems, real life experience, common area of interest and building a personal relation type networking. Under the open source community some programs are popular for web application like PHPBB.

Blogs: Web blogs are popular nowadays and any organizations are utilizing this tool to create awareness and evolve opinions on different issues. Blogs can be hosted in any organization internet or any popular blogs site like www.blogsspot.com; it can Be used to give a platform to the common people to post their view.

Expert System: Expert database with profile updating can be kept for the public view and queries can be posted to specific experts based on the areas of domain and expertise of the experts. This helps in creating innovations and learning culture in a community or society.

Network Development in India"[20]

The growth of Indian library networks may be traced to the efforts made during the last four decades. The 1958 Scientific Policy Resolution adopted at the instance of Pandit Jawaharlal Nehru emphasized the fostering of scientific temper in people. In pursuance of this agenda, several committee and commissions were appointed to look into specific issues and come up with necessary recommendations. e.g. the Sinha Committee Report (1959), Ranganathan Report to UGC (1965), Peter Lazar Report and V. A. Kamath Report (1972). In the 1980's organized efforts were made to collect and disseminate information. The 1983 Technology Policy Statement emphasized the need for technology information basic. In July, 1984 the Working Group of Planning Commission headed by Dr. N. Seshagiri recommended to the Government the need for modernization of library services and informatics during the Seventh Five Year Plan of 1985-1990.

It may be important to refer to the report of the Working Group of the Planning Commission on Libraries and Informatics for the Ninth Five Year Plan 1997-2002 which was prepared under the Chairmanship of Mr. B. P. Singh, Secretary Department of Culture. It is an important report as it has come at a stage when the Indian libraries have to face the challenges of the 21st century due to unprecedented developments in information technology, networking and internet. The report includes the following major recommendations for the networking and modernization of libraries.

- Should be creating a network for all libraries in the domain of Humanities with particular reference to Arts including MS libraries.
- Should be establish a National Library System (NLS) which included National Library of India, National Depository Libraries in Delhi, Mumbai and Chennai, National Science Library, National Medical Library, DESIDOC, NISCAIR, NASSDOC, SENDOC and such other libraries of national importance.
- The modernization of libraries using ICT should create of standard bibliographic databases to avoiding duplication and optimism uses and availability to scholars, researchers and public.
- All the university and college libraries should be automated and databases created using international standards and UGC provide financial assistance for creation of database of retrospective collection;
- Each university should establish Local Area Network (LAN) and provide terminals in each teaching Department for quick access to the resource of the library;
- National Subject Libraries, four recipient libraries under the DB Act and libraries of national importance should merge their data in a common database following uniform standards, uniform/compatible software's and computer systems on the pattern of OCLC. The databases may include books, periodicals, non-book materials, reports, standards etc and also non-print materials in electronic form. In this database the complete catalogue of the National Library, Calcutta in all languages should become available online using standard international format.

- All the participating libraries in the NLS should be networked for which necessary infrastructure should provided. The NIC may act as the agency for ensuring development and proper facilities;
- Promotion and creation of bibliographic databases should be done in all Indian languages and DELNET is responsible for that;
- NIC should be financed to support the infrastructure requirements of national, regional and local networks and it may be devise ways for interlinking networks to achieve better access to resources.
- It has been has found that DELNET has emerged as an operational library network in India. It has developed the online union catalogue of books and periodicals. It is recommended that DELNET be supported to create National Database and develop the OCLC pattern and other city networks viz CALIBNET, MALIBNET be financially supported to undertake creation of databases at state and city levels;
- INFLIBNET should coordinate with the existing networks and institutions so that duplication in various categories may be avoided;
- All government libraries including research and official libraries., documentation/ information centres, public libraries should be join a library network and follow the standards for database creation, information retrieval;
- Library networks and institutions with requisite ICT's facilities should provide and assisted to provide short term training courses to the staff and trained staff between units ought to be encouraged;
- Development of Information Highway should be given priority for institutions, libraries, information centres and individuals scattered all over the country are inter liked via teleconferencing and Interne;
- A National Centre on Informatics and Libraries should be set up for coordination of networks at the national level.

Public Libraries Networking in Madhya Pradesh

In order to achieve resource sharing on local, regional, state and national levels to develop of LAN and WAN for libraries is an urgent need. Public Libraries Network from State Central Library to Village/Rural Libraries, the overall efforts of Public Libraries system shall be keeping the pace with the changing scenario. The networking is a major thrust area for Public Libraries services. The networking major concern area of public libraries services in the state. A library network means more than two libraries interrelated by a common operation or service. The main area of any library networking is library co-operation and resource sharing. The network is working in a particular city/area, subject, or research based institute networks, but there is no network's active at state level and especially public libraries. A network is a set of technologies (including hardware, software and cabling) that can be used to connect computers together, enabling them to communicate, exchange information and share resources in real time. Networks allow many users to access shared data and programs at one time.

Under the networking from State Level to District Level to Block level to Panchayat Level to village Level shall be provided with ICT's network facilities. The network located and established via State Central Library shall be interconnected with Divisional Libraries, Divisional Libraries shall be interconnected with District Libraries, District Libraries shall be connected with Block Libraries, Block Libraries shall be connected to Panchayat Libraries and Panchayat Libraries shall be connected with Rural / village Libraries. The networking shall be eradication duplication of reading materials and optimum utilization of resources in the region as well as national level through sharing of resources.

The Recommendations of the Committee on National Policy of Library and Information System for Public Library Network[21]

- All the libraries should form part of a network from the community libraries of the village through intermediary levels to the district and to the State Central Library and these state consortia should connect with the national level;
- The State Central Library/Directorate of Public Libraries has to perform as the coordinating agency for the public libraries in the state;
- The District Library will take the leadership in establishing linkages between all other public libraries of the district and work towards resource sharing within the area;
- Use of ICT's for developing local library and information network has to be supported for resource sharing. Any user should have ready access to documents/information wherever he/she is located

"National Knowledge Commission 2006 offers Guidelines for Networking of Public Libraries as follows".[22]

- Networking of Public Libraries should be undertaken in a phased manner. There are approximately 54,000 public libraries in existence;
- Phase-I: 1,000 of these will be networked in Phase-I as a pilot project, by Delnet and Inflibnet each covering about 500 libraries in 12-18 months;
- Phase-II: Based on the experience of Phase-I, up to 10,000 libraries will be covered in one year;
- Phase-III: The remaining libraries may be networked in the third and final phase in three years. This project should be completed by 2011.
- Raja Rammohan Rai library foundation for Public Library may give the necessary infrastructural support for the above activity and co-ordinate it;
- The networking agencies should ensure state-of-the-art technology with the following features;
- Open source software, which also supports multi-lingual environment with multi-user and multimedia content creation capabilities;
- Storage dissemination and replication of the data through mirror sties, gateways, portals and inter-library loan facilities;
- Capability of conducting exhaustive training programmes.

Types of Networks

"Computer networks exist in different shapes and sizes. Over the years, the networking industry has coined terms like 'LAN' and 'WAN' attempting to define sensible categories for major types of networks designs. The precise meaning of this technology remains lost on the average person,. However, for historical reasons, the industry refers to nearly type of network as an "Area network". The most commonly discussed categories of computer networks include the following". **23**

- Local Area Network (LAN)
- Wide Area Network (WAN)

- Metropolitan Area Network (MAN)
- Storage Area Network (SAN)
- System Area Network (SAN)
- Server Area Network (SAN)
- Small Area Network (SAN)
- Personal Network (PAN)
- Desk Area Network (DAN)
- Controller Area Network (SAN)
- Cluster Area Network (SAN)

Of the above networks, the most widely used and known a network is LAN, WAN and MAN and here we gain our knowledge.

- **Local Area Network (LAN):** A LAN is a number of related computers that share information over a transmission media. A typical us of LAN is to tie together personal computers in an office so that they cal all use a single printer and a file server. The LAN can be within a building or a campus wide network.
- **Metropolitan Area Network (MAN):** Attempts are being made to develop this type of network in metropolitan areas such Delhi, Calcutta, Bangalore, Madras etc.
- **Wide Area Network (WAN):** It is established in different cities and countries are referred to as WAN, which is specially designed to inter correct data transmission devices between wide geographical areas.

Library Networks

Networking is the linkage of working procedures for the exchange of resources. Information sharing may be understood as a mode of operation, whereby resources are shared by a number of participation having same objectives. Some of the essential prerequisites for effective sharing include possession of shareable resources by the participating libraries. There are many common resources and services which can be shared among the libraries like:

- To provide a national platform designed to bridge the gap among the libraries and establish links among organizations, professionals and users involved in R & D;

- Establish local, regional, national and international network for exchange of information and expertise through the network;
- Evolve and implement programmes on user education and training of information scientists responsible for handling of information and its application to education, research and development;
- To prepare union catalogue and databases and to develop relevant information handling tools and techniques;
- Assessment of information requirements, create and improve necessary infrastructure and provide informatics based support and services to the specialized community of users working in various subject areas;
- Enhance access to the collections of the participating libraries;
- Sharing of resources and services including inter-library loan bulletin boards, SDI service, on line union catalogue of books, periodicals, reprints, documents delivery, information retrieval and dissemination, exchange of materials and information;
- On line access to foreign databases, to the user's to pay the cost;
- Building a low cost library information system which can possibly be used as a model for future expansion;
- Consultation on professional issues and promote cooperation among libraries on inter library activities and improvement of any libraries;
- Create understanding and confidence among professional and authorities.

Library Networks in India

"Here we discuss about some important Library Network of India. **24**

ADINET: Ahmedabad Library Network

It was inaugurated in February 1995 when a MOU was signed between NISSAT and ADINET at Ahmedabad. ADINET has ten institutional members, five associate institution members and two professional members. A centralized database has been created at ADINET which contains institute master, journal master and book databases. It also organized six work and training programmes. ADINET provided e-mail connectivity to 30 libraries of Ahmedabad.

BALNET: Bangalore Library Network

The network was set in 1995 with support from JRD Tata Memorial Library with collection of Bangalore University with initial membership of 100 libraries. Bangalore University has 3 constituent colleges and 532 affiliated colleges. The university has a central library with a rich collection of resources relating to science, technology, humanities and social sciences and a branch library at the central college campus. All the affiliated colleges' libraries have computerized and created bibliographical databases of their collections.

BONET: Bombay Library Network

It was set up by the Department of Electronics at the National Centre for Software Technology (NCST), Bombay with the objectives to build a new library information system which can possibly be used a model for future expansion of this service even outside of Bombay. It was established on 6 November, 1992. It offer training related to library and information science, library computerization networking.

CALIBNET: Calcutta Library Network

The network was inaugurated on 21 December 1993 with the support of NISSAT with the help of own library software "Maitrayee". It provides services like online/CD-ROM based global information search and retrieval services, full text document delivery and database services. The network links 38 science and technology libraries in the Calcutta region.

MALIBNET: Madras Library Network

It was set up by the INSDOC in 1991 to interconnect libraries and information centres in Madras with the objectives to take faster growth in the LIS profession in India, establish appropriate links to national and international libraries and networks, creation of free e-journals database, and facilitate resource sharing and information dissemination through network. The network has connected more than 60 libraries located in Madras.

MALIBNET: Mysore Library Network

It was set up at Central Food Technological Research Institute (CFTRI), Mysore on 12 June, 1995 with financial assistant NISSAT in association with Mysore City Library Consortium (MCLC). Most of the libraries are within Mysore city. Out of the total 116 were affiliated to University of Mysore and of 34 colleges are located within city.

PUNNET: Pune Library Network

Presently 30 libraries and information centers of Pune city which are accessing not only databases, but also use e-mail and internet facilities; It provides access to NICNET database e.g. MEDLANS, AIDS, US patent information and union catalogue of books available in British Libraries in India.

Conclusion

The libraries play an important role in every area to related education and information especially e-information. The e-information is very essential part of human being, so libraries is also changes their role and important and all the information is available in e-form so electronic libraries play a significant role in store, delivering the e-information among the users. Due to increase the pricing of books and shrinking the library budget, it is compulsory for any library to share their resources via network among the library users at local, regional, national and international levels. Resource sharing a tool for libraries to serve their clientele and gave the pin pointed information.

References

1. books.google.co.in/books
2. www.sunmicrosoft.com
3. www.sunsite.berkeley.edu
4. www.en.wikipedia.org/iiita_Library
5. www.en.wikipedia.org/digital library definitions
6. www.en.wikipedia.org/goals of digital/electronic library_html
7. www.en.wikipedia.org/digital/electronic library_html
8. Verma, A. "The Use of Web in Libraries". (New Delhi: Akansha Publications, 2004), 107.
9. Malvya, A. "Electronic Libraries". (New Delhi: Ess Ess Publications, 1999), 172.
10. Kaul. H. K. "Library and Information Networking NACLIN 1999". (New Delhi: DELNET, 1999), 36.
11. Kaul. H. K. "Library and Information Networking NACLIN 2003". (New Delhi: DELNET,2003), 144-45.
12. http://ncsi.iisc.ernet.in/pipermail/lis-forum/2005-June/002281.html
13. ibid
14. ibid
15. http://infosciencetoday.rog/type/article/networking-of-agriculrtual-informacation-systems-in-bangladesh-bd-agrinet-a-del, html.2
16. World Encyclopedia of Library and Information Services. 3rd ed. (Chicago: American Library Association, 1993), 482. http:books.google.co.in.
17. Potter, W. "Recent Trends in State Wide Academic Library Consortia", Llibrary Trends, 45(3(2007):417-419.
18. Ibid.
19. www.ala.org
20. http://ncsi.iisc.ernet.in/pipermail/lis-forum/2005-June/002281.html
21. Ibid.
22. www.knowledgecommission2005.nic.in
23. Kaul. H. K. "Library and Information Networking NACLIN 2003". (New Delhi: DELNET, 2003), 144-45.
24. http://en.wikipeida.org/wiki/Network

Chapter Ten

Historical Background of GIAN (GENERAL INFORMATION ACCESS NETWORK) 1

"It is project for upgrading the State Library and District Libraries by incorporating electronic content through GIAN or General Information Access Network;

Objectives of GIAN
The objectives are given below points.
- Reposition these existing libraries as knowledge centers of the 21st century by modernizing them with new media of knowledge storage and dissemination like electronic media and thereby goes beyond print that is the only form of knowledge stores in these libraries
- Create ownership for the libraries through transferring their management to local communities of interested people. This could include donors and private sector support for selected services
- Create a "revenue model" for the unit so that an income stream is generated to keep the GIAN in an effective condition and not be dependent on grants
- Utilize the grant provided by the 11th finance commission to enable the improvement of the Public Library System through incorporation of GIAN.

Background

Libraries stimulate the imagination of a society and make it grow. Governments have recognized this and therefore have gone about setting up libraries and supporting them with grants. In fact good libraries were set up even by rulers in pre-independence days though the conscious effort to spread them across the state has been a post-independence phenomenon. Libraries that were created and sustained by pre-independence patronage systems also passed into government hands. Over the years these libraries got "departmentalized" with their health depending on capacitates of the funding streams. Allocations remained by and large static while costs began to amount. Actual funds left for books and periodicals became meager. Libraries deteriorated. Post upkeep also affected morale of staff. Today many of these libraries represent a very sad picture of the provision of a vital public service.

New Context

Today the world is driven by intellectual capital. The key resource for development and economic growth has become knowledge. These libraries are potential power house for providing public access to knowledge. New technologies have now enabled wide spread sharing of knowledge especially through the internet. The role of public libraries therefore becomes very important because the best of world's knowledge can be accessed by the ordinary citizen only through a public access point like the library. Therefore there is an urgent need to upgrade and reorient these libraries using the revolutionary potential of information technologies to transform the world of knowledge storage and knowledge sharing.

New Opportunities:
Grants from the Eleventh Finance commission

In this context the decision of the 11th finance commission to provide a corpus to upgrade the State libraries and the District Libraries could not have been timelier. A budget provision of 50 Lakhs is available for upgrading the state library and 20 Lakhs for the district level libraries. The Government of Madhya Pradesh proposes to create a new stream of GIAN (Knowledge) or General Information Access Network, which would consist of a refurbished public library with state-of-the information technology support including a unit to 10 computers with internet connectivity.

GIAN: Implementation

A Core Group for management would be set up at the state-level to manage the programme. This core group will in turn create District level Management Teams. The composition of the Core Management Group at the State-level is given on Annexure I. This State-level Team will be advised by a Technical Advisory Group whose composition is given up Annexure 2. The composition of the District Management Team is given on Annexure 3. The task of the District Management Team will be three fold:

- Create public ownership for the library through a plan implemented by this forum;
- Ensure timely completion of refurbishing work and incorporation of GIAN package of electronic content;
- Create a Revenue stream to make GIAN self Financing.

Activities to implementation GIAN and increase public ownership of Public Libraries at District-level

Each Library must have a Mission statement on its modernization plan and resources must be located from grants and local efforts to implementation the plan;

- Each Library must have a Collection Statement on its stock and plants to augment;
- Each Library must create a Local Development fund through contributions;
- Each Library must fix a charge for use of GIAN unit for internet use at reasonable rates and the fund should flow into the local fund;
- Members of the District Management Committee must catalyze a "Friends of the Library" movement;
- Library should set apart a place as a Children's Corner: People should be encouraged to volunteer time to read to children;
- Libraries must organize discussions in literature, theatre, cinema etc;
- Technical personnel must be requested to volunteer services as Friends of the Library;

- There has to be 100% training of staff on handling electronic content. This training will be organized through vendors who supply hardware as part of the tender condition.

For implantation of the plan the state library would be treated on par with the District Library and will be different only a term of resource availability.

Support to Districts to Implement GIAN

- In the State government, the implementation unit of GIAN will be the Department of School Education, which today manages the library system. Through GIAN the effort is to reposition the libraries as District entities owned and supported by Districts. Establishment costs like salaries and other expenses incurred presently will continue to be provided by the School Education Department;
- Technical Support to implement GIAN will be organized through Sarve Shiksha Mission which in turn will nodalise such support through MAPIT;
- Technical configuration will be standardized through MAPIT and districts would be abide by that advice;
- Funds would be placed with Districts for Implementing the modernization plan;
- Each district will be draws up its plan for a self financing model for GIAN and inform the state government.

Gensis of GIAN (General information Access Network)

It was started in January 2000, Gyandoot (translated as 'Messenger of Information') is a Madhya Pradesh Government initiated project aimed at setting up an intranet system that connects rural cyber kiosks throughout Dhar district. There are three entities involved in Gyandoot: Gyandoot Samiti (NGO), the Government and the Kiosk Managers. Funding for the project is through village committees (Panchayats) and community or private entrepreneurs. Gyandoot (which means 'purveyor of knowledge') aims to empower local people in Dhar District by giving them access to a village-level intranet (computer network). The network has grown to include a total of 82 information kiosks, which are either privately run by small entrepreneurs, or located in local schools. The project has been well-publicized, and is considered one of the leading examples of community-based tele-centres in India.

Objectives of GYANDOOT

The long-term objective of the project has been to use innovative e-governance, ecommerce and e-education techniques as a tool of social change and development through the wired villages in the district.

Objectives and Goals

- To ensure equal access to emerging technologies for marginalized segments of the society.
- To create a cost-effective, replicable, economically self-reliant and financially viable model for taking the benefits of IT to the rural masses.
- To implement a new grass-roots entrepreneurial model with the participation of groups of non-traditional entrepreneurs.
- To provide self-employment through entrepreneurship to local rural youth.
- To improve the quality, speed and sensitivity of the state delivery apparatus towards the needs of local citizen-customers.
- To impact IT on the government-citizen interfaces as the thrust area, so that the benefits of the knowledge economy directly reach the marginalized have-nots and know-nots.
- To search for the potential of rural markets in the digital domain.
- To analyze the processes and modalities involved in the socio-cultural environment while taking technology to the deprived communities.

Institutional Agreements

Organization roles /responsibilities/constraints;

SOOCHAK (Manager/owner of the kiosk)

- The person operating the Soochanalaya is a local matriculate operator and is called Soochak. A soochak is not an employee but an entrepreneur. Soochak only needs maintenance and numeric data entry skills most of the software is menu-driven;

- In the Gyandoot™ scheme of things, each of the 35 centres, where Soochanalayas have been established, caters to surrounding 25-30 villages. Soochanalayas have been established in the buildings of Gram Panchayats that are located either at block headquarters or at haat bazaar (weekly marketplace in tribal areas) or are prominent villages on major roads (e.g. bus stand points). In Soochanalaya include approximately 15 Gram Panchayats and 25-30 villages. The coverage of network wide-ranging information needs of the villagers. Every Kiosks established within 10 km in Dhar town, serving the urban population;
- In January 2000, 35 kiosks were opened, 20 were opened by the Gram Panchayat (village council), and 15 were private. The Gram Panchayat provided the building, telephone, electricity connection and furniture for the every kiosk. Each kiosk connects to the Pentium 3 Remote Access Server (RAS) which is housed in the computer room of the Zila Panchayat (District Council). The district authorities provide this space free of charge, as well as for the Gyandoot project manager and support staff of four.

Target Groups

The main target group is the villagers who require the information. The majority (87%) of people in Dhar District depend on agriculture, with cotton, wheat and soyabean being main crops. It is estimated that 60% of the district population live below the poverty line.

Participation of Users

The services/facilities on Gyandoot have been chosen through a participatory process involving the community; government officials and the Gyandoot team.

Format of Information

The information is provided in the local language-Hindi so, increasing accessibility to the local population.

Gender

84 per cent of users are men (average). Higher % men in rural areas; the urban Cyber Cafe served more women than men (70—30).

Information and Communication Technology (ICT)

Opting for a simpler dial-up network using modems over existing telephone lines (POTS or Plain Old Telephone System). Initially the soonchanalayas (information kiosks) only provided access to the local Gyandoot network, with email being limited to other local users. However the entrepreneurs (soochaks) over time have demanded full Internet access, which has been progressively rolled out using Wireless in Local Loop (WiLL) and WiLL who has been installed in 8 kiosks, with a further 10 being added by December 2002, offers higher bandwidth, always-on connectivity, plus opportunity for the managing entrepreneurs to generate revenue by offering local telephone services.

GYANDOOT Equipment

- The server: Configuration P-III, 128 Mb RAM, 18 Gb HDD, Serial port card;
- Programming languages used HTML, ASP, JAVA;
- Four computer operators under District Information Officer of NIC of Dhar District.

KISOK Equipment

- A computer with multimedia facilities, modem, UPS with 4 hour back up, printer and a telephone;
- Dial up connectivity through OFC/Wireless in Local loop developed by IIT Chennai;
- Via 4 computer operators within the NIC

Common cause of failure of GYANDOOT:

- Limitations of connectivity;
- Bandwidth;
- Load shedding etc—the kiosks have suffered unreliable power supplies. Fluctuating levels of voltage and planned outages have made it difficult to use the installed UPS (uninterruptible power supply).

- Low purchasing power (40% population below the poverty line): Continued drought for three years has further reduced the disposable income;
- High percentage of reluctant tribal population;
- Illiteracy among the tribal community;
- Lack of support for the government;
- Lack of ICT's awareness among the community

Financing-Budget
- The network has been set up at a total initial cost of Rs. 25 lakhs ($ 50,000) with additional investment from private parties for expansion of the project;
- The average cost incurred by the village committee and the community in establishing a single kiosk was Rs. 75,000 ($ 1,500).

No.	Item	Cost (Rupees)
1	Multimedia PC (Pentium 3)	32,000
2.	Modem	3,500
3.	UPS	9,500
4.	Printer	10,000
Total Set Up Costs		57,000

Electricity	6,000 pa
Stationery	4,000 pa
Contingency	2,000 pa
Estimated Annual Running Costs	12,000 pa
Estimated income pa **Estimated annual running costs**	12,000 pa
Gyandoot revenues	12,000 pa
Publishing work (eg PC desktop)	15,000 pa
Training in PC skills (ten students @ 200rs/month)	24,000 pa
Estimated total income pa	51,000 pa
Annual income (without loan repayment)	39,000 pa (3250/month)
Annual income (with loan repayment of 1500/month for five years to repay set up costs and Year 1 running costs = 69,000 rupees)	51,000 pa

Table 10.1 Estimate Budget of Gyandoot Project

Cost Recovery
- The 11 centres started as private enterprise, the Soochak is the pays Rs. 5,000 as a license fee for one year to district council. Each Soochak is expected to earn a net income of at least Rs. 36,000 per annum at conservative projections;
- The Soochanalayas provide user-charge-based services to the rural people;
- The services carry a charge based on the principle of opportunity cost. Some of the services are: On-line Registration of Applications (Rs. 10), On-line Public Grievance Redressal (Rs. 10);
- The Soochanalaya is run on commercial lines. The Soochak has an initial one-year agreement with the village committee. She/he does not receive any salary and all the Soochaks comfortably earning their livelihood. Finance is available from the banks for new Soochanalaya units. Three new Soochanalaya units are sanctioned by the banks for financing units;

- The entire expenditure for the Gyandoot network has been borne by Panchayats (village committees) and the community or private entrepreneurs;
- The Soochak bears the cost of stationery, maintenance and electric and telephone bills. She/he pays 10% of income as commission to the Zila Panchayat (District Council) for maintaining the intranet Training/Upgrading and replacing Gyandoot is currently evaluating a solar power pack at two kiosks, used alongside the national grid, which is likely to cost some $2,000 per installation.

Current Intranet Services Given under GYANDOOT
E-Governance
- Registration of Applications (Rs. 10): The villagers can file applications for land records, driving licenses, caste/income/domicile certificates or for getting demarcation done etc. through the kiosk. They also get intimation when the certificate is ready for collection. The service leads to time and money saving for citizens. It also helps in lowering of corruption, as everyone has to work in deadlines, and there is a minimum interaction between the customer and the department official;
- Public Grievance Redressal (Rs. 10): Complaints ensure a pro-active and super-efficient department;
- Information regarding government Programmes;
- E-mail facility on social issues, eg. Child marriage and child labour;
- Opinion polls on development administration and services;
- Application and processing of pension schemes

E-commerce
- Auction prices of agricultural commodities;
- Online Village Market – anyone can post or search for information on items for sale;
- Anyone can send and receive mails in local language;
- Yellow pages facility where you can post information of shops, hospitals etc. on the network;
- Purchase of vermi-compost;

- Dating Agency where customers can posting and surf for data on eligible bachelors.

E-education
- Sawaliram se puchiye – Career Advise service;
- Access to exam paper example;
- Personality tests;
- General Awareness Questionnaires;
- Computer training courses.

E-agriculture
- Information on good cultivation practices of important crops grown in the district;
- Information for making vermi-compost and practices of organic farming;
- Information for judging the quality of seeds and rates of certified seeds of various crops;
- Consultancy available for any problem related to agriculture.

Other Services
- Information on time tables of nearby railway and bus station;
- Telephone directory of important people in the district;
- Information on ambulance service: Its availability and rates;
- Training and Education facilities information;
- Job alert.

Key Linkages
- Through mass media campaigns using posters/pamphlets, TV cable network, newspapers, playing of audiocassettes etc;
- Gyandoot does have links to NGO's, but kiosks do not offer other community development services (i.e. Governments authorities/ agencies are not making use of Kiosks to any great extent); and Gyandoot realize they need NGO's and agencies to promote Gyandoot to rural poor;

- Gyandoot has affected political decision-making in resource allocation with the Member of Parliament allocating Rs 25,00,000 to set up information kiosks in 3432 schools for e-education;
- The state IT policy has been re-oriented after the impact of the project to provide fruits of the IT to the rural masses through similar project model. Gyandoot project finds mention in the State IT policy.

Intermediaries

- Not applicable to their project. Information is not controlled or edited at any point.

Users

- The majority of men and women in Dhar District are not literate. In rural areas only 16 per cent of women and 42 per cent of men are literate, with these figures rising to 54 and 79 per cent respectively for urban areas.
- Village committees and the local community selected the Soochaks for the initial 20 centres. The community selected three panels of members to receive training, at their own cost, at the District Council. At the end of the training, the best trainees were selected out of a panel of three as Soochaks;
- The Soochak (The Information provider) is a local person who is 10th passes trained by Gyandoot Samiti to run the computer as well by advanced training of their own.

User Training

- Student of classes 9-12 are taken to the nearest Soochanalaya for a study tour and demonstration of the Gyandoot system and its facilities.

Development benefits

- Gyandoot describes a number of examples where farmers have been able to secure better prices for their crops by taking their goods to a local market offering the highest prices, and by cutting out local middlemen. Farmers in Bagadi village, for example, were getting a rate of 300 rupees ($6) per quintal from local traders for their potato crop. On getting the rate slip from their local Gyandoot information kiosk, they could not believe that the current rate in Indore Market was 400 rupees ($8) per quintal. So they hired a truck to take their produce to Indore—one hour away;

- There has been increased awareness about computers and IT in rural areas, which resulted into opening of new private computer training institutions and the enrolment in such institution, has increased by 60%.;
- Results have been impressive: introducing transparency and accountability into the inner working of local government. The efficiency level in the functioning of the government departments has increased;
- Self Help Groups in the rural areas are getting more organized and empowered due to transparency brought about in the government services and rural economy.
- The lower government functionaries have become computer-savvy. This is apparent from increased number of applications for computer loans from Employees Provident Fund and increased number of officials who have joined computer-training classes;
- Computer literacy has increased in the rural areas. This is evident from the fact that around 120 rural youths are getting trained in the Soochanalaya in the remote areas;

Gyandoot project is being replicated in all the districts of the state;

Reference:

1. Sarve Shiksha Mission GIAN (General Information Access Network): Madhya Pradesh (Bhopal: Sarve Shiksha Mission, 2022).
2. www.GYANDOOT.nic.in

Chapter Eleven

Sarve Shiksha Mission

Brief Physiography of Madhya Pradesh

Madhya Pradesh, in its present form, came into existence on November 1, 2000 following its bifurcation to create a new state of Chhatisgarh. The undivided Madhya Pradesh was founded on November, 1956. Madhya Pradesh because of its central location in India has remained a crucible of historical currents from North, south, East and West. Paleolithic, Mesolithic, Neolithic, Chalcolithic and Iron Age culture have flourished in the state along Narmada Valley and other river valleys. Rich archaeological wealth has been unearthed in various parts of the state throwing light on its history. Evidences of earliest human settlements have been found in bhimbethika and other places of Raisen district. Over 600 rock shelters have been found in bhimbethika. About 500 caves have rock paintings, which depict the life of pro-historic cave-dwellers. Sanchi in Raisen district is a world renowned Buddhist centre known for its stupus, monuments, temples and pillars dating from 3rd century B.C. to 12th century A. D. The most famous Sanchi stupas were built by the Mauryan Emperor Ashoka, then governer of Ujjain. Bhojpur, in the same district is famous for its incomplete but marvelous Shiva temple, built by legendry Parmer king of Dhar, Rajaj Bhoh (1010-53). Khajuraho in Chhatrpur district is renowed the world over for its unique temple. Built by Chendla rulers from 950-1050 A. D., in a truly inspired burst of creativity these temples are a unique gift of world. Orchhna in Tikamgarh district is medieval legacy in stone built by Bundela rulers in the 16th

and 17th centuries. This land is hollowed by the memories of the great warrior Chhatrasal who illumined the pages of history by his heroic deeds. Madhdya Pradesh has a number of important pilgrimage centres. While Ujjain and Omkareshwar have special significance due to Shrines having two of the twelve jyotirlingas, Maheshwar, Maldeshwar, Amarkantak, Hoshangabad are also important in their own rights. Madhya Pradesh has produced great men nd women who are also held esteem due to their great deeds. India's immortal poet-dramatist Kalidas belonged to Ujjain and great musician Tansen to Gwalior. Bravery of great women like Durgawati, Avantibai, Kamlpati and Devi Ahilya Bai is inscribed in golden letters in history. Madhya Pradesh is the second largest Indian state in size in area.

No	Name of District	Total Population	Area (Sq. Kms.)	Males	Females	Rural	Urban	SC	ST	Literacy Rate	Males	Females
1	Shepourer	5,59,495	-	2,95,297	2,64,198	4,70,924	88,751	90,240	1,16,986	46.40%	61.76%	29.07%
2	Morena	1,592,714	11,594	8,74,089	7,18,624	1,249,409	3,43,305	3,35,305	10,464	64.74%	79.89%	46.24%
3	Bhind	1,428,559	4,459	7,80,902	6,47,657	1,089,62	3,38,933	3,06,786	6720	70.52%	68.19%	55.23%
4	Gwalior	1,632,109	5,214	8,83,317	7,48,792	6,49,101	9,83,008	3,08,664	5,69,48	69.38%	80.36%	56.40%
5	Shivpuri	1,441,950	10,278	0	6,65,760	1,202,277	2,39,673	2,70,864	1,61,393	58.86%	74.11%	40.84%
6	Guna	1,666,767	11,65	8,84,202	7,82,747	1,311,954	3,54,813	2,93,527	2,03,742	59.55%	74.13%	42.88%
7	AshokNagar	6,88,904	4.673.90	-	-	-	-	-	-	-	-	-
8	Datia	6,28,240	2,038	3,38,232	2,90,008	4,90,691	1,37,549	1,56,732	9,977	71.73%	84.29%	5.23%
9	Dewas	1,30,822.3	7,020	6,77,866	6,30,357	9,49,876	3,58,347	2,38,934	2,151,51	60.94%	75.74%	45.03%
10	Ratlam	1,21,539.3	4,861	6,20,862	5,94,531	8,46,959	3,68,434	1,63,001	3,147,04	67.17%	79.52%	54.28%
11	Shajapur	1,29,068.5	6,196	6,69,852	6,20,833	1,05,145,5	2,39,230	2,83,639	35,302	70.86%	83.29%	57.42%
12	Mandsaur	1,18,372.4	9,791	6,05,119	5,78,605	9,63,020	2,20,704	2,12,262	37,526	70.31%	85.24%	54.73%
13	Neemuch	7,26,070	-	3,72,419	3,53,651	5,23,100	2,02,970	91,088	61,790	66.16%	82.53%	48.99%
14	Ujjain	1,71,098.2	6,091	8,82,871	8,28,111	1,04,819,5	6,62,787	4,22,882	53,230	70.86%	83.05%	57.87%
15	Dhar	1,74,032.9	8,153	8,90,416	8,49,913	1,45,214,5	2,88,189	1,12,916	9,484,34	52.45%	65.75%	38.57%
16	Indore	2,46,582.7	3,898	1,28,935.2	1,17,647.5	7,35,464	1,73,036.3	3,88,459	163872	75.15%	84.60%	64.81%
17	Alirajpur	-	-	-	-	5,65,857	-	-	-	-	-	-
18	Jhabua	1,39,456.1	6,782	7,02,053	6,92,508	1,27,353,0	1,21,031	39,290	1,211,116	36.89%	47.97%	25.70%
19	Khargone	1,53,056.2	13,450	-	-	-	-	-	-	-	-	-
20	Badwani	1,08,144.1	-	5,48,609	5,32,832	9,23,466	1,57,975	68,426	7,247,35	41.53%	50.96%	31.82%

No.	District											
21	Khandwa	7,50,662	10,779	-	-	1,24,783,8	4,60,332	-	-	-	-	-
22	Bhurhanpur	6,34,883	2,472.50	-	-	-	-	-	-	-	-	-
23	Betul	1,39,517,5	10,043	7,09,956	8,65,219	1,13,605,6	2,59,119	1,47,604	5,49,907	66.38%	76.81%	55.58%
24	Hoshangabad	1,08,426,5	10,037	5,71,774	5,12,491	7,49,871	3,34,394	1,70,780	1,640,49	70.00%	80.83%	77.94%
25	Harda	4,74,416		2,47,226	2,27,190	3,73,249	1,01,167	76,200	1,263,22	66.71%	57.83%	54.06%
26	Bhopal	1,84,351,0	2,772	9,72,649	8,70,861	3,60,792	1,48,271,8	2,581,73	60,561	74.61%	81.94%	66.37%
27	Sehore	1,07,891,2	6,578	5,65,137	5,13,775	8,85,172	1,93,740	2,21,077	1,161,22	63.07%	77.28%	47.36%
28	Raisen	1,12,515,4	8446	5,98,247	5,26,907	9,18,354	2,06,800	1,84,234	1,77,139	72.16%	81.58%	61.30%
29	Rajgarh	1,25,408,5	6,154	6,49,106	6,04,979	1,03,676,3	2,17,322	2,18,706	47,370	53.70%	69.14%	37.10%
30	vidhisha	1,21,485,7	2,742	6,47,838	5,67,019	9,54,490	2,60,367	2,41,131	59,323	61.83%	74.23%	47.40%
31	Sagar	2,02,198,7	10,252	1,07,320,5	9,48,782	1,43,108,0	5,90,907	4,15,374	1,964,72	67.73%	79.41%	54.35%
32	Damoh	1,08,394,9	7,306	5,70,229	5,13,720	8,79,598	2,04,351	2,11,258	1,361,75	61.75%	74.67%	47.30%
33	Panna	8,56,558	7,135	4,50,549	4,06,009	7,48,374	1,08,184	1,71,353	1,213,13	61.36%	73.33%	47.97%
34	Chatarpur	1,47,472,3	8,687	7,88,933	6,85,790	1,15,042,8	3,24,295	3,429,90	51,593	53.26%	65.28%	39.26%
35	Tikamgarh	1,20,299,8	5,048	6,37,913	5,65,085	9,90,265	2,12,733	2,921,71	51,957	55.73%	68.68%	40.99%
36	Jabalpur	2,15,120,3	10,160	1,12,730,4	1,02,389,9	9,23,863	1,22,734,0	2,739,53	3,228,90	75.69%	84.56%	65.88%
37	Katni	1,06,416,7		10,63,689	5,15,799	8,38,906	2,25,271	1,22,171	2,455,18	63.56%	77.94%	48.24%
38	Narsinghpur	1,16,660,8	5,133	5,88,750	5,77,858	1,04,592,1	1,20,687	1,20,657	4,291,04	65.21%	77.18%	53.82%
39	Chindwara	1,84,928,3	11,815	9,47,337	9,01,946	1,39,708,0	4,52,203	2,142,01	6,414,21	65.81%	76.45%	54.63%
40	Seoni	1,16,660,8	8,758	5,88,750	5,77,858	1,04,592,1	1,20,687	1,206,57	4,291,04	65.61%	77.18%	53.82%
41	Mandla	8,94,236	13,269	4,47,956	4,46,280	8,02,322	91,914	41,305	5,117,98	59.61%	73.72%	80.63%
42	Balaghat	1,49,796,8	9,229	7,40,749	7,57,219	1,30,399,6	1,93,972	1,160,70	3,265,40	68.72%	45.49%	57.18%

43	Reewa	1,97,330,6	6,314	10,166,87	9,56,619	1,65,274,3	3,20,563	3,0723,5	2,540,61	62.01%	75.65%	47.58%
44	Singrauli	1,84,033,8	-	-	-	-	-	-	-	-	-	-
45	Sidhi	1,83,115,2	10,256	9,47,830	883322	1570121	2,61,031	2,1702,6	5,47,375	52.27%	67.36%	35.98%
46	Satna	1,87,010,4	7,502	9,71,396	898708	1484551	3,85,553	3,0421,7	2,681,04	64.61%	77.14%	51.05%
47	Umaria	5,15,963	-	2,65,128	250835	432830	83,133	35,126	2.2725,0	59.13%	72.89%	44.54%
48	Dindori	5,80,730	-	2,91,716	289014	553860	26,870	33,848	3,744,47	54.17%	69.95%	38.24%
49	Shahdol	1,57,530,3	14,028	8,04,988	770315	1177149	3,98,154	1,159,04	7,000,651	58.71%	71.80%	44.99%
50	Annuppur	6,67,255	-	-	-	-	-	3,096,24	48,476	57.75%	69.55%	45.45%

Table 11.1 Physiography of State of Madhya Pradesh 1

Population (Census 2001)	60348 (In Thousand)
Male (Census 2001)	31444 (In Thousand)
Female (Census 2001)	28904 (In Thousand)
Scheduled Tribes (Census 1991)	12,233 (In Thousand) (19.44 %)
Scheduled Caste (Census 1991)	9155 (In Thousand) (15.40 %)
Area (in sq. kms.)	308,000
Districts	50
Tehasils	272
Development Blocks	313
Total Villages	55,393
Populated Villages	52,143
Gram Panchayats	23,051
Literacy	64.1 Percent
Male	76.5 Percent
Female	50.6 Percent
Density of Population	196 per sq. kms.
Male-Female Ratio	920: 933

Table 11.2 Information about the Madhya Pradesh[2]

"The Districts of Madhya Pradesh in ten Divisions":[4]

No	Name of Division	No of Districts
1.	Chambal	03 viz Sheopour, Morena and Bhind.
2.	Gwalior	05 viz Gwalior, Shivpuri, Guna, Ashoknagar and Datia.
3.	Ujjain	06 viz Dewas, Ratlam, Shajapur, Mandsour, Neemuch and Ujjain.
4.	Indore	08 viz Dhar, Indore, Alirajpur, Jhabua, Khargone, Badwani, Khandwa and Burhanpur.
5.	Narmada Puram	03 viz Betul, Hoshangabad and Harda.
6.	Bhopal	05 viz Bhopal, Sehore, Raisen, Rajgarh and Vidisha.
7.	Sagar	05 viz Sagar, Damoh, Panna, Chhatrpur and Tikamgarh.
8.	Jabalpur	07 viz Jabalpur, Katni, Narsingpur, Chindwara, Seoni, Mandla and Balaghat.
9.	Reewa	04 viz Reewa, Singrauli, Sidhi and Satna.
10.	Shahdol	04 viz Umaria, Dindori, Shahdol and Anuppur.

Table 11.3 Divisions of Madhya Pradesh District Wise

Detailed Information
about Districts of Madhya Pradesh

Here we get the information about the Districts of Madhya Pradesh:

Sheopour District

Sheopur is located at northern part of Madhya Pradesh. Some of the main locations are Vijaypur, Karahal and Baroda. Major tourist attraction is Palour (kuno) wildlife sanctuary. The well known kaketa reservoir is located in this district. The important rivers like chambal, seep and kuno drain the district.

Morena District

The district is drained by the important rivers like Chambal, Kunwari, asan and Sank. National Chambal Sanctuary is in three states of Madhya Pradesh, Uttar Pradesh and Rajasthan. Wheat is the most important food grain grown in the district. Mustard is the most important oil seed grown in the district.

Bhind District

The Bhind district of Madhya Pradesh is geographically is known for its rivers. As per the history the district is named after the Bhindi rishi (Sage Bhindi). It is well known fact that the region has been subjected to depredations of dacoit's robbers or thugs since ages. The soil of bhfertile and is well drained by the chambal and send rivers and the tributary streams of the kowari and puhuj.

Gwalior District

Gwalior city is a District in Madhya Pradesh State near Agra. It is the site of factories production cotton, yarn, ceramics, chemicals and leather products. The old city is covered with white sandstone Mosque, Palaces, rock temples and status of archaeological and architectural interest.

Shivpuri District

The district is bounded on the north by Morena, Gwalior and Datia districts, on the east by Jhansi district of U. P. on the west by Kota district of Rajasthan and on the south by Guna District.

Guna District

Guna gateway of the Malwa and Chambal is located on the northern-eastern part of Malwa platue, between parbati and betwa. The western boundary of the district is well defined by the river. The parbati is the main river flowing along the western boundary touching Rajgarh district and jhalawarh and Kota district of Rajasthan.

Ashoknagar District

The Ashoknagar is located on the northern-eastern part of Malwa platue between Sindh and Betwa. The eastern and western boundaries of the District are well defined by the rivers. The betwa flows along the eastern boundary separating from Sager District, and lalitpur and Jhansi District of Uttar Pradesh. Chanderi is famous for its exquisite and delicate muslin industry is a part of the district.

Datia District

Datia is the districts headquarter of the Datia District. It is ancient town, mentioned in the Mahabharata as Daityavakra. Handlooms' weaving is an important industry. Data is a famous for the seven stories places built by Raja Bir Singh Deo in 1614. A pilgrim spot for devotes, Datia has the sidhapeeth of Sri Peetambara Devi, Buglamukhi Devi Temple and Gopeshwar temple. About 15 KM from Datia is the Sonagiri, a scared Jain hill

Dewas District

It is situated on the Malwa plateau in the West-Central part of state. The tropic of cancer passes through the district near Nemawar village south of Khategaon town. It is situated on the Bombay-Agra National highway No. 3 and is also connected by broad-gauge railway line of western Railways.

Ratlam District

Ratlam is one of important District of Madhya Pradesh, which is situated in the North-west part of the state, "The Malwa Region". The new town of Ratlam was founded by caption borthwick in 1829 with regular and broadened streets and well built houses. Ratlam was once one of the first Commercial towns in central India being the center of an extensive trade in opium, tobacco and salt. It was also famous in Malwa for its bargains called Sattas.

Shajapur District

The district is identified from the Headquarters town Shajapur names after honor of Shhjahan the Mughal Emperor who halted in 1640. It is said that the original name was Shajahanpur, which subsequently reduces to Shajapur.

Mandusar District

Mandusar is rich in historical and archeology about what make it famous is the temple of lord pashupati nath located in the bank of shivina. Its iodi has parallel only in Nepal. The most common language is malwi (rajasthani and Hindi mix). It is also famous for large production of opium around the world. The state pencil industry is the main industry of district.

Neemuch District

Neemuch has been declared as a separate district by M P Govt as on 30 the June, 1998. Earlier it was a part of the Mandsour district. District Neemuch is situated in the North West border of Madhya Pradesh and south-East of Rajasan. Broad gauge railway and road routes are available to reach Neemuch District.

Ujjain District

Mahakala of Ujjain is known among the twelve celebrated Jyotirlinas in India. The glory of Mahakaleshwar temple has been vividly described in various puranas. Starting with kalidas many Sanskrit poet have eulogized this temple in emotive terms. The tradition of Mahakala in minds of the people is eternal Ujjain used to be center point of the calculation of the Indian time and Mahakala was considered as the distinctive presiding deity of Ujjain.

Dhar District

The district extends over three physiographic divisions. They are the Malwa in the north, the Vindhyachal range in central zone and the Narmada valley along the southern boundary. However, the valley is again closed up by the hills in the south-western part.

Indore District

Indore is situated on the Malwa plateau at an altitude of 553 m above sea level, on the bank of two small rivers the Saraswati and the Khan. They unite at the Centre of the city where a small 18th century temple of Sangamnath or indershwar exists. The name of Indore is due to this diety. It is the largest city in Madhya Pradesh state in central India. It is commercial capital of the state of Madhya Pradesh. Indore city presents a happy blend of historical past and promise of rapid future modernization.

Alirajpur District

Alirajpur is situated on the Malwa plateau and border of Gujarat. It is new district of the state. It was formed in the year of 2005.

Jhabua District

Jhabua is a predominately tribal district located in the western part of Madhya Pradesh. It is surrounded by Panchamahal and Baroda district of Gujarat. The adivasi dominated district situated in hilly area is full of natural resources. The district has an agricultural based economy. The main crops are of the area are Maize, Jowar, Bajra, Cotton, Wheat, Urad, Arhar, Groudnout and Gram. Limestone, Dolomite, calside etc minerals are found here. Meghnagar is the developing industrial area of the district.

Khargone District

The Khargone district formerly known was West Nimar. But the formation of Madhya Pradesh it was known as a west Nimar. But due to administrative problems was also divided into parts as Khargone and Badwani.

Barwani District

Barwani is situated on the southern west side of Madhya Pradesh as well as holy river Narmada. District is surrounded by Satpuda (in south) and Vindhyachal (in North) forest range. District Barwani was formed on 25th May 1998. The name of Badwani originated from the forests of Bad which have surrounded the city in old time. Wani is the old word for the garden and hence city got its name Badwani which means garden of beds. Before independence Barwani was known as The Paris of Nimar.

Khandwa District

District has lack of irrigation-means and results in monsoon dependent agricultural production. The major crops of the districts are soybean, cotton, Jowar, ground nut, banana, wheat, sugarcane, chilly etc. Major occupation is agriculture.

Burhanpur District

Burhanpur is situated on the bank of river Tapti in the state of Madhya Pradesh India. This historical city was founded in about 1400 AD. By princes Nasir Khan. The city is surrounded by rampart and has several huge gates. It was once the capital during the Mughal (Akbar) rule in India. It has a number of mosques, tombs and Places of historical values. The famous is the Jama Masjid in the heart of the city. The Asirgarh fort was known as without winning this fort it was impossible to have control on southern India.

Betul District

Betul is one of the marginally located southern districts of Madhya Pradesh, lying almost wholly on the Satpura plateau. IIt forms the southernmost part of the Bhopal Division. These enclaves lie on the Northern bank of the Tapti.

Hoshangabad District

The district takes its own name from the head quarters town Hoshangabad which was founded by "SULTAN HUSHANG SHAH GORI", the second king of Mandu (Malwa) in early 15th century. Hoshangabad district lies in the central Narmada Valley and on the northern fringe of the Satpura Plateau. In shape, it is an irregular strip elongated along the southern banks of Narmada River.

Harda District

In the 'Mugal' History prosperous village Handiya was situated on the west of Harda. After some years the area of Harda and Mahemudabad get increased. Harda got situated by combining KulHarda and Mehmudabad Villages. After getting the Railway line Harda gets developed rapidly.

Bhopal District

Bhopal, the capital of Madhya Pradesh, is a fascinating amalgam of scenic beauty, old historic city and modern urban planning. It is the 11th century city Bhopal founded by Raja Bhoj but the present city was established by an Afghan soldier, Dost Mohammed (1707-1740). His descendants build Bhopal into a beautiful city. The two lakes of Bhopal still dominate the city, and are indeed its nucleus. Bhopal today presents a multi-faceted profile; the old city with its marketplaces and fine old mosques and palaces still bears the aristocratic imprint of its former rulers, among them the succession of powerful Begums who ruled Bhopal from 1819 to 1926. Equally impressive is the new city with its verdant, exquisitely laid out parks and gardens, broad avenues and streamlined modern edifices. It is greener and cleaner than most cities in the country.

Sehore District

The lacquer bangles of the district are a coveted adornment of the Gond, Bhiala, Nad, and Korku tribes of the region. Bhavai, the traditional dance of these tribes is an excellent example of their artistic proclivities. In tribal area of Sehore the Bagoria dance, with its vigorous drum beating, is still performed around the Holi festival. This dance is occasion for tribal girls& boys to have run away marriage.

Raisen District

Raisen District lies in the central part of Madhya Pradesh. It is bounded in the west by Sehore district, in the north by Vidisha district, in the ease and south-east by Sagar district, in the south-east by Narsinghpur district, and in the south by Hoshangabad and Sehore district. Raisen District takes its name from massive Fort. This fort is built on a sandstone hill, at the foot of which settles the town. The name is probably a corruption of Rajavasini or Rajasayan, the royal residence.

Rajgarh District

Rajgarh district is located in the Northern part of Malwa Plateau. It forms the North Western part of division of Bhopal Commissioner. It has a quadrangular shape with the Northern and Western sides respectively. The zigzag boundaries of the district resemble a pear. Rajgarh district is bounded by Shajapur district in the south as well as west. The district of Sehore, Bhopal, Guna and Jhalawar (Rajasthan) enclose it from the South-East, East, and North-East and North directions.

Vidisha District

The District Vidisha lies on the Vindhyachal plateau of the main Vindhyachal Range, which throws several spurs towards North and North-East. The plateau slopes towards the North and it is drained by a number of rivers. These rivers have formed their valleys between the spur fanges. Most of the Vidisha lies in the valleys of Betwa River which flows from South to North.

Sagar District

The origin of the name comes from the Hindi word SAGAR meaning lake or sea, apparently because of the large and once beautiful lake around which the town of Sagar has been built. Sagar was founded by Udan Singh in 1660 and was constituted a municipality in 1867. A major road and agricultural trade centre, it has industries such as oil and flour milling, saw-milling, ghee processing, handloom cotton weaving, bidi manufacture and railway and engineering works. It is known in all over India due to its University named as Dr. Harisingh Gaur University and Army Cantonment and recently it has come into lime light due to "Bhagyodyay Tirth" a charitable hospital named after a Jain Sant Shri VidyaSagarji Maharaj. It is known for Police Training College which are only two in Madhya Pradesh other one is in Indore. Head quarter of Forensic Science Lab is also in SAGAR. Sagar lies in an extensive plain broken by low, forested hills and watered by Sonar river. Wheat, chickpeas, soghum, and oilseeds are chief crops of the region, there is extensive cattle rising. Sandstone, Limestone, iron ore and asbestos deposits are worked. The archaeological site nearby Eran has revealed several Gupta inscriptions. District Sagar is predominantly a Scheduled Caste/Backward class district. These together form about 75% of the district. The district has sizable population of tribals who are named as Rajgonds after their kingdom.

Damoh District

In the struggle for freedom from Brithishers, Damoh kept pace with national devotions and under the leaderships of Thakur Kishore Singh of Hindoria, Raja Devi Singh of Singrampur, Pancham Singh of Karijog, Gangadhar Rao, Raghunath Rao, Mejban singh, Govind Rao, and some others fought against the British rule in its rebellion in 1857. According to legends Damoh got its name from the name of the Queen of Narvar Rani Damyanti, wife of Raja Nal.

Panna District

Panna is located in the north-eastern part of Madhya Pradesh with the headquarters at Panna town. Originally a Gond settlement up to the 13th century, Panna was made the capital by Raja Chhatrasal Bundela. The only Diamond City in India is Panna. Panna is beautifully calm and serene roll-on meadows dotted with evergreen trees, hills, forests Panna is famous for its temples which strikes a very fine blend of Hindu and Muslim architecture. Panna is the most sacrosanct pilgrimage for the followers of the Pranami sect world over. With a sanctuary for rare wild life and avifauna & a diamond mine, Panna has transformed a royal past into a vibrant and lively.

Chhatrpur District

The District Chhatarpur was known after the name of the great warrior of the region Maharaja Chhatrasal. The District is situated at North East border of Madhya Pradesh.

Tikamgarh District

Tikamgarh district lies in the northern part of Madhya Pradesh. The early history of Tikamgarh district is however not chronicled, though as suggested by the numerous ruins of buildings and other old remains lies scattered at various places, viz Orchha, Garh Kudar, Prithvipur, Barana, Lidhoura, Digora, Mohangarh, Baldeogarh and Tikamgarh, it must be having a glorious past. The district was the part of vast empires successively ruled by the Mauryas, the Sungas and the imperial Guptas. The Orchha records trace the descent of the Bundela Kingdom of Orchha from Garh Kudar chiefs of Benaras Hemkaran, also known as Pancham Bundela.

Jabalpur District

The city of Jabalpur was the capital of the erstwhile medieval Gond rulers. It is the only an important historical place, but it is also famous for the Marble Rocks gorge on Narmada river, near it. It is an administrative and educational center and is the gateway to important wildlife sanctuaries around it. It is one of the largest cites of Madhya Pradesh. The origin of Jabalpur goes back to ancient times. It was then known as Tripuri and was governed by Hayahaya rulers.

Katni District

Katni is conglomeration of culture from three different cultural states viz. **Mahakausal, Bundelkhand**, and **Baghelkhand**. There are three different stories which reveals why Katni is called Mudwara. Katni junction is having half circular Mode (turn) from wagon yard. So people call it "Mudwar".

Another story is that there was a village call Modwar that has been given as a reward of bravery for cutting Mud (heads). The new town has been given the same name. At one side of this fort a court is available, Other side is of a beautiful building known as *RANGMAHAL* there are stone at various part of the fort designed from *KARITALAI*. This is the most beautiful fort in Katni district.

Narsinghpur District
Narsinghpur district is situated in the central part of Madhya Pradesh. It attracts special attention because of its natural situation as well. On the Northern ends Vindhyachal & on the southern ends throughout the lengths are Satpura ranges of Mountains. In the Northern part river Narmada flows from East to West. Which is a sacred as holy as river Ganga. Narsinghpur district has received many natural gifts as Narmada Kachhar. In the Eighteenth Century Jat Sardars got constructed a large Temple, in which Idol of Lord Narsimha placed & worshiped & so in the name of Lord Narsimha.

Chindwara District
Chhindwara district was formed on 1st November 1956. It is located on the South-West region of 'Satpura Range of Mountains'. This district is bound by the plains of Nagpur District (in Maharashtra State) on the South, Hoshangabad and Narsinghpur Districts on the North, Betul District on the West and Seoni Districts on the East.

Seoni District
Seoni is primarily a tribal dominated district formed on 1st November 1956. The district name Seoni has the origin from the word "SEONA" (or gudina arborea), a species of tree belonging to the verbanaleal family which was commonly found in this area. The wood of this tree is used in manufacture of "DHOLAK". The district is situated on a narrow, North-South section of satpura plateau in the South of Jabalpur Division. Seoni district is rich in timber resources. Teak is most important tree growing in and around Seoni district. Wainganga River is the lifeline of Seoni district. It originates at "Mundara" village in Seoni district. Asia's largest mud dam has been built on this river at Bhimgarh village in Chhapara block of the district.

Mandla District

Mandla is a tribal district situated in the east-central part of Madhya Pradesh. The district lies almost entirely in the catchments of river Narmada & its tributaries. A district with a glorious history, Mandla comprises of numerous rivers and endowed with rich forests. The world's famous Tiger Sanctuary, Kanha National Park located in the district, is one of the hottest targets for both the domestic as well as foreign tourists.

Balaghat District

District Balaghat looks like a flying bird and is situated in southern part of Jabalpur division. It occupies the south eastern region of the Satpura and Upper Wainganga Valley. District Balaghat is bounded by Rajnandgaon in the East, Seoni in the West, District Mandla in the North and District Bhandara of Maharashtra State in the south. The Wainganga River separates the district from Seoni while the rivers Bawanthadi and Bagh define the inter-state boundary.

Reewa District

The district is bounded on the north and east by the state of Uttar Pradesh, in the south Sidhi district and in the west with Amarpatan and Raghurajnagar tahsils of Satna district. In shape the district can be compared to an isosceles triangle, with its base along the Satna border and the two longer arms converging towards Mauganj in east. The district derives its name from Rewa town, the district headquarters, which is another name for Narmada river. The district with present boundary came into existence in 1950 after the promulgation of the Provinces and states (Transfer of ENCLAVES) order 1950.

Singrauli District

Singrauli is the 50th district of Madhya Pradesh. It was ranted district status on 24th May 2008; with headquarter at waidhan to fulfill the aspirations of people of this place. It has been formed after dividing it from Sidhi district. Singrauli has three tehsils and blocks namely Singrauli, Deosar and Chitrangi. Singrauli is fast emerging as the power hub of India, especially for electric, power and coal and therefore locally it is also call as Urjanchal (a Hindi word which means land of energy). The total installed capacity of all thermal power plants at Singrauli is around 10 % total installed capacity of India.

Sidhi District

Sidhi district is a reflection of proud history of the state of Madhya Pradesh. It makes the North-Eastern boundary of state. Sidhi district is a repository of natural, historical and cultural history. This district is known for luxuriant natural resources with the rive sone draining the district. On one side the spectrum of its floristic socio cultural diversity and ethnic history of tribal, the district has a panoramic view of the Kaimur, Kehejua and Ranimunda hills blazing with flowers of flame of forest and intoxicated by the sweet smell of mahua flowers.

Satna District

The district takes the name from Satna the headquarters town which in its urn takes it from Satna Reewa which flows near the town. In the north the district boundary marches with that of Banda district of Uttar Pradesh. Eastern Bombay of the district runs with the Teonther, Sirmour and Huzur tehsils of Reewa district.

Umaria District

Umaria district is located to the North East of Madhya Pradesh. The district has extensive forest; about the 42 % of the total area is covered by forests only. The district is rich in minerals. The most mineral found in the district is coal and as a result 8 mines are being operated by South Eastern Coalfield Limited in the district. The famous bandhavgarh National Park and Sanjay Gandhi Thermal Power Station are located in the district.

Dindori District

It touches Shahdol in east, Mandla in west, Umaria in north and Bilaspur district of Chhattisarh state south. The holy river Narmada passes through the district. Dindori has many historical as well as spiritual places. The Kanha Tiger National Park is 180 Km and Bandhavgarh National Park is 140 Km away from the district headquarter. It was created on 25th May, 1998 The Baiga are very particularly Vulnerable Tribal groups which can be found only in this district. The Baigas are known as the "National Human".

Shahdol District

The etymology of the name ascertained from the residents points to its derivation from the name of the one Shahdolwa ahir of Sohagpur village. The district headquarter was shifted from Umaria to Shahdol after the merger of princely states took place in 1948. With lush green forests, natural wealth of coal, minerals and with primitive tribal population, the district Shahdol is situated among the range of Vindhyachal and heading fast in development track. The district has vast reserves of local mines.

Anuppur District

In Anuppur District Amarkantak a sought after the destination for the nature lover, the pilgrims as well as for the adventure seeker, many mythological stories relating to Lord Shiva and his daughter Narmada have been woven around this mystical town of Amarkantak. Amarkantak is known primarily as a religious place. The holy river Narmada sone originate from here, another important river Johilla, too originate from here. There are about 12 temples here devoted to Narmada maiyya.

Genesis of Sarva Shiksha Mission

Constitutional commitment to ensure free and compulsory education for all children up to the age of 14 years, It provision of Universal Elementary Education has been a. salient feature of National Policy. It was recommended by National Policy of Education (NPE) and the Programme of Action (POA) 1992. It is combine effort scheme of Operation Blackboard, Non Formal Education, Teacher Education, Mahila Samakhya, Primary Education Project (APPEP) Andhra Pradesh, Education Project, Bihar, Lok Jumbish Rajasthan, Education for All Project Uttar Pradesh; Shiksha Karmi Project Rajasthan; Mid Day Meal, District Primary Education Programme (DPEP).

Need of Elementary Education

Elementary education is essential part of any education system and we can not imagine any education system without elementary education. Elementary education provides social justice and equity and also providing basic education for all. The elementary education improves the level of human being especially with regard to life expectancy, infant mortality, and nutritional status of children and also contributes to economic growth in any country.

Constitutional, Legal and National Statements for Universal Elementary Education

Constitutional mandate 1950: The State shall endeavor to provide, within a period of ten years from the commencement of this Constitution, for free and compulsory education to all children until they complete the age of'14 years.

National Policy of Education 1986: It shall be ensured that free and compulsory education of satisfactory quality is provided to all children up to 14 years of age before we enter the twenty first century.

Unnikrishnan Judgment, 1993: Every children/citizen of this country has a right to free education until he completes the age of fourteen years.

Education Ministers' resolve, 1998: Universal elementary education should be pursued in the mission mode. It emphasized the need to pursue a holistic and convergent approach towards UEE.

National Committee's Report on Universal Elementary Education in the Mission Mode: 1999: Universal Elementary Education should be pursued in a mission mode with a holistic and convergent approach with emphasis on preparation of District Elementary Education Plans for Universal Elementary Education. It supported the fundamental right to education and desired quick action towards opeartionlization of the mission mode towards Universal Elementary Education.

Development of Education

The number of schools in the country increased fourfold-form 2, 31000 in 1950-51 to 9, 30,000 in 1989-99, while enrolment in the primary cycle jumped by about six times from 19.2 million to 110 million. At the upper Primary stage, the increase of enrolment during the period was 13 times, while enrolment of girls recorded a huge rise of 32 times. The Gross

Enrolment Ratio at the Primary stage has exceeded 100 percent. At the primary stage, 94 percent of the country's rural population has schooling facilities within one kilometer and the upper primary stage it is 84 percent, but another side is that out of the 200 million children in the age group of 6-14 years, 59 million children are not attending school. Of this, 35 million are girls and 24 million are boys. There are problems relating to drop-out rate, low levels of learning achievement and low participation of girls, tribal and other disadvantaged groups. The country is yet to achieve the elusive goal of UEE, which means 100 percent enrolment and retention of children with schooling facilities in all habitations.

Sarva Shiksha Abhiyan (SSA) 6
The Sarva Shiksha Abhiyan is a historic initiate by Indian Government towards achieving the goal of Universlization of Elementary Education (UEE) through a time bound integrated approach, in partnership with States. It promises to change the face of elementary education sector of the country, aims to provide useful and quality elementary education to all children in the 6-14 age group by 2010.

Objectives of Sarve Shiksha Mission:
- All children in school, Education Guarantee Centre, Alternate School, to School' camp by 2003;
- All children complete five years of primary schooling by 2007;
- All children complete eight years of schooling by 2010;
- Focus on elementary education of satisfactory quality with emphasis on education for life;
- Bridge all gender and social category gaps at primary stage by 2007 and at elementary education level by 2010;
- Universal retention by 2010.

Structure for Implementation
The programme is being established with the Prime Minister as the Chairperson and the Union Minister of Human Resource Development as the Vice Chairperson and in the States to establish a state level Society for DEE under the Chairmanship of Chief Minister and Education Minister. It

ensures that there is functional decentralization down to the school level in order to improve community participation.

Coverage and Period
The SSA will cover the before March 2002 and upper limit for the programme period has been fixed as ten-years up to 2010.

Strategies Central to SSA programme

Institutional reforms: The states will assessment of their previous education system including educational administration, achievement levels in schools, financial issues, decentralization and community ownership, review of State Education Act, rationalization of teacher deployment and recruitment of teachers, monitoring and evaluation, education of girls, SC/ST and disadvantaged groups, policy regarding private schools and ECCE.

Sustainable Financing: It is based on the premise that financing of elementary education interventions has to be sustainable and financial partnership between Central and the State.

Community ownership: It is based on community ownership of school based interventions through effective decentralization and involvement of women's groups, VEC members and members of Pancliayati Raj institutions.

Institutional capacity building: The SSA play a crucial role in capacity building role for national and state level-institutions like NIEPA/NCERT/NCTE/SCERT/SIEMAT.

Improving mainstream educational administration: It is based on institutional development infusion of new approaches, and by adoption of cost effective and efficient methods.

Community based monitoring full with full transparency: The Programme will have a community based monitoring system. The Educational Management Information System (EMIS) will correlate school level data with community based information from micro planning and surveys. **Habitation as a unit of planning:** It is based on a community based approach to planning with habitation as a unit of planning and it will be plan on the basis for formulating district plans.

Accountability to community: The cooperation between teachers, parents and PRIs, as well as accountability and transparency.

Education of girls: Education of girls, especially those belonging to the SC/ST.

Focus on special groups: It will be focus on the religious and linguistic minorities' disadvantaged groups and disabled children.

Pre Project phase: SSA will implemented entire country with a well planned pre project phase that provides for a large number of interventions for capacity development to improve the delivery and monitoring system.

Thrust on quality: It is a special focus on education at elementary level useful and relevant for children by improving tile curriculum, child centered activities mid effective tackling methods.

Role of teachers: It recognizes critical role of teachers and advocates a focus on their development needs, setting up of BRC/CRC, recruitment of qualified teachers, opportunities for teacher development through participation in curriculum related material development, focus on classroom process and exposure visits.

District Elementary Education Plans: It will be preparing a District Elementary Education Plan reflecting all the investments being made in education sector.

Components of SSA

The components of Sarva Shiksha Abhiyan:
- Appointment of teachers and teacher training;
- Qualitative improvement of elementary education;
- Provision of teaching learning materials;
- Establishment of Block and Cluster Resource Centres for academic support;
- Construction of Classrooms and school buildings;
- Establishment of education guarantee centres;
- Integrated education of the disabled and distance education.

Requirement of Financial Resources for UEE

Rs. 60,000 crores is required for next ten years from the budget of the Central and the State level, this assessments made by the Department of Elementary Education & Literacy. The Sarva Shiksha Abhiyan (SSA) has two aspects:

I. It provides a framework for implementation of Elementary Education schemes;
II. The budget provision to achieve Universlization of elementary education is set by Government.

Financial Norms

- Financial assistance could be 85:15 sharing basis for IX plan, and 75-25 for X plan and 50:50 after between the Central and State Governments.
- The base year allocation for fund for elementary education is 1999-2000 for the States.
- The Government would be released fund and installments (except first) to the States/Union Territories, after the previous installments has been transferred to the State Implementation Society;
- For teacher's salary appointed under the Mission could be 85:15 sharing basis for IX plan, and 75-25 for X plan and 50:50 after between the Central and State Governments.
- All legal agreements for the externally assisted project will continu basis until project consultation with foreign funding agencies;

- All elementary education of the Department (except National Bal Bhawan and NCTE) will cover after the IX Plan. Mid Day Meal would remain on district intervention, transportation cost would share by Centre and cost of cooked meals by States.
- District Education Plan would clearly show the funds allocation for various schemes like, JRY, PMRY, Sunishchit Rozgar Yojana, Area fund of MPs/MLAs. State Plan, foreign funding and NGO;
- The funds would be used for up-gradation, maintenance, repair of schools, Teaching Learning Aids and local management to be transferred to School Management Committees;
- The distribution of scholarships and uniforms will be part of the State Plan.

Intervention	Norm
Teacher	One teacher=40 children in Primary and upper primary schools and 2 teachers for Primary school
School/Alternative Schooling facility	Within one Kilometer.
Upper Primary Schools	It based on the number of children completing primary education for one upper primary school for every two primary schools
Class Rooms	One room each for teacher in Primary & Upper and also for Head Master in upper Primary school.
Free textbooks	To all girls, SC, ST children at primary & upper primary level or Rs. 150/—per child
Civil Works	Ceiling of 33% of funds, BRC/CRC construction.
Maintenance and Repair of School Buildings	Up to Rs. 5000 per year as per a specific proposal and also involve community contribution of specific area.
Up gradation of EGS to regular school and TLE for upper primary	Provision for TLE @ RS. 10,000/per school for teacher & classrooms @ Rs. 50,000 per school for uncovered schools.

School	Rs. 2000/—per year per primary/upper primary school for replacement
Teacher grant	Rs. 500 per teacher per year in primary and upper primary
Teacher training	20 days in service for all teachers, 60 days refresher courses for untrained teachers and 30 day orientation for freshly trained recruits Rs. 70/—per day
State Institute of Educational Management Administration and Training	One time assistance up to Rs. 3 crore
Training of community leaders	For 8 persons in village for 2 days @ Rs. 30/—per day
Provision for disabled children	Up to Rs. 1200/—per child for disabled children as per proposal.
Research, Evaluation, supervision and monitoring	Up to Rs. 1500 per school per year By creating pool of resource persons, providing travel grant and honorarium for monitoring, generation of community based data, research studies, cost of assessment and appraisal terms & their field activities
Management Cost	Not to exceed 60% of the budget of a district plan
Innovative activity for girls' education, early childhood care & education, interventions for SC/ST community, computer education specially for upper primary level	Up to Rs. 15 lakhs for each innovative project and Rs. 50 lakhs for a district will apply for SSA
Block Resource Centres/Cluster Resource Centres	Rs. 6 lakh ceiling for BRC construction Rs. 2 lakh for CRC construction; Deployment of up to 20 teacher in a block with more their 100 schools Provision of furniture etc. @ Rs. 1 l for BRC and Rs. 10,000 for a CRC Contingency grant of Rs. 12,500 f BRC and Rs. 2500 per CRC per

Interventions for out of school children	Norms already approved under Education Guarantee Scheme & Alternative and Innovative Education providing. Setting other alternative schooling models Bridge Courses, remedial courses, to School Campus with a focus on mainstreaming out of school children into regular schools.
Preparatory activities for micro planning, household surveys, studies, community mobilization, school based activities, office equipment, etc.	As per specific proposal.

Table 11.4 Financial Norms for Sarva Shiksha Mission

Conclusion

Sarve Shiksha mission play an important role to eradication of illiteracy in state, it gives significant result of educational programmes which stated by government of India as well as Government of Madhya Pradesh and plays another important role in library field, the e-libraries established under the project GIAN in year 2002.

References:

1. www.mp.nic.in
2. www.mp.nic.in
3. www.mp.nic.in
4. www.mp.nic.in
5. www.mhrd.nic.in
6. www.ssa.mp.nic.in

Chapter Twelve

Model for Integrated Public Libraries System for Madhya Pradesh

In the Public Libraries all people can go without any distinction of caste, religion, sex and creed. S. R. Ranganthan also corroborated in this philosophy and propounded his five laws. His first law is "Books are for use". Charles Darwin's biological principal "Survival of the Fittest", is truly applicable to the modern society also. Hence significance of the libraries is all the more necessary to make one's mind superior. Significance of the libraries has realized that without supports of the public libraries there can be no true democracy, no real freedom of mind or of body.

There is a need to establish, maintain and develop an integrated library system and adequate public library services in the state. The detail proposed Integrated Public Library System for Madhya Pradesh plan is given herein under. To cater information need of the people of State a network of libraries be spread which compasses basic components for library services, structure of libraries, recruitment of professional staff, financial support, library services to all. To get a work done in right manner proper plan has to be developed first and accordingly implementation of the same is also essential.

Integrated Public Library System

The Integrated Public Library System should be establish and develop an adequate library service in the state. State Library System consisting of the

(1) *Ministry of Public Libraries;*
(2) *State Central Library & Knowledge Centre;*
(3) *Divisional Libraries & Knowledge Centre;*

(4) *City Libraries & Knowledge Centre, Ward Libraries,*

(5) *e-Libraries;*

(6) *State Institute of Library Education Research and Training*

(7) *District Libraries & Knowledge Centre;*

(8) *Tehsil Libraries and knowledge Centre;*

(9) *Block Libraries & Knowledge Centre;*

(10) *Panchayat Libraries & Community Information Centre;*

(11) *Village Libraries & Community Information Centre;*

(12) *Distribution Centres and Mobile Libraries and Reading Room;*

Structure of Integrated Public Library System for Madhya Pradesh
The proposed structure of libraries in the state shall be as under:

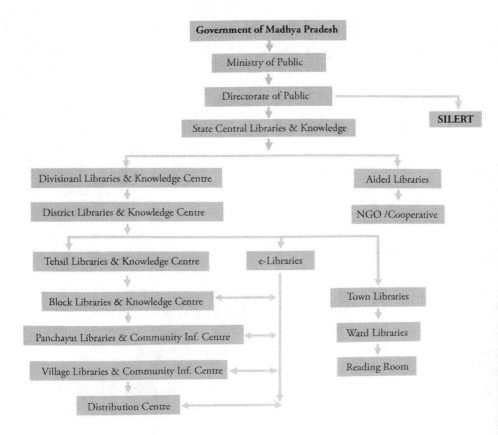

**12.1 Proposed Integrated Plan
for Public Libraries of Madhya Pradesh**

State Library Council

For the purpose of organizing and promote a library system in under the Ministry of Public Library will be. A State Library Committee is constituted for the purpose of advising the State Library Authority. It shall consist of the following members.

Composition of State Library Council

The State Library Council shall consist of following members:

(i) The Minister of Public Libraries, who shall be the Chairman of Council;

(ii) The Secretary, who responsible for the Libraries shall be the Vice-President;

(iii) The Director, Primary and Secondary Education or nominee Member;

(iv) The Director of Panchayat Raj or nominee, Member;

(v) The Director of Tribal or nominee Member;

(vi) President, Madhya Pradesh Library Association, Member;

(vii) Chairman, Raja Rammohun Roy Library Foundation, Calcutta or his nominee, Member;

(viii) Two eminent educationists (Lib Sci), socialist nominated by the committee, Members;

(ix) Chairperson, Madhya Pradesh Women Commission, Bhopal or his nominee, Member;

(x) Chairman, INFLIBNET, Ahmedabad or his nominee, Member;

(xi) Sr. University Librarian, M P Universities, Members;

(xii) Librarian, State Central Library, Member Secretary.

Functions of State Library Council

Following functions shall be undertaken by the State Library Council.

(i) The council shall report to the Government every year its findings, relating to the Implementation of the public library act and achievement of standards every year.

(ii) The council may appoint committee (s), working group (s) if necessary;

(iii) The council shall accept gifts, donations, endowments for development of library services;

(iv) The council shall advise the State Government on all matters to relate to promotion and development of library services in the State;

(v) The council shall general responsible for the supervision of the Integrated Public Library System.

It shall be establish nomination and develop an integrated, Comprehensive and efficient library service in the State;

(vi) To provide for an adequate library service;

(vii) To develop library institutes;

State Central Library & Knowledge Centre

The State Central Library shall be the apex of the library of entire library state of Madhya Pradesh. The library shall function as a repository for the library system of the state.

The Function of Sate Central Library & Knowledge Centre;

(i) Information and reference centre of the state;

(ii) Be a depository of less used materials deposited with them by other libraries in the state;

(iii) Share their resources with them, through resource sharing and library network;

(iv) Compile state bibliography of book and journals published out of the state in any language and as well as their collection;

(v) Provide bibliographic and documentation services in the form of articles of the state and state official documents;

(vi) Conservation and preservation of rare book and manuscripts of books;

(vii) Develop special collection and serve special categories of reader such as children, blind and handicapped etc.

(viii) To acts as a state centre of Audio-Visual materials, its production, storage and distribution to State Public Library System;

(ix) To provide adequate information service, SDI service, Data-base service, Documentation service, Translation, Bibliographical. News Paper Clipping service, Reprographic service.

(x) To collect all publications related to Madhya Pradesh literature, its History, culture and art;

(xi) To act as a State Dormitory Library of at least one sound copy of a book weeded out by any library in the state;

(xii) To centralize all technical work such as classification, cataloguing of books and other resources;

(xiii) To perform other such function as are assigned by the council;

Responsibilities of State Central Library & Knowledge Centre

The Responsibilities of Sate Central Library & Knowledge Centre;

(i) Information Service;

(ii) e-learning;

(iii) Knowledge Management;

(iv) Knowledge Centre Activities;

(v) Content Creation and Management;

(vi) Subject Gateways;

(vii) Content Analysis;

(viii) Collaborative Publishing;

(ix) e-Governance;

(x) Training.

Aided Libraries

The library that operates library services by any non governments such as NGO's, cooperative societies, or autonomous bodies and special libraries (children libraries, women libraries, prisoner's library and libraries for physical handicapped and mentally retreated children's) will be open with help of NGO's.

State Institute of Library Education Research and Training

The function of the SILERT shall be follows;

- Provide in-service training programmes for library personnel is the state;
- Organize continuing professional activities and programmes such as seminars and conferences, refresher courses, specialized courses, extension lectures, workshop etc;
- Sponsor research work and activities relating to library an information services;

- Advise in technical and professional matters;
- To carry out research in the area of library and information science.

Divisional Libraries & Knowledge Centre

The Divisional Library shall be function as apex library in the Division to perform the functions same as *State Central Library & Knowledge Centre*. The administrative control of Divisional Libraries is *District Libraries & Knowledge Centre, Tehsil Libraries and Knowledge Centre, Block Libraries & Knowledge Centre, Panchayat Libraries & Community Information Centre, Village Libraries & Community Information Centre, Distribution Centres and Mobile Libraries and Reading Room, Town Libraries and Knowledge Centre* and *e-Libraries* functioning in the Division, it is responsible for take care of information and needs of the public resides in entire Division.

District Libraries & Knowledge Centre

District libraries shall be function as apex library in the District. These libraries shall be Perform all library services to the people reside at District area. Book Deposit Centres shall work under *District Libraries & Knowledge Centre*. ICT's infrastructure will be provided to these libraries merge the e-libraries to provide e-services through establish a **KISOSKS** Centre for urban people.

District Library Committee

(i)   The District Collector shall be the President;
(ii)   The Zila Pramukh shall be the Vice-President;
(iii) District Education Officer, Member;
(iv)   One person nominated by the Madhya Pradesh Library Association, Member;
(v)   Two eminent educationists, socialist nominated by the committee, Members;
(vi)   One woman, nominated by the committee, Member;
(vii) District Librarian shall be Member Secretary.

Functions of District Library Committee
The functions of the District Library Committee shall be as follows:

(i) To advise the committee on the working of library service under the area;

(ii) To promote co operation among libraries and other educational libraries;

(iii) To assist and advise the committee and help fulfillment of the objectives of Integrated Public Library System in the region;

(iv) To recommended budget proposals for strengthening libraries and services in the District;

(v) To discuss, accept and prepare annual report of the working libraries in District.

Responsibilities of District Library and Knowledge Centre
The Responsibilities of District Library & Knowledge Centre;

(i) Information Service;

(ii) e-governance;

(iii) Content Development;

(iv) Co-Ordination of Rural Knowledge Centres.

E-Libraries

This library was established under the Sarve Shiksha Mission in 2002. The main objectives of these project was upgrade the existing facilities State Central Library and District Public Libraries of the state to become effectives Knowledge Dissemination Centers and hubs of Intellectual activity and effective use of these libraries in the interest of common people of state. These libraries were established at District levels. These libraries will be merging with existing District Public Libraries to provide existing infrastructure of e-libraries to District Public Libraries and Knowledge Centers.

Town Libraries and Knowledge Centre

To cater information need of urban community where more than one lac people are reside, the city library establish to render library services. The library shall have well equipped with all the ICT's infrastructures and with e-resources to meet the need of urban people.

Responsibilities of Town Library and Knowledge Centre
The Responsibilities of Town Library & Knowledge Centre;
 (i) Lending of books;
 (ii) Reference Services;
 (iii) Inter-Library Loan
 (iv) Web-Based Services such as e-learning, Banking and Insurance;
 (v) Community Information;
 (vi) Content and Database Creation.

Branch Libraries and Knowledge Centre
It shall establish a library for the sub urban unit where population in between 25,000 to 50,000. This library shall be provides its service to sub urban society. The Nagar Nigam and Nagar Palikas library shall be a part of branch libraries and each and every Nagar Nigam and Nagar Palikas have their ward libraries also.

Reading Rooms
Reading rooms shall be function a branch of branch libraries it is depends on the population. The library provides newspapers, magazines, and light reading materials to sub urban people. The population in between 5,000 to 25,000

Tehsil Libraries & Knowledge Centre
The library shall function as an effective agency to meet all the information need of the rural people of a Tehsil. The *Tehsil Libraries & Knowledge Centre* has all kind of reading materials of local people. ICT's infrastructure shall also be provided to these libraries to provide e-services through establish a KISOSKS centre.

Tehsil Library Committee
 (i) The Tehsil Pramukh shall be the President;
 (ii) The Nayab Tehsildar shall be the Vice-President;
 (iii) One person nominated by the Madhya Pradesh Library Association, Member
 (iv) Two eminent educationists, socialist nominated by the committee, Members;

(v) One women representative nominated by the committee, Members;

(vi) Tehsil Librarian shall be Member Secretary.

Functions of Tehsil Library Committee
The functions of the Tehsil Library Committee shall be as follows:

(i) To advise the committee the working of library service under the area;

(ii) To promote co operation among libraries and other educational libraries;

(iii) To assist and advise the committee and help fulfillment of the objectives of Integrated Public Library System in the region;

(iv) To recommended budget proposals for strengthening libraries and services in the Tehsil;

(v) To discuss, accept and prepare annual report of the working libraries in Tehsil.

(vi) closed co-operation with Block Public Library.

Block Libraries & Knowledge Centre

The library shall function as an effective agency to meet all the information need of the rural people of a Block. The *Block Libraries & Knowledge Centre* has all kind of reading materials of local people. ICT's infrastructure shall also be provided to these libraries to provide e-services through establish a KISOSKS centre.

Block Library Committee

(i) The Block Pramukh shall be the President;

(ii) The Block Development Officer shall be the Vice-President;

(iii) One person nominated by the Madhya Pradesh Library Association, Member

(iv) Two eminent educationist, socialist nominated by the committee, Members;

(v) One women representative nominated by the committee, Member;

(vi) Block Librarian shall be Member Secretary.

Functions of Block Library Committee
The functions of the Block Library Committee shall be as follows:

(i) To advise the committee on the working of library service under the area;

(ii) To promote co operation among libraries and other educational libraries;

(iii) To assist and advise the committee and help fulfillment of the objectives of Integrated Public Library System in the region;

(iv) To recommended budget proposals for strengthening libraries and services in the Block;

(v) To discuss, accept and prepare annual report of the working libraries in Block.

(vi) closed co-operation with District Public Library.

Panchayat Libraries & Community Information Centre

The library shall function as an effective agency to meet all the information need of the rural people of a Panchayat level. The reading materials will also available and ICT's infrastructure shall also be provided e-services through establish a **Village Knowledge Centre** to rural community.

Panchayat Library Committee

(i) The Sarpanch shall be the President;

(ii) One person nominated by the Panchayat, Members;

(iii) One person nominated by the Madhya Pradesh Library Association, Member

(iv) Two eminent educationists, socialist nominated by the committee, Members;

(v) Panchayat Librarian shall be Member Secretary.

Functions of Panchayat Library Committee
The functions of the Panchayat Library Committee shall be as follows:

(i) To advise the committee the working of library service under the area;

(ii) To promote co operation among libraries and other educational libraries;

(iii) To assist and advise the committee and help fulfillment of the objectives of Integrated Public Library System in the region;

(iv) To recommended budget proposals for strengthening libraries and services in the area;

(v) To discuss, accept and prepare annual report of the working libraries in area;

(vi) To close co-operation with Tehsil Public Library.

Responsibilities of Village Library and Community Information Centre. The Responsibilities of Village Library and Community Information Centre;

(i) Lending of books;

(ii) Web-Based Services such as e-learning, Banking and Insurance;

(iii) Panchayat-Level Information;

(iv) e-Governance;

(v) Community Information;

(vi) Content and Database Creation.

Village Libraries & Community Information Centre

Village library to establish at every village of the state these will be extend service as one of the important units of the state public library system is village library. The library shall have all kinds of reading materials and basic information resources to meet local needs of village community to related information like agricultural information, weather related information, pesticides, water resources etc. The reading materials will also available and ICT's infrastructure shall also be provided to these libraries to provide e-services through establish a **Village Knowledge Centre** to rural community.

Village Library Committee

(i) The Pradhan shall be the President;

(ii) One person nominated by the Gram Panchayat, Members;

(iii) One person nominated by the Madhya Pradesh Library Association. Member;

(iv) Two eminent educationists, socialist nominated by the committe Members;

(v) One women representative nominated by Gram Panchayat, Member;

(vi) Village Librarian shall be Member Secretary.

Functions of Village Library Committee
The functions of the Village Library Committee shall be as follows:

(i) To advise the council on the working of library service under the area;

(ii) To promote co operation among libraries and other educational libraries;

(iii) To assist and advise the committee and help fulfillment of the objectives of Integrated Public Library System in the region;

(iv) To recommended budget proposals for strengthening libraries and services in the area;

(v) To discuss, accept and prepare annual report of the working libraries in area;

(vi) To close co-operation with Panchayat Library.

Distribution Centre and Mobile Library

This Distribution Centre will be attached to **District Public Libraries & Knowledge Centre** with facility of Mobile Library to spread the library service in the entire area. The mobile libraries are use to satellite technology for use enable internet access. It is also enhances services by providing real time catalogue access. The new satellite technologies mean that the mobile libraries can stop anywhere for used.

Administration set up of Libraries

The Minister of Public Library, Directorate of Public Libraries, State Librarian, Divisional Librarians, District Librarians, Block Librarians, Tehsil Librarian, Panchayat Librarian, and Village Librarian shall be the administrators.

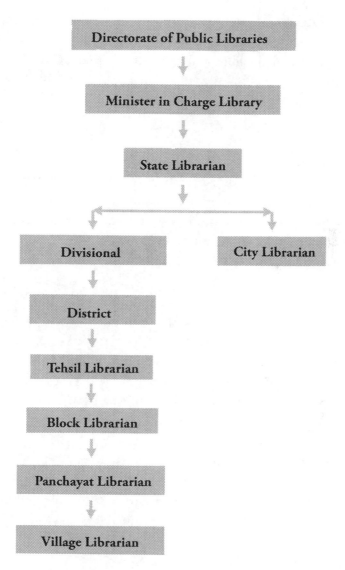

12.2 Administration of Public Libraries

Functional set up of Propsoed Integrated Public Library System for State
The functional set up of proposed Integrated Public Library System for state
in given below points:

Collection of Reading Materials

The collection of reading materials in public and e-library in state is sufficient to serve their library users, but e-resources are not available in public library and as well as e-library in state, so it will be improved in proposed IPLS for MP.

Manpower

The available manpower is not sufficient to serve library users in ICTS environment. It will be propsoed the further required manpower is 117612 to serve library users, but it is not possible in one phase, so it will be implemented in phase manner in four or five phase. I proposed, First phase recruit around 20,000 library professionals for IPLS and so on. It is urgent need to in act to Library Legislation in MP for PL

Finance

It is main concern of any organization, without finance nobody can not proper serve to their library user; it will be proposed that if we assume that, 3 Rupees per capita for library development in Madhya Pradesh. It will be collect around 180000000 in one year and proposed a budget for public library of Madhya Pradesh. The total finance requirement to recruit manpower is around (34561587000)

Physical Infrastructure (Building)

It one area that, the physical infrastructure is available for public libraries and e-library in state, but it also required further 29016 library building, but it not big matter, so it will be improved in different phases.

Library Equipments and ICT Infrastructure

If merger the both libraries public library and e-library in IPLS-MP, so it will be eradiate these problem of public library. E-library has latest equipment to serve library users and public libraries don't have any latest equipment.

Requirement to Establish a New Network

It discuss in Chapter No.9. What is requirement to establish a new network and essentials component of any network and given approx price of equipment to establish a library network. Detailed are given in Annexure IV.

Proposed Network (GIAN Network) for Public Library in Madhya Pradesh

Objectives:

The libraries/knowledge is best places of dissemination of information regarding Government policy, plans and various schemes;

- To form a network for Public Libraries and e-libraries of Madhya Pradesh;
- To form a network for Rural and Village Libraries of Madhya Pradesh;
- To convert these public libraries as a Knowledge and Information Centers, dissemination and promote uses of information among the libraries in the form of electronic form as well as traditional form;
- To promote sharing of resources public libraries by developing a network of libraries under these GIAN—Network, by collecting, storage, sharing and disseminating the information, promote and develop computerized services to their users;
- To develop local databases in local languages to fulfill the local needs of local peoples at local level;
- To create awareness among peoples in the filled of information technology through conducting seminars, workshops, training programmes with the help of local authorities;
- To conduct surveys for government policy, social problems and give feed back to local authorities and government for their policies and give suggestions time to time for better implementation for policies in the interest of peoples;
- To generate revenue by providing information services, consultancies and provide any information to users need with minimum charges will be applicable.
- To promote Research and Development activities and develop technical support centre to fulfill objectives of GIAN network;
- To prepare the Union Catalogue of reading materials books, journals, magazine which exist in public libraries of Madhya Pradesh;
- To promote exchange of information between the public libraries in Madhya Pradesh and as well as national and international lev networks;

- To offer computerized services to users, participating libraries and cumulative effort for collection development for unnecessary duplication;
- To create a centre or state centre in the filled of Archive "rare book";
- To purpose the plan for library on the finance purpose and how we generate "Local Development Fund" for library activities;
- To generate new services at state level which used at local level and improve existing ones.

Function of Network Public Libraries of Madhya Pradesh (GIAN Network)

Functions of such proposed GIAN network would be:

- To create awareness amongst peoples utilization of various local resources;
- Collection development of various types of resources which are useful to local peoples;
- To provide latest information about any field of knowledge, which Information wants by people;
- To encourage people to use scientific approach with the help of IT for solving their problems;
- To encourage people to use of GIAN network for information and Communication Needs;
- To develop various types of Local Databases information in local languages, which provides better communication and information to the local peoples;
- To gave the information about government policy, schemes and planning at GIAN network centers;
- These GIAN Consortia centers are develop as information and dissemination centers for the people;
- GIAN network combination to develop, dissemination and storage of information in traditional form as well as in electronic form;
- GIAN network provide information about the culture heritage, social and traditional Values to our people;

Frame Work of Network for Public Libraries of Madhya Pradesh

The State Central Library, Bhopal and four Divisional Central Libraries at Indore, Gwalior, Reewa and Jabalpur and 50 District Public Libraries, 50 e-Libraries are working. Madhya Pradesh is divided in nine Divisions i.e. Bhopal, Jabalpur, Indore, Gwalior, Jabalpur, Rewa, Narmada Puram, Shahdol and Ujjain, so Where Divisional Libraries, the leading library of their Divisional, i.e. Indore, Jabalpur, Rewa and Gwalior and Narmada Puram, Shahdol and Ujjain, where District Library is leading library, after that Block Library, Tehsil Library, Panchayat Library and Village Library. The frame work of GIAN Network is given below figure.

Indore Division	Rewa Division
Divisional Library	Divisional Library
District Library	District Library
Block Library	Block Library
Tehsil Library	Tehsil Library
Panchayat Library	Panchayat Library
Village Library	Village Library
Gwalior Division	**Jabalpur Division**
Divisional Library	Divisional Library
District Library	District Library
Block Library	Block Library
Tehsil Library	Tehsil Library
Panchayat Library	Panchayat Library
Village Library	Village Library
Bhopal Division	**Chambal Division**
District Library	District Library
Block Library	Block Library
Tehsil Library	Tehsil Library
Panchayat Library	Panchayat Library
Village Library	Village Library
Ujjain Division	**Narmada Puram Division**
District Library	District Library
Block Library	Block Library
Tehsil Library	Tehsil Library
Panchayat Library	Panchayat Library
Village Library	Village Library
Sagar Division	**Shahdol Division**
District Library	District Library
Block Library	Block Library
Tehsil Library	Tehsil Library
Panchayat Library	Panchayat Library
Village Library	Village Library

Server at State Central Library Bhopal

Frame Work of GIAN Network

Conclusion

The libraries specially the public libraries have certainly their role in the spreading the education and uplifting of its standard among the rural people. The present time has global impact on all aspects of the life of the society. Therefore, the information generated swiftly exchanged and communicated. The idea of networking of public libraries will certainly have its importance in this direction and it is also beneficial community at local level the community feel newness of library services.

Steps for Implementation of Proposed Network

To smooth conducting to library services in Madhya Pradesh, I recommended that six steps:

Step No One: In first phase connect all Divisional Library and Knowledge Centre with State Central Library and Knowledge Centre.

Step No Two: In second phase connect all District Library and Knowledge Centre with Divisional Library and Knowledge Centre and State Central Library and Knowledge Centre.

Step No Three: In Third phase connect all Tehsil Library and Knowledge Centre with District Library and Knowledge Centre, Divisional Library and Knowledge Centre and State Central Library and Knowledge Centre.

Step No Four: In fourth phase connect all Block Library and Knowledge Centre with Tehsil and Knowledge Centre Library, District and Knowledge Centre Library, Divisional Library and Knowledge Centre and State Central Library and Knowledge Centre.

Step No Five: In fifth phase connect all Panchayat Library and Community Information Centre with Block Library and Knowledge Centre, District Library and Knowledge Centre, Divisional Library and Knowledge Centre and State Central Library and Knowledge Centre.

Step No Six: In sixth phase connect all Village Library and Community Information Centre with Panchayat Library and Community Information Centre, Block Library and Knowledge Centre, District Library and Knowledge Centre, Divisional Library and Knowledge Centre and State Central Library and Knowledge Centre.

Chapter Thirteen

Suggestion and Recommendations

Weakness and Rectification of Public Libraries:
Here discuss about the weaknesses of Public Libraries how ease these problems. Detailed re discuss in given below points.

Collection of Reading materials and Non-Book Materials
Collection of Reading materials: It is one area where the Divisional Public Libraries, District Public Libraries and e-library have bigger advantage to serve their users. The reading material of the libraries is not sufficient, as far as present scenario because there is no library committee to purchase reading materials and there is no provision included for suggestion of library users.

Rectification: For this purpose, it should be form a library committee in each and every library and also included suggestion of library users and it should also implement, *"1854 Book and Registration Act"* to compile for public libraries in state. If the merge the above libraries in proposed Integrated Public Library System for Madhya Pradesh or GIAN Network, than available average reading materials to every person would be increased and it is about the *about 0.17%,* so it is very beneficial for reader to availability to more reading materials and variety. **Facts is given in Table 4.4**

Non-Book Materials: There is one another area should be improved very fast, is that collection of non-book materials. The non-book material is n available in most libraries. The percentage of non-book materials compa to the total collection of *Divisional Public Libraries* in insignificant is % and *District Public Libraries* in insignificant is mere about *0.08 %*

Rectification: In non-book materials included CD-ROM, Audio-Video cassettes, educational CD's, e-lecture, e-books and e-journals. The e-libraries having ICT infrastructure and internet connection. If merge the libraries, than we access e-information via network, we can say that library is called Hybrid Library or Public e-Library. It is combination of traditional library and electronic library; further also create a library network at state level and resource sharing among the different networks at local national and international level.

Manpower

That most library manpower of Divisional Public Libraries and District Public Libraries has experienced, but it is not aware uses of ICT's and latest technology is being not used in most libraries, but other fact that manpower of e-libraries is aware and used frequently ICT application in libraries, on the basis of facts given in *Table No.5.2, 5.3, 5.4, 5.5, 5.6, 5.7.* I concluded that the available manpower is satisfactory. The shortage of professional qualified persons in public libraries, but overall situation appears too satisfactory for the availability of professional staff compared to the non-professional staff.

Rectification: The proper combination of experiences and knowledge of ICT's is very useful for any organization, so that combination is being used in recruitment. If the merge libraries under the proposed Integrated Public Library System for Madhya Pradesh or GIAN Network, then available of manpower is called Hybrid manpower; **Facts given in Table 5.8.** The professional staff of a library with proper technical education, training and certificates alone should be allowed to be employed for performing technical and supervisory function in Public Library.

National Knowledge Commission 2006 is also some recommendations to recruit manpower for Public Libraries. These recommendations are; library and information handling skills; ICT knowledge skills; communication and training skills; marketing and presentation skills; understanding of cultural diversity; knowledge mapping skills.

Through various skills are required but the skill needs depend on role context of the parent organization. As all skills do not relate to everyone, a summarized set of skills three broad categories of skills, i. e. generic skills, managerial skills and professional skills; **Facts given in Annexure No. III**

Finance

After the analysis and interpretation of budget allocations of Divisional Public Library, District Public Library and e-library, it shows that budget allocation for libraries is very poor. In state Libraries is totally depends on governments aids, there is no other alternatives financial resources.

Rectification: The better solution of problem is should be enact Public Library Act in state. In library legislation, there are so many alternative arrangements for financing for libraries, the financial resources for public libraries is given **in Table No 6.1** The public libraries need a permanent source of finance both from the State and Central Government. The State government should be continuing contribution to RRRLF matching scheme and also used the *Per Capita Method* for budget provision for Public Libraries. *As far as concern Per Capita Method used in Madhya Pradesh for budget allocation for Public Libraries, so average cost is 0.77*

Physical Infrastructure (Building)

Analysis and interpretation of data for physical infrastructure (building) of Divisional Public Libraries, District Public Libraries and e-libraries, the present condition of library building is satisfactory. Due to building (physical infrastructure) libraries can't gave proper services their users.

Rectification: Planning for new or expanded library facilities is a major undertaking. It is vital that planning be done with a long-term view of future needs. A library building should have a useful life of twenty years or more.

In 2003 a joint publication between Resource and the Centre for Architecture and the Environment (CABE) looked at the issue of library building. In their publication better Public Libraries they featured a table highlighting what they perceived to be the differences between traditional architecture and modern library architecture. **Facts given in Table No. 7.1**

And also guidelines and financial assistance from the RRRLF for public libraries for space. The object of this matching scheme is to render matching assistance to Government run or aided public libraries for increasing accommodation. This scheme is known as **"Matching Scheme of Assistance to Public Libraries towards Increasing Accommodation".**

The extent of assistance will be as follows:
- Rs. 100.00 lakh (one-time) for State Central Library;
- Rs. 50.00 lakh for Divisional/Mondal/District Library/City Central Library (once in 10 (Ten) years);
- Rs. 25.00 lakh for Sub-Divisional/Taluka/Municipal Library (once in 10 (Ten) years);
- Rs. 10.00 lakh for other libraries (once in 10 (Ten) years).

Equipments

Analysis and interpretation of data available on equipments in Divisional Public Libraries, District Public Libraries and e-libraries; Divisional Public Libraries have equipments like computer, printers and scanners, only few District Public Libraries have equipment like computers and printers, but e-libraries have latest and essential equipments like computers, printers, servers, modem, LCD projector, photocopier, scanners and Internet Connection (Broadband).

Rectification: The solution of ease the problem, If merge the Public Libraries and e-libraries under the proposed Integrated Public Library System for Madhya Pradesh or GIAN Networkthan all the equipment of e-libraries as also available for public libraries. **Facts given in Table no 7.11 and Table No. 7.12**

And another solution is **Assistant Scheme of RRRLF Scheme of Matching Assistance to Public Libraries to Acquire Computer with accessories for library Application and TV, CD player, DVD player for Educational Purposes;** Assistance under this scheme will be available for purchase/up-gradation, as the case may Be, for either of the following items, once in five years;
- One TV set with accessories together with CD Player/DVD Player/ CDs /DVD for educational purposes;

- Computer system as per requirement and on the basis of Feasibility Report consisting of one Server, Clients, UPS, Printer, System Software, Application Software, Anti-virus, Net-work equipment and other accessories;
- Cost of LAN and Power Cabling;
- Cost of Retro-conversion;
- Cost of Computer furniture;
- Eco friendly Generator/ Power backup system;
- Cost towards Public Library Network ((**Separate proposal supported by the Project prepared by NIC or State authorized Agency should be submitted**);
- LCD Projector with accessories will be provided only to State Central Libraries and District Libraries on the recommendation of SLC/SLPC;

Library Services

The Divisional Public Libraries and District Public Libraries is offered different *fundamental services* like lending document for home reading, lending within the libraries, reference service, searching through catalogue cards and referral services to their users, but it can't offered *applied services like* Current Awareness Service (CAS), Selective Dissemination of Information (SDI), Bibliography, Inter Library Loan, Online Searching, Indexing Service, Abstracting Service, Document Delivery Service, Translation Service, Online Services, Bibliography information of document, Blogs, feedback of library and Resourcing Sharing due to library automation. **Facts given in Table No. 8.3**

Rectification:

It is another area needed should be improved is very fast. There is no library network is presence among the public libraries in state, so libraries can't give *IT based information services* or *applied services like* Current Awareness Service (CAS), Selective Dissemination of Information (SDI), Bibliography, Inter Library Loan, Online Searching, Indexing Servic[e], Abstracting Service, Document Delivery Service, Translation Service, Onl[ine] Services, Bibliography information of document, Blogs, feedback of lib[rary] and Resourcing Sharing due to library automation to their clientele.

the problem is that a proposed plan for resource sharing and library network between public libraries and e-library in state is discussing in **Chapter twelve.**

The another way to improve the services of public libraries to established **Knowledge KISOSKS/ Centers** and it should be attached with **Divisional Libraries, District Libraries and Tehsil Libraries,** a Knowledge Information Centres or KIOSKS, it should be established in public libraries and managed by public libraries authorities. The KOSOSKS provided information about the books, news papers, journals, gray literature, educational CD's, audio cassettes, internet facilities at cheapest rates, education based databases, latest information related government policies, announcement.

The another way to improve the services of public libraries to established **Community Information Centres** and it should be attached with **Block Libraries, Panchayat Libraries and Rural Libraries,** for transforming the rural libraries into active community information centres the infrastructure of these libraries has to be improved. They may be provided one set of computer, printer, scanner, UPS, fax and photocopying machines and internet link. The improved facilities will also enable them to serve as literacy centres in rural areas. This will not only help in improving the literacy rate, but also sustaining the literacy of the neo-literates and thereby promoted the objectives of the National Literacy Mission.

Services provided by the Community Information Centre to users:

Information on Government information and procedures; information on education and training; information on health information and different area of health aspects; information about community information; information on consumer information and services; information on historical and tourist information; information on business; information on current affairs; information on various government schemes for different community; information on future plan of government; information for agriculture and allied subjects like which seeds more production, crops that an fetch more profit, technical information about the cultivation system d marketing of the products.

Findings:
The following conclusion has been stated out for the finding of the study;

- The library staff of Divisional Public Libraries and District Public Libraries is males and a few place females and they have also experienced.
- The library staff of Divisional Public Libraries and District Public Libraries has not knowledge and awareness about Information Communication & Technology.
- The present library staff of Divisional Public Libraries and District Public Libraries is not adequate; the staff members are not offered in-service training or deputed for training programmes.
- The Divisional Public Libraries and District Public Libraries have their own Physical Infrastructure (Building) with sufficient accommodation.
- The Divisional Public Libraries and District Public Libraries, so behind implementation & uses of Information Communication and Technology in daily routine work of library.
- The present status of library automation and network is equal to nil, they are neither connected to other public libraries in state not they linked other public libraries of India.
- The Divisional Public Libraries and District Public Libraries have good collection of books, and also subscribed journals, magazines and newspapers for fulfill requirement of their clientele and also hasn't non book material in their collection.
- The finance allocation of Divisional Public Libraries and District Public Libraries is worse conditions.
- The Divisional Public Libraries and District Public Libraries still follow closed access system by not allowing the users to physically browse through the stack section and to select the books required for them by feeling the books.
- The Divisional Public Libraries and District Public Libraries is still hasn't proper classification; cataloguing system for library materials and also used ledger system to issues the reading materials to their users.

- The status of essentials equipments like Photo Copier, TV, OHP, and LCD is not available in Divisional Public Libraries and District Public Libraries
- The Divisional Public Libraries and District Public Libraries has provides old library service, so it is not fulfilling information requirement their clientele.
- No evidence of Divisional Public Libraries and District Public Libraries playing a major role in Inter Library Loan or Intra Library Loan for their members due to library automation.

The Findings of e-Libraries:
- The library staff of e-libraries is males and a few place females and they have also experienced.
- The library staff of e-libraries has adequate knowledge and awareness about Information Communication & Technology.
- The e-Libraries have their own Physical Infrastructure (Building).
- The e-Libraries have an ICT's Infrastructure and also Internet connection to fulfill thrust of information to their clientele.
- The e-Libraries have good collection of books for fulfill requirement of their clientele and haven't non book materials in their collection.
- The equipment status like scanners, photo copier, TV, OHP, LCD, DVD writer is available in e-Libraries.

Suggestions

is hoped that the following suggestions may bring some changes to the
ent scenario of Public Libraries.
- A separate Directorate for Public Libraries should be created under the Ministry of culture. The Director should be library professional.
- A task force headed by a retried library and information science professional should be appointed to give suggestion to upgrade the public library system in state.

  The existing public libraries should be further strengthened with sufficient budget. The public libraries need a permanent source of finance both from the State Government. The State government may continue contribution to RRRLF matching scheme.

- The public libraries and e-libraries should be merging and functions cohesively as one unit and the people should be change of newness in its services. The system would disseminate, storage the information through a network, but it can also provide job opportunities to the youngster's right in their own villages and it is also beneficial in term of manpower.
- The library should be function as independent with its set objectives and functions to serve its own clientele.
- In order to e-governance plan of the state government and the role of public libraries to serve as a bridge between government and citizens. In existing District Public Libraries should be established a kioskc is serve as knowledge centre and in rural /village libraries should be established a kioskc is serve as community information centre.
- The public library should be merging with e-libraries and should create a local library network between the libraries and named should be GIAN Network, it provides the library services like current awareness service, selective disseminate of information, abstract service, translation services and document delivery service to their clientele.
- The resource sharing should be implemented through a strong network and the users shall be in position to used services of others libraries.
- The uses of ICTs should increase the efficiency of the library and steps taken to computerize to meet the challenges of an information society with necessary hardware and software.
- Qualified and professional staff should be recruited for smooth functioning of library services.
- Library staff both professional and non-professional needs to be fully oriented towards applications of ICT's. The authority should organize in-service training and refresher course to acquire latest development and knowledge of computer application.
- In order to develop effective public libraries system in the state it is very essential to enact library act in the state.
- To develop reading habit among the people and encourage stude and youth to make optional use of libraries;

- It is quite difficult for readers to visit library from time to time especially in far flung areas, so library should be start mobile library service which provide an essential service in remote areas.
- The good number books, journals, magazine and online publications like e-journals, e-books, e-magazine and efficient arrangements would help attracting more users to the public libraries.
- The book adds on science and technology, children encyclopedias and books need to be added to attract children between the age group of 10-18.
- Library must be located in calm areas with natural surroundings, provision of mineral water with nominal fee, cleanliness and proper sanitation to be maintained.
- Awareness to be created amongst the public to attract more users by celebrating library Week from time to time
- Need of a strong state library association;
- Library extension services like book exhibition, workshop/seminar, library lecture, audio-video programme, story house may be organized with emphasis to promote library services.
- Separate sections for children, senior citizen, women and disabled person should be established and a section on Career Guidance may be also established for library users.

Recommendations for Further Research:

There is a massive scope for further research. The study can be done as given below:

- Comparison between public libraries among two and more state and as well as e-library where it exist;
- Service comparison between by public libraries in India, state and as well as two states;
- Status of ICT's in public libraries in India and as well as two states;
- Status of library automation public library in between two states;
- Rural public library as a community information centres;
- Effect of social media on public library services;
- Inclusive education and public library.
- Manpower status of public library;
- Role of public library in eradication of illiteracy;

- Role of public library in special education;
- Status of finance in public library.

Afterward:

In the present study has been grouped under twelve major chapters.

Chapter one names **Introduction** is gaves information about the library, purpose of library, definiations, objectives and function of public library and types of public library in general ways.

Chapter two names **Genesis and Development of Public Libraries in India,** it describe the brief information about the library from the age of Vedas and also gaves brief information of some important library like National Library, Kolkata; Khuda Bakhsh Oriental Public Library, Patna; Rampur Raza Library, Rampur; Thanjavur Maharaja Serfoji's Sarasvati Mahal Library, Thanjavur; and Harekrushna Mahtab State Library, Bhubaneswar. The chapter depicts also highlited abou the growth and Development of Public Library in Five Year Plans, Recommendations of Various Library Committees viz, National Policy on Library & Information System (NAPLIS); National Knowledge Commission and Raja Rammohan Roy Library Foundation and Public Libraries. The further describe the review literature related present study in India.

Chapter three names **Administrative Organization of Public Libraries in Madhya Pradesh** it describe Public Libraries (Divisional & District) governed by Directorate of Public Instructions, Rural Libraries governed by Panchayat and Social Welfare and e-libraries and Rural Libraries is governed by Sarve Shiksha Mission in Madhya Pradesh.

Chapter four names **Status of Collection of Reading Materials** is depicts about the Categories of Library Materials in Public Library, Format of Library Materials in Public Library, Standards for Book Collections as per IFLA guideline. It is further describing Collection of Reading Materials of Divisional Public Libraries, District Public Libraries, e-libraries and compares libraries as per IFLA standards. In state these libraries governed by three different enties, so if it should be merge a one entity is called Integrated Public Library System (IPLS) or GIAN Network, so it should increase different types of reading materials availability for the common people of region.

Chapter five names **Status of manpower** depicts about the New Skills Required for Library Professional in IT environment, Staff Formula for Library, IFLA standard and guidelines evolved by Raja Rammohun Roy Library Foundation (RRRLF) for library staff, It is further describing status of manpower (professional and non professional) of Divisional Public Libraries, District Public Libraries, e-libraries and compares libraries as per RRRLF standards and also proposed required manpower proposed as per recomendataion of National Knowledge Commission, 2005 for Integrated Public Library System (IPLS) or GIAN Network.

Chapter six names **Status of Financial Organization** is explaine resources of Finance for Public Libraries, source of funding as per IFLA Guidelines, Various Committee Recommendation of Public Library Finance in India, It is further describing status of finance Divisional Public Libraries, District Public Libraries, e-libraries and compares libraries and public libraries how generate revenue from different sources in present conditions. It is also further proposed required finance and finance for manpower Integrated Public Library System (IPLS) or GIAN Network.

Chapter seven names **Status of Infrastructure (Physical and ICT)** is depict Standard for Library Buildings, RRRLF Guidelines for Public Library, major Equipment for Public Libraries as per IFLA Guidelines, it further describing status of Infrastructure (Physical and ICT), status of library automation, uses of computers and Internet availability of Divisional Public Libraries, District Public Libraries, e-libraries and compares as per RRRLF standards. It is also proposed required Infrastrcutre (Physical and ICT) for Integrated Public Library System (IPLS) or GIAN Network.

Chapter eight names **services offered by libraries** Services to users, Service provision for Public Libraries, Existing Status of Member of each and every library, The Divisional Public Libraries and District Public Libraries is offered different *fundamental services* but it can't offered *applied services like or IT based information services,* so for these purpose proposed Integrated Public Library System (IPLS) or GIAN Network to provide IT based information serices to their users.

Chapter nine names **resource sharing and network** it provides information about what is e-library, its characteristics, objectives, functions, advantages and limitations. It is also gave information about resource sharing and present status of library network in India.

Chapter ten names **Historical Background of GIAN (GENERAL INFORMATION ACCESS NETWORK)** it discuss about the GIAN (General Information Access Network), Genesis and development GIAN and discussing about the GYANDOOT Project.

Chapter eleven names **Sarve Shiksha Mission**, it gave information about Madhya Pradesh District wise, the role and function of Sarve Shiksha Mission in Madhya Pradesh, its objective, targets and future planning.

Chapter Twelve names **Model for Integrated Public Libraries System** discuss about the proposed plan for networking and resources sharing between public libraries and e-libraries in the form of IPLS.

Chapter thirteen names **suggestions and recommendataions,** it depicts about finding, recommendations, weakness and rectification of the problems of public libraries of Madhya Pradesh.

Conclusion:

It was a great learning period and journey for me in the form of book **'Integrated Indian Public Library System'**. The entire study gave me a huge benefit to gain my knowledge towards public libraries and electronic library, which help to me in future, when I was direct interact to user of both libraries to collect the data in the real world, it gave a life time learning opportunity to me and change my entire thinking about the public libraries. I have study entire public library system in different aspect. Public library system is very broad area of library and information science in term of study.

The present book is containing each and every aspect which related public libraries and electronic library, both libraries is governed by two different entities and also compare with each other different parameter (The Public Library Service: IFLA/UNESCO Guidelines for Development **and Raja Rammohun Roy Library Foundation (RRRLF) guidelines for manpower/infrastructure (building)** and proposed an Integrated Public Library System. It is also proposed required different areas viz. collection of reading materials, status of manpower, status of financial organization, status of Infrastructure (Physical and ICT), Services offered by libraries, status of library automation. The present book presented scenario of public library and electronic library in state. I think it is very beneficial document for official, academicians, researcher, students and also those, who want gain knowledge about the public library.

About the Author

Dr. Kapil Singh Hada, presently working as a Junior Teachnical Assistant (Library), Faculty of Education, Banasthali Vidyapith, Rajasthan, since Dec, 2010. He was born on 8 July 1976 at Ratlam, Madhya Pradesh. He earned B. Lib. & Inf. Sci. from MCNUJ & C, Bhopal, M. Lib. & Ins. Sci. Dr. Hari Singh Gour Vishwavidyalay, Sagar), M. Phil (Lib. Sci) and Ph. D. (Lib. Sci.) from MGCGVV, Chitrakoot, Satna (Madhya Pradesh). He has 14 years experience in his field. He started his professional career in 1999-2000 as a School Librarian at Delhi, after these works as Asistant Librarin at Crescent Insititute of Management, Bhopal (2001-2003). After he was jointed TIT Group of Institute, Bhopal as Librarian and Incharge (2003-2010). He has also contributed 35 research articles published/ presented in National/International seminars/conferences and journal reput and participated in many conferences, seminars and workshops for presenting his research papers. His area of interest is Public Library, Digital/ Electronic Library, ICT's, Research Methodology Information Literacy and Library Automation. It is the first book of author.

Dr. R. P. Bajpai, working as Associate Professor, Department of Library and Information Science, Mahatma Gandhi Chitrakoot Gramodaya Vishwavidayalaya, Chitrakoot, Satna (Madhya Pradesh), under his guidance 6 scholars has got Ph.D. and 8 are registered.

48 research papers have been published and presented in various International; National referred journals, seminars, conferences and workshops.

Dr. Bajpai has much experience as a teacher of Library and Information as well as library professional, especially rural community information system. Beside that Dr. Bajpai is recognized as subject expert in various Universitie in India.

Dr. Bajpai has credit of being in-charge University Librarian from 1995 to till now at Mahatma Gandhi Chitrakoot Gramodaya Vishwavidayalaya, Chitrakoot, Satna (Madhya Pradesh).

Dr. Bajpai also completed three project i.e. Library Automation, Networking and conservation and preservation of manuscript under the Ministry of Culture, Government of India. It is the fourth of author. Contact him: rpbajpaimgcgvv@gmail.com

Appendics-I

Minimum Required Hardware and Network

Item	Configuration	Quantity	Rate (Rs)	Total (Rs)
Server	Pentium IV 16 GHz or above/845 chipset/256 KB Cache/400MHz FSB/256 MB SDRAM, 133MHz /40GB/ATA Hard Disk Drive/52X CD ROM/ 3PCI Slots/1AGPS/ 5 Bays/3 DIMM Slots/ 16 MB Graphics Performance Accelerator/ Integrated NIC/Integrated Audio with External Speaker/ Keyboard/ Mouse/15" Color Monitor/ Windows 2000 Pro	1	60000	60000
Desktop System		9	55000	49500
Laser Printer		1	20160	20160
Scanner		1	5585	5585
UPS		2	31200	62400
Modem		1	2616	2616
Hub		1	9009	9009
UTP cable	UTP CAT 5 CABLE (PER BOX OF 300 M)	1	3628	3628
Into Outlet	INFORMARTION OUTLE/ SURFACE MOUNT BOX (DUPLEX)	10	340	3400
Mounting Cord 7ft	CAT 5.7 FT MOUNTING CORD	10	136	1360
Jack Panel	JACK PANEL 247 MAX 24 PORTS	1	4761	4761

Rack	RACK WITHACCESSIOSIES	1	3822	3822
Cable Laying Charges with Conduit	COST AND LAYING OF CONDUCT/METER	300	6	1800
Software				
Application Software(s)	Web/ Interest Based Application Software			50000
Site Requirements				
Built Up Area renovation				50000
Furniture, OHP & LCD				3000000
Total				**1073541**

Appendics-II

List of District Public Libraries and e-Libraries

No	Divisional Public Libraries	District Public Libraries	e-Libraries
1.	Gwalior	Damoh	Bhopal
2.	Indore	Dewas	Gwalior
3.	Jabalpur	Gwalior	Indore
4.	Rewa	Hoshangabad	Jabalpur
5.		Jabalpur	Sagar
6.		Khargone	Umaria
7.		Panna	Betul
8.		Rajgarh	Vidisha
9.		Ratlam	Shivpuri
10.		Sagar	Ratlam
11.		Satna	Ujjain
12.		Sidhi	Rewa
13.		Tikamgarh	Guna
14.		Ujjain	Tikamgarh
15.		Vidisha	Panna
16.		Bhopal	Jhabua
17.		Khandwa	Hoshangabad
18.		Shivpuri	Mandla
19.		Shajapur	Dhar
20.		Betul	Sidhi

21.		Narsinghpur	Harda
22.		Morena	Neemuch
23.		Guna	Khargone
24		Datia	Satna
25.		Mandusar	Damoh
27.		Sehore	Dewas
28.		Raisen	Morena
29.		Chhindwara	
30.		Dhar	
31.		Jhabua	
32.		Shahdol	
33.		Mandla	

Appendics-III

Category of Library	Responsibilities of Library	Common Interest of all Libraries	Skills required to full filling this changing role	Staff Pattern in Public Libraries
State Central Library & Knowledge Centre	a. Information service b. e-learning c. knowledge management d. knowledge centre activities e. content creation and management f. subject gateways g. content analysis h. collaborative publishing i. e-governance j. training.	a. training, b. sharing of databases and contents, c. problem solving, transaction analysis d. gathering of information towards developing uniform standards and modeling of inspection of need, access and dissemination, e. inspection of progress of knowledge based activities f. identifying weaknesses in the system,	i. Library and information handling skills. ii. ICT knowledge skills. iii. Communication and training skills. iv. Marketing and presentation skills. v. Understanding of cultural diversity. vi. Knowledge mapping skills.	**i. Managerial Staff (Group A)** a. State Librarian b. Deputy Library Director c. Assistant Library Director (presently designated as Information Officer) **ii. Professional/ Technical Staff (Group B)** a. Information Assistant b. Junior Information Assistant c. Data Entry Operator **iii. Para-professional/ Support Staff (Group C)** a. Library Attendant **iv. Administrative Staff** a. Administrative Officer b. Stenographer c. Cashier **v. Administrative Support Staff** a. Night Watchman, Cleaner, Mali, Driver, Book Binder, Sweeper, etc, to be outsourced

District Library & Knowledge Centre	a. Information service b. e-governance c. content development d. co-ordination of rural knowledge centres.			**i. Managerial Staff (Group A)** a. District Librarian **ii. Professional/ Technical Staff (Group B)** a. Information Assistant b. Data Entry Operator **iii. Para-professional/ Support Staff (Group C)** a. Library Attendant **iv. Administrative Staff** a. Night Watchman, Cleaner, Mali, Driver, Book Binder, Sweeper, etc, to be outsourced
Sub Divisional/ Town Library & Knowledge Centre	a. Lending of books b. reference services c. inter-library loan d. web-based services such as e-learning, banking and insurance, community information, content and database creation.			**i. Managerial Staff (Group A)** e. a. Town Librarian **ii. Professional/ Technical Staff (Group B)** f. a. Data Entry Operator **iii. Para-professional/ Support Staff (Group C)** g. a. Library Attendant **iv. Administrative Staff** h. a. Night Watchman, Cleaner, Mali, Book Binder, Sweeper, etc, to be outsourced
Rural Knowledge Centre/ Community Information Centre:	a. Lending of books b. web-based services such as e-learning, banking and insurance c. Panchayat-level information d. e-governance e. community information f. content and database creation.			**i. Professional/ Technical Staff (Group B)** a. Information Assistant **ii. Para-professional/ Support Staff (Group C)** a. Library Attendant **iii. Administrative Staff** a. Village Level Volunteers

Responsibilities of Public Libraries
as per Recommendation of National Knowledge Commission

An Information Officer is needed to look after and co-ordinate the activities of clusters four to six District Libraries and their Knowledge Centres.

Glossary

Blogs: Blogs can be hosted in any organization internet or any popular blogs site like www.blogsspot.com; it can be used to give a platform to the common people to post their view.

Data Base: A centre organ machine should be installed for creating a union catalogue, comprising catalogues of all participating libraries. A centre organ that can accommodate about a bibliographic record with work space for data handling, system software, communication software, application software will be used. The physical records of all the data are stored in Main Server. This data base is made available to all "Authenticate" users logging in through their respective state centres. The data base is 24 hours online and is updated periodically.

Discussion Board or Forum: A virtual community can be created using Web-based discussion boards. Different sections or areas can be created for discussions. This is an ideal solution for different locations, different areas, different geographical areas, but have a common area of interest. They can share their problems, real life experience, common area of interest and building a personal relation type networking. There are so many readymade programs available in the market and one of them can be deployed for our requirement. Under the open source community some programs are popular for web application like PHPBB.

Expert System: Expert database with profile updating can be kept for the public view and queries can be posted to specific experts based on the areas of domain and expertise of the experts. This helps in creating innovations and learning culture in a community or society.

Extensible markup language: Which allows designers to customize formatting (tags), to greater definition, achieves transmission, validation, and interpretation of data between applications and organizations.

HTML: An abbreviation for hypertext markup language. A specific set of tags used to dercribe the structure of hypertext documents that make up most web pages. Web browsers interpret these tags to display test and graphics. HTML is an application of SGML.

Knowledge management: It is managing organizational knowledge to solve the organizational problems. It includes managing tacit as well as explicit knowledge.

LAN Switch: The LAN switch interfaces all the terminal points in the network centre. It configured depending on the number of nodes required.

Metadata: Metadata is the data that describe the content and attributes of any particular item in a digital library. This is data about data or a catalogue to web document as catalogue card is to print documents.

Network Architecture: The network centre will have all the member libraries linked with these network host system through telephone line or V-SAT links. The member libraries are routed through Regional Centre. This is done primarily considering the poor communication infrastructure especially the non-reliability of the telephone lines and also to lower cost of using telephone lines. This will eliminate the need to pay STD charges as the State Centre is located close to the libraries or another way to wireless telephone are also used for these purpose. The libraries can have their own LAN set up.

Public e-Library: Public e-library for the people, by the people, of people and via electronic way

Remote Access Server (RAS): The RAS should have a minimum 6 ports, enabling a minimum of 6 logins simultaneously. Depending on the traffic the capacity of RAS could be increased in future.

Resourcing Sharing: The resource sharing among the libraries will be books, periodicals, journals, online journals, databases, thesis, serials and other e-document.

Standardization: The problem with different classification schemes, cataloguing codes and subject headings for libraries have to solved for effective functioning of any network, the network can adopt the CCF, AACR-2 and LCSH for standardization in information heading activities of any network system.

Telephone Lines: The network centre should have adequate number of telephone lines to enable the remote server to login ay any part of the day or night.

Text Encoding Initiative (TEI): Text Encoding Initiative (TEI) is an international effort, the goal of which is to define a set of generic guidelines for the textual material in electronic form. It is basically concerned with two things: one is what textual feature should be encoded in electronic environment to make it more explicit and second is to, how encoding should be represented for loss-free, platform independent interchange.

V-SAT Connectivity: Very small apparatus terminal usually provided by the telephone company but there are many private service providers offering this facility.

Web Portal: Web site can be developed uses for this network. Access can be restricted by login or password systems. Users with different levels of permission can access contributions/articles. This type of system helps in sharing practices, experiments, innovations, failure stories etc. Web portal are developed with database supporters to keep the records of authors, members, visitors and many other things.

Z 39.50: It is a standard developed by National Information Standard Organization (NISO) for information retrieval that allows any library using a Z 39.50 compatible automated library system to access remote library collection. It specifies a response protocol between client and server.

Bibliography

Books

(1) Arms, W, Digital Libraries (New York: MIT Press) 2000.

(2) ALA (1986). *ALA World Encyclopedia of Library and Information Services*. Chicago, USA: American Library Association.

(3) Ashburner, E. H. *Modern Public Libraries: Their Planning and Design.* (New Delhi: Reliance Publishing House, 1986)

(4) Chakravarty, N. C. *A Note on Finance for Public Libraries in India.* (1961).

(5) Guruswaminidu, N. *Public Library Finance.* (New Delhi: Ess ss Publications, 1999).

(6) Harrod, L. M. (1987). Librarian's Glossary and Reference Book. London: Gowar Publishing.

(7) Gupta and Khular. Handbook of Libraries, Archives and Information Centres in India. New Delhi: National Archives of India.

(8) Mittal Publications. *History and Development of Libraries in India.* (New Delhi: Mittal Publications, 1995).

(9) Harrison, K. C. *Public Libraries Today.* (London:Crosby Lockwood Sons td, 1963).

(10) *Secondary Education Commission Report, 1953*, prepared by Publication Division (Delhi, 1953).

(11) *University and College Libraries, 1965* prepared by Ministry of Human Resourced and Development in corporation with the University Grants Commission (New Delhi: 1965).

(12) *University Education Commission, 1948-49*, prepared by Ministry of Education (Delhi: 1949).

(13) *National Policy on Library and Information System-A Presentation, 1986*, prepared by the Cultural Department in corporation with the Ministry of Human Resource Development (New Delhi:1986).

(14) *Advisory Committee for Libraries*, 1961, prepared by the Ministry of Education (Delhi: 1961).

(15) *Education Commission, 1964*, repared by the Minitry of Education (New Delhi: 1966).

(16) *Report of the Working Group of the Planning Commission on Modernization of Library Services and Informatics,* 1984, prepared by Planning Commission of India. (New Delhi: 1984).

(17) Handbook of Libraries, Achieves and Information Centres in India: Library Development in India. Vol. 16; New Delhi, India: Segment Books.

(18) Kalia, D. R. *Public Libraries: Years Library and Information Services in India.* (Delhi: Shipra Publication).

(19) Kumar, P. S. G. *Indian Library Chronology.* (Delhi: Metropolitan Books, 1977.)

(20) Hindustan Publishing Cooperation. *Library Movement in India: An Introductory Essay.* (Delhi: Hindustan Publishing Cooperation, 1962).

(21) Mishra, Jagdish. *History of Libraries and Librarianship in Modern India Since 1850.* (Delhi: Atma Ram and Sons, 1979)

(22) Kaul, H. K. *Library Resource Sharing and Networking.* (New Delhi: Vigro Publications, 1999).

(23) *Guidelines of Public Library Systems and Services* Submitted to RRRLF. (Calcutta: RRRLF).

(24) Malvya, A. *Electronic Libraries.* (New Delhi: Ess Ess Publication, 1999).

(25) Mookerjee, S. K. *Development of Libraries and Library Science in India.* (Delhi: Asia Publishing House, 1969).

(26) Mahaparta, P. K. and V. K. Thomas, *Public Libraries in Developing Countries; Status and Trends.* (New Delhi: Vikas Publishing House, 1969)

(27) Nair, Raman. *Public Library Development.* (New Delhi: Ess Ess Publications, 1993).

(28) Parashar, R. G. and Harisingha Gour. *Managing University Libraries* (New Delhi: Today and Tomorrow, 1991).

(29) Rath, P. *Public Library Finance.* (Delhi: Pratibha Publication, 1996.)

(30) Sharma, P. S. K. *Public Library in India.* (New Delhi: Ess Ess Publications, 1990).

(31) Shastri, D. P. *"Bharat Mai Pusastkalaya Ka Udhbhav aur Vikas".*

(32) Sharma, S. K. *Public Libraries in India*. (Delhi: Ess Ess Publications, 1991).

(33) Sincliar, John. ed (1987). *Collins Dictionary*. London: Collins Sons.

(34) Swaminathan, S. *Libraries in India: Yesterday and Today, Library Science Today:* Ranganthan Festschrift, Vol 1. (Calcutta: Asia Publishing House.1965).

(35) Rose, Ernestine. *Public Libraries in American Life*. (New York: Columbia University Press, 1954).

(36) Taher, Mohammad. *Libraries in India's National Development Perspective: A Sagaof Fifty Years since Independence*. (New Delhi: Concept Publishing Company, 2001).

(37) The Madras Public Libraries Act, 1948.

(38) The Andhra Pradesh Public Libraries Act, 1960.

(39) The Mysore Public Libraries Act, 1965.

(40) The Maharashtra Public Libraries Act, 1967.

(41) The West Bengal Public Libraries Act, 1979.

(42) The Manipur Public Libraries Act, 1988.

(43) The Kerala Public Libraries Act, 1989.

(44) The Haryana Public Libraries Act, 1989.

(45) The Gujarat Public Libraries Act, 2002.

(46) The Orissa Public Libraries Act, 2002.

(47) The Rajasthan Public Libraries Act, 2006.

(48) Thomas, V. K. *Public Libraries in India: Development and Finance*. (New Delhi: Vikas Publishing House, 1997).

(49) Trehan, G. L. *Modern Public Library Movement and Library Legislation for Punjab*. (Chandigarh: Library Literature House, 1967).

(50) Vashistha, C. P. et al., *New Horizongs in Library and Information Sciences*. (Madras: I. R. Publications, 1994).

(51) Vyas, S. D. *Public Library System*. (Jaipur: Panchsheel Prakashan, 1998).

(52) Vyas, S. D. *Library and Society*. (Jaipur: Panchsheel Prakashan, 1993).

(53) Vyas, S. D. *Public and School Library System in Rajasthan*.(Delhi: Indian Book Press, 1990).

(54) Verma, L. N. and U. K. Agarwal. *Public Library Services in India*. (Udaipur: Himanshu Publication, 1994.)

(55) Ramannair, R. *Public Library System: A Model Outlook on in Principles and Practice in National Information Policies and Programme.* (New Delhi. Indian Library, 1991).

Journals

(1)   Barua, B. P. "Universal Accessibility to Information role of a Public Library in the Indian Context," *Granthana (Indian Journal of Library Studies,* 1.1 (1990)

(2)   Kalia, D. R. "Guidelines for Public Library Systems and Services", *Granthana: India Journal of Library Studies,* 2.11: 31-84. (1991)

(3)   Kaula, P. N. "A Study of Public Library and Development and Services for Rural Upliftment", *Herald of Library Science,* 39. 3-4 (2000).

(4)   Oppenheim, C. and D. Smithson. "What is the Hybrid Library?", *Journal of Information Science* 25.2: 97-112.

(5)   Weinstein, Joshua I. "The Market in Plato's *Republic.*" *Classical Philology* 104 (2009): 439–58.

(6)   Pradhan, Mohan Raj. "Developing Digital Libraries: Technologies and Challenges". *Library Herald.* 42.2 101 (2004).

(7)   Rajashekar, T.B. "Digital Libraries". *Information Studies* 4.1. 223-38. (1995).

(8)   Rangathan, S. R. "Model State Library Act". *Herald of Library Science,* 11.3: 232-33. (1972).

(9)   Ranganthan, S. R. "Model Public Library Act, 1972 in Public Library System", *SRELS,*(1973).

(10)   Saracevic, T. "Digital Library Evaluation: Towards of Concepts". *Library Trends,* 49.2: 350-69. (2000).

(11)   Singh, Mohinder. "Progress of Librarianship in India, 1911-1978'.Libri 29:160. (1979).

(12)   Tilaiynagyam, "Bharat Mai Jai Pusastkalaya ka Viakas", *Grathalaya Vigyan,* 2:26-39.

(13)   Uheegu, A.N. "Information Communication Networking in Rural Communities: The Case of Women in IMO State, Nigeria", *Journal of Information Science,* 26.1:51-59. (2000).

Conferences/Seminars:

(1) Nagar, B. R. "'Digital Library: Issues Related with Digitization and Sharing of Resources' (paper presented at the 48th Indian Library Association Electronic Information Environment and Library Services: Bangalore, 2003).

(2) Trehan, G. L. "'Developing Society and Its Library Needs'.(paper presented at the 28th All India Library Conference: Seminar Papers. Delhi: Indian Library Association, 1982).

Web Site:

(1) "UNESCO, IFLA, ICA", Guidelines of Digitization Projects for Collection and Holdings in the Public Domain Particular those held by Libraries and Archives. 2 Retrieved from http://Set.ifla.org/VII/s19/pubs/digit-guide.pf

Index

Infrastructure, 5-6, 12
Information Infrastructure Technology and Applications (IITA), 143
Khuda Bakesh Oriential Public Library, 33
KISOK, 170
Kitab Ghar, 28
Library Fund, 42, 97, 99, 100-102
Library Networks 151-152, 156, 158, 210
Maharah Takiji Rao Holkar-II, 29
Manager of Information, 165
Manpower 41, 43, 78, 82-87, 91-92, 100, 149-150, 213, 219, 225-230
National Library of India, 29, 40, 156
Network Component, 154
National Knowledge Commission, 41, 82, 92, 159, 219, 228, 235
Panchayat, 40, 47-48, 64-65, 94, 95, 98-100, 109, 117, 158-169, 168-169, 172-173, 182, 201, 202, 205, 209-211, 216-217, 222, 228
Per Capita Method, 104, 107, 220
Infrastructure Physical (Building), 111
Public Library Manifesto, 21, 24
Public Library Network, 24, 133, 159
Rampur Raza Library, Rampur, 33, 228
Ranganthan, 22, 96, 107, 111, 201
Resource Sharing, 52, 98, 100, 108, 140, 146-153, 158-159, 163
RRRLF, 40, 44-46, 108, 220, 221, 225, 228-230
RRRLF Guidelines for Public Libraries, 92, 112
Services Offered, 24, 133-134, 229, 230
Sarve Shiksha Mission 64-65, 76-77, 91, 107, 117, 124-125, 129, 137, 137, 167, 207, 228, 230
Staff Formula, 81, 228
SOOCHAK, 169-170, 172-173, 175
Tanjore Saraswati Mahal Library, 27
Taluka Library, 24-25
UNESCO, 30, 77, 230
Village Library 41, 101, 118, 208, 215
V-SAT, 154, 237-238